WOMEN'S VOICES
1880–1918

THE NEW WOMAN

EDITED BY
JULIET GARDINER

FOREWORD BY
VICTORIA GLENDINNING

COLLINS & BROWN

First published in Great Britain in 1993
by Collins & Brown Limited
Mercury House
195 Knightsbridge
London SW7 1RE

1 3 5 7 9 8 6 4 2

British Library Cataloguing-in-Publication Data:
A catalogue record for this book
is available from the British Library.

ISBN 1 85585 159 8 (paperback edition)

Conceived, edited and designed
by Collins & Brown Limited
Editor: Mandy Greenfield
Designer: Clare Clements

Typeset by Falcon Graphic Art Limited
Printed and bound in Great Britain
by Cox & Wyman Ltd, Reading

CONTENTS

WRITERS AND PERIODICALS
FEATURED IN THE BOOK

FOREWORD

I was quite shaken after reading this book, chiefly because of its immediacy. Direct experience and first-hand opinion, conveyed in the 'voices' of women from the past, hit the spot in a way that whole libraries of feminist social history never quite can. These voices, from every age-group and social class, express every possible attitude to women's lot – from desperation, pain, anger, bewilderment and militancy, to humour, resignation and embattled defence of the status quo.

For it becomes clear that the New Woman of a century ago was as hard to pin down as the New Man is today. Men and women were no more homogenous as groups then than they are now. Those who questioned the conventions were not, in the first great period of the women's movement covered by this book, all after the same thing. There is in these pages the 'blue-stocking', who prides herself on not being able to cook and sew, and the ascetic, 'thinking high thoughts, living simply'. But there is also 'the Girl of the Period', in skimpy frocks and make-up, whose behaviour seemed, to disapproving observers, little better than a tart's. This disagreement about what exactly constitutes sexual liberation has become an unresolved subtext in feminist dialectic.

The most eloquent voices, however, are those which simply lay before us their daily lives. The farm servant's day puts paid to any residual feeling that work in the country was somehow better than sweated labour in the industrial towns, though the testimony of the employee in the brush-making factory is enough to make one weep with outrage, too. In this context, the well-meaning lady who exhorts well-off girls to visit the poor, bringing the priceless gifts of their 'gay chat' and 'the halo which rest and refinement give in the eyes of the work-worn and rough-living', is stupid to the point of criminality.

Marie Corelli may have thought that women's suffrage would be 'nothing less than a national disaster', but progressive men and women felt that getting the vote was the key to women's liberation. It was achieved soon after the period covered by this book, but it did not transform women's lives overnight.

There have been huge improvements since then in public attitudes, in career and educational opportunities for women, and in the conditions of working women's lives. But it is sickening to realize how much underlying prejudice and injustice remains. These voices describe the exhaustion involved in combining work and domestic duties, the problems of childcare, and society's pressures on women to provide support-systems for men, in terms that still apply today. In their jokes, analyses and blueprints for improvement some of the women seem actually more radical than are most modern women, particularly about marriage.

I know now why I find the book disturbing. It is because I feel that we have, with our compromises and complacency, let these women down. But we can listen to their voices, and think again.

Victoria Glendinning

INTRODUCTION

The self-conscious label of *'fin-de-siècle'*, with its overtones of decadence and decay, stuck uneasily to many of the women of the 1880s and 1890s. In a period when it has been said 'men became women and women became men' and the word 'feminism' first gained currency, for those women concerned with such matters, the age seemed one of genesis rather than decline, of opportunities to be fought for, boundaries to be re-drawn, categories to be re-named.

'We are now at the swing of the pendulum in the "woman question",' wrote the novelist Sarah Grand in an article that appeared in 1894. The 'woman question', which, throughout the nineteenth century, had been concerned with the debate over women's legal and political rights, took on a new coloration as the century drew to its close.

By the 1880s the hard-won battle for the recognition of women's rights in two of the most fundamental areas of their lives – marriage and motherhood – had reached a certain plateau. The map of women's lives could be traced afresh from the foothills of these achievements, and the implications of the slow movement towards the vindication of women's rights and their emancipation could begin to be discerned.

The hard-wrung concessions over women's education were central to this new topography. If women were to be educated outside the home, skilled in more than the domestic arts, what was to be the purpose of their education? If not trained only as helpmeets, wives and mothers, what was the role in life for which they were being prepared? And how would this affect

1

their 'womanliness', if the definition of womanliness comprised dependence and joyful servitude? If they were to be educated like men, what was to stop them beginning to think like men, and even act like men? What were the determinants of the feminine?

If women could earn their own living and find fulfilment in work and society outside the home, how would they come to view marriage? If they were no longer to be economically dependent on a husband, would they want to trade terms for new conditions within marriage? Or reject marriage altogether? And what of the sexuality of women outside marriage? Was their stance to be one of celibacy, a silent reproach to the excesses and sexual double standards of so many men? Or were they to follow the new breed of sexologists and proclaim themselves, too, sentient beings, with sexual needs and demands that had a right to be satisfied within marriage – or without?

If a large number of women were not to marry – some through choice – how was the present situation of political representation to continue to be justified?

These were the concerns that exercised women's voices from the end of the nineteenth century until the First World War – and beyond. 'This consciousness of self is of recent growth ... unknown to our mothers and grandmothers,' wrote a male critic in 1897. The explosion of magazine and periodical publishing aimed at women, *The Englishwoman's Review*, *The Freewoman*, the *Girl's Own Paper*, *Women's World* and later the political periodicals, *The Suffragette*, *Votes for Women* and *The Common Cause*, provided new outlets for women's writing; and the burgeoning of fiction magazines – including *The Yellow Book* (with a female assistant editor, Ella D'Arcy) – gave women writers new opportunities to perfect the genre of the short story with its vignettes of women's lives, to dramatize and fictionalize their dilemmas.

It was at this time that many women who are now regarded as among the finest writers of our century – Virginia Woolf, Katherine Mansfield, Olive Schreiner, May Sinclair, Dorothy Richardson, Rebecca West – first found their voices, in a vivid expression of women's feelings and needs, and in their calls for recognition and change.

But to imagine that the chronicles of such sensibilities rested

2

entirely with these particular writers is to obscure both the depth and breadth – and the sheer quantity – of women's writing in the forty-odd years between 1880 and 1918. The Victorian age, and the years that followed, were the great period of novel-writing. In his *Companion to Victorian Literature*, John Sutherland has estimated that probably around 7,000 Victorians could properly call themselves 'novelists' – and of these many were women writing with urgency, with irony, with resignation or passion. They fashioned their experiences and observations into novels that could be as 'emancipated' as their actions and demands.

Women's writing published at the *fin de siècle* and the years beyond includes, among many others, work by Ménie Muriel Dowie, who travelled throughout Europe alone at twenty; Gertrude Bell, who ventured where no Englishwoman had ever before trodden in North Africa and the Middle East; Sarah Grand (Frances Elizabeth Clarke), who drew on the experiences of her husband's work in an institution for prostitutes with sexually transmitted diseases to write sensationally successful novels with a strong social message; 'George Egerton' (Mary Chavelita Dunne), who eloped with a bigamist to Norway, became fluent in the language and translated Knut Hamsun's novel *Hunger*; Ada Leverson, whose wit caused Oscar Wilde to dub her 'the Sphinx'; Elizabeth Robins, founder of the Actresses' Franchise League and the Women Writers Suffrage League; Cicely Hamilton, who wrote more than twenty plays on issues affecting women; Ella Dixon, author of *The Story of a Modern Woman* (1894), in which she wrote, 'All we modern women mean to help each other now. If we were united, we could lead the world'; Lady Florence Dixie, who explored Patagonia on horseback and worked tirelessly for anti-imperialist causes in South Africa and for Home Rule for Ireland.

The very success of such novels as Sarah Grand's *The Heavenly Twins* and *The Beth Book* and Iota's *A Yellow Aster*, which dealt with questions of women's emancipation and the scourge of venereal disease; of Olive Shreiner's *The Story of an African Farm*; of the work of Grant Allen in *The Woman Who Did* (though never a popular book with feminists); of George Egerton's short story *The Regeneration of Two*; and of Nesta Syrett's *Nobody's Fault*, which narrated the option of free love and the rejection of marriage, testified to the power of fiction as an alternative means of exploration and a manifesto for change. Indeed, Beatrice Webb, writing in 1895, expressed a wistful recognition of the power of literature to change attitudes:

> For the last three months an idea had haunted me that after we have ended our shift on trade unionism I would try my hand at pure 'fiction' in the form of a novel dated 'Sixty Years Hence'. It should not be an attempt to picture a utopia. It should attempt to foreshadow society as it will be eighty years hence if we go on 'evoluting' in our humdrum way.

And Ann Veronica's father, in H.G. Wells's novel, knew where to put the blame:

> ... it's these damned novels. Those sham ideals and advanced notions, Womens Who Dids, and all that kind of thing ...

Women's voices did not, of course, form a chorus of accord at this, as at any other, period. There were many like Mrs Oliphant, Marie Corelli and, most notoriously, Mrs Eliza Lynn Linton who inveighed against these forward women, the 'anti-marriage league', who were as intent on subverting the genre of women's writing as they were the fabric of women's lives.

And there were those women whose voices were heard not in debate but in the recounting of experience. The eloquent 'New Woman', who campaigned publicly for educational opportunities and claimed the right of professional recognition and sexual freedom; who took on the medical Cassandras in challenging the essence of 'womanliness', chancing that her body would not wither on the vine if her mind was allowed full exercise; who advocated 'rational dress' and the freedom from constraint symbolized by wearing the clothes that enabled her with ease to mount and ride the newly introduced bicycle – this woman was in the vanguard of an unsettled and unsettling middle-class minority, some of whose number turned their minds to the plight of their working-class sisters.

In their own writings and in their conversations with writers and researchers, these women (and those who investigated their lives) showed the continuing hardship endured by most working-class women at the start of the twentieth century.

INTRODUCTION

The New Woman is an attempt to present a selection of women's voices from a wide spectrum of feminists, anti-feminists, observers and polemicists. The majority of extracts – whether fiction or non-fiction – fulfil the journalist W.T. Stead's criteria for 'the modern woman novel' as being:

> not merely a novel written by a woman, or a novel written about a woman, but . . . a novel written by a woman about women from the standpoint of Women.

There is, however, one male voice included: an extract from Grant Allen's influential book *The Woman Who Did*.

Brief biographical notes – where known – are given after the first excerpt from each writer's work; cross-references to other excerpts by the same author will be found on pp. vi–vii.

In reading and selecting the material for this book, I have been grateful for the suggestions of family, friends and colleagues. In particular, I should like to thank Henry Horwitz for book suggestions and book collection; Holly Jones for discussion and research; Mandy Greenfield, my editor at Collins & Brown; the staff at the London Library, where shelf upon shelf of late Victorian and Edwardian fiction reposes; and the staff at the Fawcett Library, in particular David Doughan, without whose encyclopaedic knowledge, so generously and tirelessly shared, this book – and, I suspect, many others – could not have been written.

In the absence of a bibliography, I should also like to recognize my debt to historians and literature specialists of the period, for insights and information gleaned from their books, in particular: Elanie Showalter's *Sexual Anarchy: Gender and Culture at the Fin de Siècle*; Gail Cunningham's *The New Woman and the Victorian Novel*; Judith Walkowitz's *City of Dreadful Delight: Narratives of Sexual Danger in Late-Victorian London*; the introductions to the Virago reprints of several of the novels quoted; and the invaluable *Feminist Companion to Literature in English* by Virginia Blain, Isobel Grundy and Patricia Clements.

Juliet Gardiner

CHAPTER ONE

THE 'NEW WOMAN'

'The energetic, independent woman of culture is frequently caricatured as the "New Woman",' wrote a columnist in 1902:

> The charge that has led to the development of this type
> may be summed up as the improved mental and physical
> development of the girl, necessarily accompanied by and
> leading to a different ideal for the woman.

It was this 'ideal for the woman' that was up for grabs in
the furious debate about the 'New Woman' that took place from
the 1880s – though the latter appellation does not seem to have
crystallized until the mid-1890s, coined in a debate between the
novelists Sarah Grand and Ouida.

On the one hand, the 'New Woman' was caricatured, in a
prize-winning poem published in 1894, as masculine, aggressive
and de-sexed:

She flounts love's caresses
Reforms ladies' dresses
And scorns the Man-Monster's tirade.
She seems scarcely woman
This mannish New Woman
The Queen of the Blushless Brigade.

On the other hand, Mrs Eliza Lynn Linton labelled her disdain-
fully as a 'girl of the period' and portrayed her as unwomanly in
a different way – forward, fast and assertive.

Both stereotypes conceded one thing: the representation of the
'New Woman', in life and literature, with her demands for

education, economic independence and sexual equality – and soon for the vote – offered a challenge and a threat to the established order. She threw certainties into dispute, threatened to disrupt family life as the Victorians liked to believe they had known it, and played the lord of misrule in a world turned upside-down by her demands.

She flouted conventions in dress – advocating 'rational', as opposed to restrictively 'feminine', dress, with its frills and flounces that were an inhibition to free movement and activity; in language; and in social behaviour, from smoking to free love and birth control.

The 'New Woman' was the target – if not the creation – of cartoons and satire, particularly in *Punch*, which seized upon the 'mannish woman' and, in her portrayal, pre-figured the 'flapper' of the 1920s. In literary debates she personified economic independence, occupational opportunities and, above all, sexual autonomy; for press and periodicals, she was a useful stalking-horse for disquiet about values that were in dispute, sexual anarchy and decadence, economic transformation and a new world of work that threatened male assumptions and certainties.

She was the heroine – or, if not the heroine, certainly the protagonist – of a new genre of novels, which struck particularly at marriage and for sexual emancipation. Sometimes this woman of principle and action was to be recognized not only figuring in novels but, in the case of women like Ménie Muriel Dowie and George Egerton (Mary Chavelita Dunne), writing them too – and living out their morality and lifestyles.

By the early years of the twentieth century many 'New Women' had come to believe that their grievances could best be redressed by having the vote, and by changing the social and legal conditions of their existence. As far as the opponents and the ridiculers went, the mannish 'New Women' merged easily into the 'shrieking sisterhood' of the suffragettes, for both made unacceptable demands. The label 'New Woman' faded, the experimental and utopian tenor of the writing became more overtly political and prescriptive in the work of writers like Elizabeth Robins and Cicely Hamilton, and it might have seemed that the public sphere had lost its private face. But it was not quite so, as a character in H.G. Wells's novel *Marriage*, which was published in 1912, candidly recognised:

> All the movements about us ... women have become
> human beings. Woman's come out of being a slave, and
> yet she isn't an equal ... We've had a sort of sham emanci-
> pation, and we haven't yet come to the new one.

WOMEN ADVENTURERS

Among the hoary, white old questions that go tottering down the
avenue of time, is one of an intermittent vitality truly surprising.
The Independence of Woman – is it right or wrong? – that is the
tremulous, doddering head of it. Is a woman the equal of a man?
May a woman engage in all that a man may? – those are its
withered skinny legs. Is a woman born to be free? Has a woman
a genuine or a sham intelligence? – those are its lean and palsied
arms. It is not, any way that you look at it, a very nice question,
and it comes wavering and stumbling along in the company of
many other questions as shrivelled as itself.

They form a long row in the avenue like pensioners out in the
bleak winter weather, shivering in workhouse blue. Winds play
about them and pluck at their poor hair, the winds of popular
opinion and prejudice, in angry gusts, but they huddle closer
and closer, picking their way with tired, bleary eyes, and crazy,
blundering steps.

Nothing much the matter but old age, you will say. Yet who
wouldn't be sorry for them – those old questions? See some rank,
blustering fellow come up, seize one by the shoulder, interrogate
it harshly, drag its clothes awry, expose its scarred skin, proclaim
the story of its sores to every gaping foot-passenger, while the
other feeble companion questions cling pitifully together, terri-
fied lest it be their turn next! Poor old pensioners in the avenue,
why not let them be? They lived their lives, fought out their day
while that day lasted and the fighting was still to do; why din the
tale into our younger ears? Leave their wounds warmly happed –
who out of heaven cares what was done at Navarino?

8

But no! We can't let them blink and babble out their lives on the long bench before the sunny wall, nor yet potter quietly through the winds of their last winter. We must catch them, spin them round in our midst, talk and tell of them, keep them ever in our sight, poor pensioners, to be in turn the pensioners of posterity.

Now in the comic paper by a hard-worked journalist, now in the dull review by a lady of title; there in the summer twaddle of a daily with the sunstroke; here in the organ of 'advanced' young manhood, or in the sheet of proudly retrograde young womanhood: but ever somewhere and elsewhere the poor old question is hawked and hustled! Shall a woman be allowed to wear a short dress and gaiters in a muddy street? If it were a new question put to a new race of intelligent beings without a congestion of conservatism in their brains, it would have, no doubt, one answer – Yes, if she wants to. As it is, we being as we are, and knowing what we know, and persistently refusing to know what we won't know – this little query raises howls of opinion; opens a dress exhibition; causes a host of persons to 'invent' what the calm people of the world have been wearing ever since they can remember; interviews (in various humours) a dozen notabilities, and – drops like a lucifer to sputter out in the mud of a stale and unsavoury grave.

Only that there is no death! What seems so is transition to the quiet obscurity of that institution where we keep such pensioners.

This is only one of the questions. There are hundreds like it. They sparkle, flicker, blaze like a candle-factory on fire, according to the time people have at their disposal at the moment of the inception. Then they die down to cold ashes, or smoulder like the autumn rubbish-heap in the middle of my cabbage-bed.

I would not have it imagined that I confound every question about Woman's Position – let us write it large – with what I have called the pensioners. Far from it.

There is the question of the franchise, which is a new question; which is, as it were, before the jury of the world at this moment, and as I am not summoned to give evidence I can reserve my comment. And there may be a newer question to-morrow or next week – a question arising out of recently constructed conditions, governed by novel exigencies, to be settled in accordance with modern conviction. Very plainly let it be seen I am not confusing these with the others.

But the old questions, the questions that are our pensioners, are those which have been asked and answered ever since there were men and women. And I contend that discussion of them is flatulent and stale; for to each man and woman whose action is to be affected by the answer – they are no questions at all! Without help of me this resolves itself into a paradox, which is only to say it resembles many other true things.

Shall women smoke? (This is a peculiarly wheezy old pensioner, but its cough does not seem to carry it off.) Look at a gipsy or a char-woman, or a fine black-haired old hawker. Shall she smoke? Why, she does smoke. And perhaps no one wants to question the admissibility of Meg Merrilees's short pipe.

So it is, Shall a lady smoke? It would be my firm conviction that every lady who wishes to smoke does smoke; and yet, for some people, this still remains a question, and is good for a biennial agitation inside the covers of this or that hungry journal.

Shall women propose? Well, if they can stand the risk of being accepted, surely yes. But it is a question. That is to say, that for the doing of these things no thoroughly seasoned convention has yet been constructed, and there is ever a big class clamouring for its construction.

From time to time the questions change the fashion of their headgear and the colour of their hair, and it makes a wonderful difference to them, so that they are hardly recognized by the crowd. At one time it seemed to be a question if women should go to the wars, when 'going to the wars' was the style and title of every young ambition in the country. And, as usual, the women who wanted to go went, in the face of an opposition perhaps sturdier than the oppositions of to-day, though not fitted with such fangs.

Bluster, swagger, and bounce are as healthy and as frequent as ever they were, and among the serene find as little encouragement; but genuine soldiery, martial instinct, and hardy enthusiasm for a cause, are as interesting as they are rare. There have been women who possessed them. Among the histories of these that have been found and handed to me some please me greatly. If they show less nervous courage and more power to take hard knocks, less hysteric heroism and more swashbuckling, I am the more for them . . .

Diving in dreary 'Miscellanies' of the earlier part of the eighteenth century, we may come on accounts of a good many curiously-behaved women; the unconventional woman wasn't a bit less popular then than she is now, and very little less common. Rarely, however, was she of the better class, and here is the singular and striking difference.

Unconventionality in the lower classes, more particularly in the middle class, is rarer to-day than a white blackbird; then it was apparently not infrequent. The Woman Adventurer – I employ the term in its narrowest interpretation – is, in this age of universal freedom for woman, likely to become extinct. At first sight such a statement may seem absurd, but a closer inspection of the terms will prove its truth. The Woman Adventurer is not a woman who has achieved some heroic deed (whether in men's clothes or not), nor yet the woman who has yielded to some single strange freak and left the beaten track for a little time; far from this, she is the woman with one inherent, dominating passion for adventure, for change, for surprise; the woman who keenly loves to be overtaken by unexpected situations; who dotes on predicaments, who revels in mischance. When do we hear of such a woman to-day? Never. Truly there are women of great bravery amongst us. (The Woman Adventurer is not necessarily brave.) There are women who will support unheard of toil and hardship to attain some object; women who have shown unexampled endurance among savages on desert islands, cast away at sea, or – who in the black moral pitch of great cities have swum strongly, and kept up not only their own heads, but those of the suffering strugglers they leapt in to save. But none of the qualities possessed by these noble women were required by the Woman Adventurer of the early seventeen hundreds. Read her story, and you will see she was of a light build – morally and mentally; and physically her toughness was half brag. She was of a coarse grimy sensuality; she had a gay, abandoned nature; loved men and ale; grumbled at privation, and fought her battles best over the pint pot, or in the blink of the dull oil footlights.

Search for her just now, fine female blusterer that she is, through the length and breadth of England, and I warrant she will not be found.

11

Perhaps it is as well! though I relinquish with sorrow the picturesqueness of her seeming, and the dashing poetry of her swagger. She was what she was through being ever at masquerade; she was passing for a man most of the time; his port and bearing she must imitate, or be 'discovered.' If she was discovered – she was lost. Of course!

And the women who step out of the ranks to-day and go forth adventuring, do it in all the cold seriousness of skirts, do it as women – as very earnest women – with no dash and little brag, and some rather fine purpose at the back which somehow stills the note of Adventure. So if the old spirit be gone out of it, the movement of women is freer than ever before. Allowed now to understand the world in which they live, and the conditions of its and of their own being, there is no longer any need for them to put on the garb of men in order to live, to work, to achieve, to breathe the outer air.

Woman was never freer. She may do what she will. It is the professions that are closed to her that we count, no longer those that are open. She may be a lawyer, or a doctor – and it has no element of 'adventure' in it – a writer or a painter. Hard work, rather than glittering and decorative opportunities, lies before her.

As reformer and politician, though not yet as legislator, as soldier in the army of temperance, or social regenerator, the spice, pungency, and romance she meets with are relegated to the region of the 'smart,' vicious, or impertinent newspaper paragraph.

It is the opinion of a lady to-day who has written and said much regarding the position of women, and whose views have attracted some attention even though they have been sparingly accepted, that the wise mother of the future will dress her girls and educate her girls as boys, playing off this rather ticklish experiment in the hope of opening for them a number of practical doors she supposes to be closed. Nature has not offered the lady an opportunity, or we might have watched with interest the success that waited on such a trial. In my idea, this would be to take a step backwards. An observation of women's success in public matters leads me to be certain that, for the moment, advantage lies with women as opposed to men. They do well to keep to their own clothes. An air of masculinity, however slight,

12

goes against the woman who would be successful in the eye of the public and on platforms. Her frills and her laces are, in the meantime, a weapon, or if not a weapon to fight with, at least an implement to work with. To have a character for enjoying tea and toast and the softnesses of life, to have it known that one is frightened at mice and spiders, assists greatly at the cordial reception of the most advanced intellectual display.

This is deeply to be deprecated, and no doubt some few women may personally have deprecated it, though they have not obtruded their deprecation for fear of discounting their success.

I look forward to the day when no howl of amazement, no blare of delight, will rise up whenever a woman chances to have evinced the bravery, the intelligence, or the foresight which is expected of men. In the meantime we must bow to these plaudits because they are inevitable, because preceding generations of women have persuaded preceding generations of men that bravery, foresight, and intelligence are not to be expected of women in a masculine degree: thus instances of it must stand on the side of minority and exception.

No very great degree of faith or prophecy is required to hope for and expect a period when the bulk of experience will be the other way; when the woman of the future shall have succeeded in blotting out the general impression of foolishness, cowardice, and imbecility of the woman of the past, with her own very different stamp. Then no undue notice will be taken of the fact that the human being who accomplishes something worthy or reasonable is dressed in skirts instead of trousers. It will be neither help nor hindrance to wear female clothing. Adventures may be sought, life tasted and work done, without the removal of a corset – if the women of a future day wear corsets.

Thus, on the page of to-morrow we shall find a clear signature, instead of the cross of ineptitude which has been 'Woman, her mark.'

From Women Adventurers: The Lives of Madame Velazquez, Hannah Snell, Maryanne Talbot and Mrs Christian Davies, *1893, edited by Ménie Muriel Dowie (1866–1945). Married to an MP, Sir Henry Norman, Dowie was an intrepid traveller throughout the Balkans and the author of several books, including the militantly feminist novel* Gallia *(1895).*

'THE NEW WOMAN'

Pausing on the century's threshold,
  With her face towards the dawn,
Stands a tall and radiant presence;
  In her eyes the light of morn,
On her brow the flush of knowledge
  Won in spite of curse and ban,
In her heart the mystic watchword
  Of the brotherhood of Man.

She is listening to the heart-beats
  Of the People in its pain;
She is pondering social problems
  Which appeal to heart and brain.
She is daring for the first time
  Both to think – and then to act;
She is flouting social fictions,
  Changing social lie – for FACT.

Centuries she followed blindfold
  Where her lord and master led;
Lived his faith, embraced his morals;
  Trod but where he bade her tread.
Till one day the light broke round her
  And she saw with horror's gaze,
All the filth and mire of passion
  Choking up the world's highways.

Saw the infants doomed to suffering,
  Saw the maidens, slaves to lust,
Saw the starving mothers barter
  Souls and bodies for a crust.
Saw the workers crushed by sweaters,
  Heard the cry go up 'How long?'

14

Saw the weak and feeble sink – neath
   Competition's cursed wrong.

For a moment paused she shuddering;–
   Her's in part the guilt, the blame, –
Untrue to herself and others,
   Careless of her sister's shame . . .
Then, she rose – with inward vision,
   Nerving all her powers for good;
Feeling one with suffering sisters
   In perfected womanhood.

Rising ever 'bove the struggle
   For this mortal fleeting life;
Listening to the God *within her*
   Urging Love – forbidding strife. –
Love and care for life of others
   Who with her *must* fall or rise.
This the lesson, through the ages
   Taught to her by Nature wise.

She has pondered o'er the teaching,
   She has made its truths her own;
Grasped them in their fullest meaning,
   As 'New Woman' is she known.
'Tis her enemies have baptized her,
   But she gladly claims the name;
Her's it is to make a glory,
   What was meant should be a shame.

Thinking high thoughts, living simply,
   Dignified by labour done;
Changing the old years of thraldom
   For new freedom – hardly won.
Clear-eyed, selfless, saved through knowledge,
   With her ideals fixed above,
We may greet in the 'New Woman'
   The old perfect law of Love.

By D.B.M. in Shafts, *January 1894, a 'progressive' feminist paper, advocate of vegetarianism and anti-vivisection, published between 1892 and 1900.*

IS THE NEW WOMAN A MYTH?

The remnant of the old order stand aghast, clinging affrightedly to their traditions; meanwhile the new order hastens forth eagerly, heralding and welcoming the fuller entrance of the New Era. That very word 'new,' strikes as it were the dominant note in the trend of present-day thought, present-day effort and aspiration.

It sounds out from every quarter. The new art, the new literature, the new fiction, the new journalism, the new humour, the new criticism, the new hedonism, the new morality. The very atmosphere contributes its quota. At a not long past meeting of the Royal Society, Lord Rayleigh and Professor Ramsay announced the discovery of the new element, argon. Lastly, more discussed, debated, newspaper paragraphed, caricatured, howled down and denied, or acknowledged and approved, as the case may be, than any of them, we have the new woman. The new man has not as yet lifted up announcing voice. But, doubtless, he too is coming; after whom, perhaps, the millennium followed by a new heaven and a new earth.

Of all these new facts and entities, the new woman appears to me to be immeasurably the first in importance, the most abounding in potentialities and in common interest. But before we can arrive at anything at all approximating to a decision on the questions: Is the nineteenth century new woman a myth, as so many people aver – a figment of the journalistic imagination, according to the *Spectator*? Is she, indeed, none other than an intensely aggravated type of the unwomanly, unlovable, unlovely, untidy, undomesticated, revolting, shrieking, man-hating shrew of all the centuries? Or is she on the other hand, verily an altogether new type of woman evolved from out the ages?

The genuine new woman is she who, with some of the ablest men of the century, has awakened to the fact that the time has

16

come when the work of the world in all departments has need of woman, that one sex cannot effectually and efficiently cope with the business and affairs of humanity; that in the intellectual sphere as in the physical there cannot be natural and healthy creation without the co-operation and amalgamation of all the mental attributes, male and female. The male superiority in philosophy, science, invention, and conception of abstract justice, blending with the female superiority in intuition, in altruism, and in the fuller and richer flow of the emotional life; the two half and incomplete individualities combining and forming the perfect whole. The new woman maintains that as the needs and desires of the world are not those of men alone, but are those of men, women, and children, so those needs and desires can only be naturally and effectually provided for by man and woman working harmoniously together for those ends. Not man for man and woman for woman, but man and woman for men and women. Before, however, that much to be desired consummation can be arrived at, before man and woman as peers, the complement of the other can go forward abreast and hand in hand for the world's regeneration, woman must first of all and of necessity work woman for woman. Which work, be it said, lies not altogether along smooth roads and through pleasant places, but over great time old mountains of prejudice and convention, not seldom through foul sloughs of cruel calumny and wilful misrepresentation, and always amid the jeers and jests of the unthinking mob. The genuine new woman neither asks nor desires sexual superiority or supremacy. Nor is she either ashamed or aweary of her womanhood. She is both ashamed and aweary, though of the poor puppet, too long her representative, who not alone must needs dance to the tune set for her by others, but must, not seldom, into the bargain pay the piper, and school herself to the belief that in so doing she is fulfilling her God-intended destiny, and she does claim in the name of justice to be allowed to be in all things what she was created for, a helpmate for man.

Another argument flung at the new woman is, that seeing the majority of women are quite content for things to remain exactly as they are, that they neither ask nor desire emancipation, the new woman is but making much ado about nothing. The apathy of the majority granted, but in all the great reforms throughout the course of civilization it has been given to the few alone, the pioneers, at first to see the need of reformation. The great bulk have been satisfied to remain in the same old groove. The argument might with equal force be applied to the status of women in Japan, where she is little better than a servant, where the wife dutifully kneels before her lord and master to feed him, and after that superior animal has satisfied his appetite, is graciously permitted to dine. Notwithstanding which state of things she looks very happy and is apparently contented.

Lastly, we have the objections of those who, in one and the same breath, revile woman for what she has been and is, and denounce and jeer at her for endeavouring to be something better. One of this class some time back waxed eloquently wrath on the subject of the new woman in an article in *The World* on 'Women's Clubs.' The following was the writer's solemn deliverance on the vexed question, and its sentiment is that of the vast multitude who are so steeped in conventions and traditions that any new form of truth affrights or shocks them till it too shall have acquired some few poor rags of conventionality wherewith to cover its simple nakedness withal:– 'Those are no true friends of woman who urge her to step down from the pedestal on which the concensus of the civilized world has placed her and smirch her white garments with the mire of the arena where man has to fight and toil for her.' In answer to which one naturally asks: What then are the tens of thousands of women to do who have no one to fight and toil for them in the arena; for whom in such case the pedestal means either degradation or starvation? Or what of those other tens of thousands already fallen or dragged off the pedestal – down, and kept down? Shall no woman leave her pedestal, risk smirching her white garments, risk even the smirching of her own good name, her character and purpose, in order to hold out a helping hand, if possible, to raise them up? Again, says the woman, are men able and willing to fight and toil for her so that she can stay a mere ornamental inutility on her pedestal, truly blessed and truly fulfilling her woman's destiny, according to one of our minor poets, 'by being beautiful, and wearing pretty things.' Supposing adversity and reverse of fortune overturn her and them, pedestal and all, what then awaits such a woman but

18

cruel realization of the fact that the pedestal was a lie, and that she had been cheated of her birthright – her right to be a free, reasoning, thinking, ever-forward, moving human soul? And what, moreover, if death snatch away the bread-winner, and the woman left, perchance, without even the wherewithal to pay for the washing of the white garments, with perhaps young children clinging to her, must of sheer necessity and perforce step down into the arena. All ignorant of its modes of warfare, of its very language, all unequipped either for offence or defence, will not the cheap chivalry that theorizes so glibly of the supreme sacredness of womanhood, put her through the grinding mill of competition wherein her labour will be cheapened by reason of her very womanhood? Will it not, if she fall to even lower, baser uses, bow its head with hypocritical resignation, and say: 'As it is, so it was, and so it must ever be.' The article concluded: 'Woman's true subjection is to dress. Every action of the normal woman is influenced by the possession of a pretty frock. Talk as she may of the high ideals of womanhood, her soul is nevertheless enthralled by fashions. To adorn her with feathers and fur, distant seas and continents are desolated. For her milliners, dressmakers, jewellers, and a thousand servants of extravagance and luxury exist and have their being. These are the gilded fetters with which man has bound her, which she hugs with delight, and which she will never allow her strong-minded sisters to unchain.'

There we have a realistic picture by a nineteenth century man of the world, of what he and hundreds of thousands like him are content for women to remain, of the poor doll they call a normal woman. Look at her, men and women – the woman on the pedestal, decked in furs and feathers and jewels, hugging the gilded fetters which so aptly symbolize her degradation – and say which is the likelier to be the nobler human creature, the more useful citizen, the fitter mother of children, the sweeter, more loyal helpmate for a true man – she or the new woman?

'Is the New Woman a Myth?' by C. Morgan-Dockrell in The Humanitarian, Vol. VIII, January–June 1896.

TO THE TEA-AND-TENNIS GIRL

DEAR ETHEL,

Your youthful face is suffused with a becoming glow of indignation – not unmixed with mortification – at the unseemly folly of these women who are clamouring for their 'rights.' You are so indignant, indeed, that you are scuttling as fast and as publicly as possible away from them, and would disclaim your association with their sex if you could: that being impossible, you can at least avow your distaste for their ideas and your utter lack of desire for any of the things for which they are shouting so rudely, and with such a complete lack of attractiveness or charm. In short, you desire to emphasize as strongly as you can that you don't want independence and you do want Man, and whatever he wants from you, you are prepared to supply.

Dear little girl: you are young and simple, and you are showing a healthy natural instinct which calls out for a mate. And because you have been trained in certain conventions, you think – quite naturally – that the best possible chance of attracting a mate is by showing him, with almost feverish haste, that *you* are his ideal, you are the woman whom he wants, you haven't any ideas in your head about dry things like votes, or responsibilities to the community, or moral questions. You flutter out, in short, at the sound of war-cries, like a crowd of pretty frightened pigeons, crying, 'We don't belong to that camp. We are the real old-fashioned frivolous girls. We look up to men and are ready to obey them, and think they are much, much, much the superior being: and we don't want to govern anyone, and we like being governed, and we don't want any responsibility or any interests outside our parents' home ... and ... and some day a dear little home of our own ... and dear little children!'

Poor frightened little pigeons, scurrying so pathetically about! For the young men who are talking so loudly in the train take precisely no more notice of you than they did before: and they continue to go on taking notice of the waitresses and barmaids and pretty clerks whom they meet in their daily life, and with whom they feel on terms of perfect freedom; while the stage still exercises its enormous fascination, and the smile of a queen of the *coulisses* still confers high honour, something to be boasted of and flaunted in Club or restaurant.

And they display exactly the same repugnance to attending your tea-parties, and they are as increasingly difficult to secure for your dances, and just as shy of dancing when you get them there, and the competition is every bit as hard . . . even harder: for a new factor has crept in, the competition of comradeship!

And here I do think you deserve sympathy. For Man – that rascally, hypocritical, turn-coat Man to whom you are offering yourself so wholly and with such entire devotion – is positively making himself agreeable to those independent, unsexed young women who are entering his professions, speaking at public dinners, taking their share in the responsibilities of Club life, forming societies for the advancement of mutual male and female interests, and sharing his work and freedom. The least that Man can do to stamp out these shameless rebels is to show his personal disgust of them as individuals.

He is doing nothing of the kind.

Instead, he is positively frequenting their society. He lunches, teas, and dines with them at their unfeminine and independent institutions – *clubs* – showing his preference, indeed, with astonishing emphasis, for these abandoned haunts to that of the rigid family drawing-room which his 'ideal' inhabits; positively seeming to prefer the companionship of the girl herself to that of the girl and her sheltering family! He talks about his men-friends to these girls, and introduces them. They even make up parties together, meet at Club, studio, or rooms, go [on] expeditions. At college, even, the learned girl students are admired and sought with just as much avidity – even more so – as if they possessed the minimum of your intelligence. These unsexed, though outwardly presentable, young females are invited to the College dances, and instead of standing partnerless, despised and mocked as an object-lesson to the home-girls, who have flocked up for the Mays, behold them surrounded with renegade young men, their friends and co-workers from lecture-room and laboratory, who show every appearance of delighting in their acquaintance.

And the galling part of the whole thing is that these brazen

21

young women are deliberately and openly disavowing all man's conceptions and wishes of what they ought to be doing and thinking. They are pursuing keen interests of their own, and while they appear to appreciate man's attention and companionship (the hussies!), they are certainly not devoting their lives to obtaining it. In fact, they appear to be paying very little attention to what he wants or desires at all.

Though they have not reached the impudent assertiveness of the American girl . . .

There is another shock! Who could be more brazenly defiant of man's laws than that apparition which flashes to our shores in hundreds, returning with the pick of our peerage and the furtive homage of every grade of Englishman? If the reign of the American girl is not so unquestioned as it was ten years ago, it is because she is being overtaken by the English girls who have followed in her footsteps, and become as bright, intelligent, and independent . . . the English girls who have gone out into the world of men and found the humbugs as appreciative of their pluck as of their American cousins. Poor little tea-and-tennis girls, alone in the evening practising in a gas-chandeliered drawing-room, with papa and mamma snoring in the dining-room, and your brothers . . . 'out' . . . just that! Mysteriously 'out'! Poor little tea-and-tennis girl! Handing cake as a religious rite at your mother's At Home days, or 'calling,' nicely gloved and best frocked, every afternoon at similar functions, to sit in an atmosphere of matronly femininity and discuss ailments, servants, local gossip, and now and then the latest novel, struggled for at the local circulating-library: and all the time with the dismal consciousness of the awful waste of time: for by no chance will the young men you are hunting be discovered there. For you know . . . and, alas! your mother knows it, too . . . your brother and his friends would be cheerfully shot before they would face the ordeal: they plead they're too busy. Yet, if an invitation came from the pretty little fashion-artist, or the smart young journalist, or even that wise, amusing woman-author (forty, if a day) those same young men would appear (rather suppressed, perhaps, and without the patronage that exudes from them when they grace by any chance *your* tennis-tea, but otherwise quite cheerful) to partake of tea at the 'impossible' hour of five o'clock, at the 'unfeminine' institution haunted by the shameless independent ones, and called their 'club.'

Well, little tea-and-tennis girl, it *is* unfair; and I could quite understand if a revolution rose up in your midst, and you all indignantly asked Man what he meant by it, and would he kindly say what he really did want, for at present his actions surely controverted his behests.

To which, alas! might come the brutal answer – if he were provoked by your rebellion, for unquestioning submission to him is his first law – that you wanted him very much more than he did you: and that, though his ideal wife was still as he described, you wanted marriage very much more than he did: and he was very sorry, but it was nature, and could not be helped, and the only proper thing for you to do under the circumstances was to keep quiet and patient, and go on being just what he wanted you to be, till one of you captured his fancy. He might also add benignly that if you wanted occupation there was no harm in your making yourself as pretty and as domestically useful as possible, as, of course, the prettier and more capable you were, the more likely he was to throw the handkerchief; but however keenly you desired him, you were on no account to run after him or show your desire, as that was unmaidenly and unbecoming, and he hated being chivvied.

And that, dear little tea-and-tennis girl, would be all the real actual satisfaction you would get: though this plain statement would, of course, be put in a pretty dress of sentiment about 'woman, the angel of the house,' 'the sanctity of the home,' 'the power of woman's indirect influence,' 'the potency of mystery between the sexes,' 'the ennobling influence of purity,' and so forth: we have neither the time nor patience to put the words together: but read this letter to any average man, and he will produce the dress of sentiment immediately.

And now, because you are an English girl, and it is not the English nature to take insults lying down, you are getting very angry, and are saying that men are selfish brutes.

But now let us look at the matter quietly and reasonably, for, believe me, you are quite wrong to be angry, and it is just as natural for the young man of your acquaintance to fly from you as it is for you – in your present conditions – to pursue.

23

For it isn't you he objects to. Meet him in a country house, or abroad, or anywhere where circumstances bring you simply and naturally together, and you will find him protective, chivalrous, and simply appreciative of your company. No: it isn't you he flies from: he flies from the trap at whose entrance your prettiness is placed as decoy-bait.

He dare not come and visit you in your parents' home! He knows too well that your whole thoughts are bent on matrimony, and that every word and act of his will be watched by a battery of eyes to see if he 'means anything.' And he gets nervous!

That's the whole truth of it! He is not prepared to commit himself, and he is afraid that a word may be misconstrued, or that if he evinces any interest in you he may be rushed into an engagement . . . that it will be 'expected' of him!

So he turns with obvious relief to the companionship of women who aren't watching every movement in the hope of seeing an indication of 'intentions,' or finding a weak spot where they can attack and capture. And he leaves you in rather humiliating isolation.

Well, little tea-and-tennis girl, it is not only unfair . . . but even silly . . . for him to encourage you so much verbally to do just what he doesn't want you to. But that is not his fault so much as the fault of his conservative ideals: and if his sentimentality is somewhat bewildering, you can take comfort in the fact that in his heart no one has a keener sense of justice or more true reverence for all that is brave and fearless and independent than this perplexing young man.

For he is even generous in the recognition of the pluck of his enemies! He may hate the suffragettes who are bullying him so unmercifully, but he takes off his hat all the same to their courage, whether he is policeman or editor or man in the street: and for all that he says about his dislike of women's independence, directly you sally out into the field of battle you will find him, to your amazement, a splendid friend, a loyal comrade, and most implicitly respectful . . . to all that is worthy of respect.

For though oriental ideals have been grafted to some extent on our social system, the English Man is not in the least oriental in his nature. He is neither slave nor tyrant. Freedom is as the breath of life to him: and when he understands that you need and want it, he will help you to gain it, and he will not love you any the less for having it.

In short, you have only to concentrate on making the very most and best of your qualities: on thinking out your duties and responsibilities, and bravely and earnestly fulfilling them, whether personal, civic, or political; and you will find that no one will appreciate you more, help you more, or be prouder of you than the young men who are upholding a long defunct ideal on one hand and the modern independent woman on the other; while they turn their backs altogether on you.

No understanding them? My dear, don't try to. Just let them alone!

From Woman: A Few Shrieks, *1907, by 'X' (Constance Smedley, 1881–1941), an illustrator and novelist. The first of her twenty or so novels,* An April Princess, *was published in 1903. In 1909 she married Maxwell Armfield and together they ran a drama school. In 1914 Smedley founded an international chain of women's clubs to cater for 'professional women of limited means'.*

WAS E'ER A ROSE WITHOUT ITS THORN?

Fate had thought fit to deny me even one advantage or opportunity, thus I was helpless. I set to work to cut my coat according to my cloth. I manfully endeavoured to squeeze my spirit into 'that state of life into which it has pleased God to call me'. I crushed, compressed, and bruised, but as fast as I managed it on one side it burst out on another, and defied me to cram it into the narrow box of Possum Gully.

The restless throbbings and burnings
    That hope unsatisfied brings,
The weary longings and yearnings
    For the mystical better things,
Are the sands on which is reflected
    The pitiless moving lake,

Where the wanderer falls dejected,
  By a thirst he never can slake.

In a vain endeavour to slake that cruel thirst my soul groped
in strange dark places. It went out in quest of a God, and finding
one not, grew weary.

By the unknown way that the atmosphere of the higher life
penetrated to me, so came a knowledge of the sin and sorrow
abroad in the world – the cry of the millions oppressed, down-
trodden, God-forsaken! The wheels of social mechanism needed
readjusting – things were awry. Oh, that I might find a cure and
give it to my fellows! I dizzied my brain with the problem; I was too
much for myself. A man with these notions is a curse to himself,
but a woman – pity help a woman of that description! She is not
merely a creature out of her sphere, she is a creature without a
sphere – a lonely being!

Recognizing this, I turned and cursed God for casting upon
me a burden greater than I could bear – cursed Him bitterly,
and from within came a whisper that there was nothing there
to curse. There was no God. I was an unbeliever. It was not
that I sought after or desired atheism. I longed to be a Christian,
and fought against unbelief. I asked the Christians around me for
help. Unsophisticated fool! I might as well have announced that
I was a harlot. My respectability vanished in one slap. Some said
it was impossible to disbelieve in the existence of a God: I was
only doing it for notoriety, and they washed their hands of me
at once.

Not believe in God! I was mad!

If there really was a God, would they kindly tell me how
to find Him?

Pray! pray!

I prayed, often and ardently, but ever came that heart-stilling
whisper that there was nothing to pray to.

Ah, the bitter, hopeless heart-hunger of godlessness none but
an atheist can understand! Nothing to live for in life – no hope
beyond the grave. It plunged me into fits of profound melancholy.

Had my father occupied one of the fat positions of the
land, no doubt as his daughter my life would have been so
full of pleasant occupation and pleasure that I would not have

developed the spirit which torments me now. Or had I a friend – one who knew, who had suffered and understood, one in whom I could lose myself, one on whom I could lean – I might have grown a nicer character. But in all the wide world there was not a soul to hold out a hand to me, and I said bitterly, 'There is no good in the world.' In softer moods I said, 'Ah, the tangle of it! Those who have the heart to help have not the power, and those who have the power have not the heart.'

Bad, like a too-strong opponent in a game of chess, is ever at the elbow of good to checkmate it like a weakly managed king.

I am sadly lacking in self-reliance. I needed some one to help me over the rough spots in life, and finding them not, at the age of sixteen I was as rank a cynic and infidel as could be found in three days' march.

From My Brilliant Career, *1901, by Miles Franklin (1879–1954). Franklin's publisher omitted the questionmark in the title, softened the book's criticism of Victorian Australian society and woman's place in it, and, against her wishes, revealed that the author was a woman.*

THANK HEAVEN FOR THE NEW WOMAN!

Thank heaven for the New Woman! Not the woman who is but a travesty of man, she is a mere ephemeral eruption on the face of progress, an eruption that will shortly fade and show the world a new complexion of things.

The veritable New Woman is at present training in our colleges, teaching in our schools, serving in our hospitals, guardianing the poor and pitiful, cycling along our roads – in all of which capacities she is broadening her horizon, facing human facts, treading conventions and social fetishism under foot, learning to be a human unit rather than a social cipher.

She will presently emerge a fine free creature, equal to, yet unlike her fellow, with a mind pure in its enlightened breadth, with emotions full and tender, with a frame whose sensitiveness is tempered and not toughened by liberty and use.

In that day her healthful mind and body shall know love for that which Nature intended, the highest issue to which life lifts, for out of it human souls leap toward perfection, on its right understanding evolution turns.

'The Dignity of Love' by Arabella Kenealy in The Humanitarian, *Vol. VIII, January–June 1896.*

LYNDALL

'Don't you wish you were a woman, Waldo?'

'No,' he answered readily.

'I thought not . . . I never met a man who did . . . It is delightful to be a woman; but every man thanks the Lord devoutly that he isn't one.'

They reached the next camp.

'Let us sit at this camp and watch the birds,' she said, as an ostrich hen came bounding towards them, with velvety wings outstretched, while far away over the bushes the head of the cock was visible as he sat brooding on the eggs . . .

'I like these birds,' she said; 'they share each other's work and are companions . . .

'This one thought stands – never goes – if I might but be one of those born in the future; then, perhaps, to be born a woman will not be to be born branded . . .

'It is not what is done to us, but what is made of us, what wrongs us. No man can be really injured but by what modifies himself. We all enter the world little plastic beings, with so much natural force, perhaps, but for the rest – blank, and the world tells us what we are to be, and shapes us by the ends it sets before us. To you it says – *Work*; and to us it says – *Seem*! To you it says – As you approximate to man's highest ideal of God, as your arm is strong and your knowledge great, and the power to labour is with you, so you shall gain all that human heart desires. To us it says – Strength shall not help you, nor knowledge, nor labour. You shall gain what men gain, but by other means. And so the world makes men and women.

'Look at this little chin of mine, with the dimple in it. It is but a small part of my person; but though I had a knowledge of all things under the sun, and the wisdom to use it, and the deep loving heart of an angel, it would not stead me through life like this little chin. I can win money with it, I can win love; I can win power with it, I can win fame. What would knowledge help me? The less a woman has in her head the lighter she is for climbing. I once heard an old man say, that he never saw intellect help a woman so much as a pretty ankle; and it was the truth. They begin to shape us to our cursed end when we are tiny things in shoes and socks. We sit with our little feet drawn up under us in the window, and look out at the boys in their happy play. We want to go. Then a loving hand is laid on us: "Little one, you cannot go," they say; "your little face will burn, and your nice white dress be spoiled." We feel it must be for our good, it is so lovingly said; but we cannot understand; and we kneel still with one little cheek wistfully pressed against the pane. Afterwards we go and thread blue beads, and make a string for our neck; and we go and stand before the glass. We see the complexion we were not to spoil, and the white frock, and we look into our own great eyes. Then the curse begins to act on us. It finishes its work when we are grown women, who no more look out wistfully at a more healthy life; we are contented . . . In some of us the shaping to our end has been quite completed. The parts we are not to use have been quite atrophied, and have even dropped off; but in others, and we are not less to be pitied, they have been weakened and left. We wear the bandages, but our limbs have not grown to them; we know that we are compressed, and chafe against them.

'But what does it help? A little bitterness, a little longing, when we are young, a little futile searching for work, a little passionate striving for room for the exercise of our powers, – and then we go with the drove. A woman must march with her regiment. In the end she must be trodden down or go with it; and if she is wise she goes.

29

... 'We stand here at this gate this morning, both poor, both young, both friendless; there is not much to choose between us. Let us turn away just as we are to make our way in life. This evening you will come to a farmer's house. The farmer, albeit you come alone and on foot, will give you a pipe of tobacco and a cup of coffee and a bed. If he has no dam to build and no child to teach, to-morrow you can go on your way with a friendly greeting of the hand. I, if I come to the same place to-night, will have strange questions asked me, strange glances cast on me. The Boer-wife will shake her head and give me food to eat with the Kaffirs, and a right to sleep with the dogs. That would be the first step in our progress – a very little one, but every step to the end would repeat it. We were equals once when we lay new-born babes on our nurse's knees. We will be equals again when they tie up our jaws for the last sleep ...

'Mark you,' she said, 'we have always this advantage over you – we can at any time step into ease and competence, where you must labour patiently for it. A little weeping, a little wheedling, a little self-degradation, a little careful use of our advantages, and then some man will say "Come, be my wife!" With good looks and youth marriage is easy to attain. There are men enough: but a woman who has sold herself, even for a ring and a new name, need hold her skirt aside for no creature in the street. They both earn their bread one way. Marriage for love is the beautifullest external symbol of the union of souls; marriage without it is the uncleanliest traffic that defiles the world.' ... 'And they tell us we have men's chivalrous attention!' she cried. 'When we ask to be doctors, lawyers, law-makers, anything but ill-paid drudges, they say, – "No; but you have men's chivalrous attention; now think of that and be satisfied! What would you do without it?" ...

'I was coming up in Cobb and Cobb's the other day. At a little wayside hotel we had to change the large coach for a small one. We were ten passengers, eight men and two women. As I sat in the house the gentlemen came and whispered to me, "There is not room for all in the new coach, take your seat quickly." We hurried out, and they gave me the best seat, and covered me with rugs, because it was drizzling. Then the last passenger came running to the coach – an old woman with a wonderful bonnet, and a black shawl pinned with a yellow pin.

' "There is no room," they said; "you must wait till next week's coach takes you up"; but she climbed on to the step, and held on at the window with both hands.

' "My son-in-law is ill, and I must go and see him," she said.

' "My good woman," said one, "I am really exceedingly sorry that your son-in-law is ill; but there is absolutely no room for you here."

' "You had better get down," said another, "or the wheel will catch you."

'I got up to give her my place.

' "Oh no, no!" they cried, "we will not allow that."

' "I will rather kneel," said one, and he crouched down at my feet; so the woman came in.

'There were nine of us in that coach, and only one showed chivalrous attention – and that was a woman to a woman.

'I shall be old and ugly too one day, and I shall look for men's chivalrous help, but I shall not find it.

'The bees are very attentive to the flowers till their honey is done, and then they fly over them. I don't know if the flowers feel grateful to the bees; they are great fools if they do.'

'But some women have power,' said Waldo . . .

'Power! Did you ever hear of men being asked whether other souls should have power or not? It is born in them. You may dam up the fountain of water, and make it a stagnant marsh, or you may let it run free and do its work; but *you* cannot say whether it shall be there: *it is there*. And it will act, if not openly for good, then covertly for evil; but it will act. If Goethe had been stolen away a child, and reared in a robber horde in the depths of a German forest, do you think the world would have had "Faust" and "Iphigenie"? But he would have been Goethe still – stronger, wiser than his fellows. At night, round their watch-fire, he would have chanted wild songs of rapine and murder, till the dark faces about him were moved, and trembled. His songs would have echoed on from father to son, and nerved the heart and arm – for evil. Do you think if Napoleon had been born a woman that he would have been contented to give small tea-parties and talk small scandal? He would have risen; but the world would not have heard of him as it hears of him now – a man, great and kingly, with all his sins; he would have left one of those names that stain the

31

leaf of every history – the names of women, who, having power, but being denied the right to exercise it openly, rule in the dark, covertly, and by stealth, through the men whose passions they feed on, and by whom they climb.

'Power! . . . Yes, we have power; and since we are not to expend it in tunneling mountains, nor healing diseases, nor making laws, nor money, nor on any extraneous object, we expend it on *you*. You are our goods, our merchandise, our material for operating on; we buy you, we sell you, we make fools of you, we act the wily old Jew with you, we keep six of you crawling to our little feet, and praying only for a touch of our little hand; and they say truly, there was never an ache or a pain or a broken heart but a woman was at the bottom of it. We are not to study law, nor science, nor art; so we study you. There is never a nerve or fibre in your man's nature but we know it . . .

'They bring weighty arguments against us when we ask for the perfect freedom of woman. . . but, when you come to the objections, they are like pumpkin-devils with candles inside; hollow, and can't bite. They say that women do not wish for the sphere and freedom we ask for them and would not use it!

'If the bird *does* like its cage, and *does* like its sugar and will not leave it, why keep the door so very carefully shut? Why not open it, only a little? Do they know there is many a bird will not break its wings against the bars, but would fly if the doors were open . . .

'Then they say, "If the women have the liberty you ask for, they will be found in positions for which they are not fitted!" If two men climb one ladder, did you ever see the weakest anywhere but at the foot? The surest sign of fitness is success. The weakest never wins, but where there is handicapping. Nature left to herself will as beautifully apportion a man's work to his capacities as long ages ago she graduated the colours on the bird's breast. If we are not fit, you give us to no purpose the right to labour; the work will fall out of our hands into those that are wiser.' . . .

'They say women have one great and noble work left them, and they do it ill. – That is true; they do it execrably. It is the work that demands the broadest culture, and they have not even the narrowest. The lawyer may see no deeper than his law-books, and the chemist see no further than the windows of his laboratory,

32

and they may do their work well. But the woman who does woman's work needs a many sided, multiform culture; the heights and depths of human life must not be beyond the reach of her vision; she must have knowledge of men and things in many states, a wide catholicity of sympathy, the strength that springs from knowledge, and the magnanimity which springs from strength. *We* bear the world, and *we* make it. The souls of little children are marvellously delicate and tender things, and keep for ever the shadow that first falls on them, and that is the mother's or at best a woman's. There was never a great man who had not a great mother – it is hardly an exaggeration. The first six years of our life make us; all that is added later is veneer; and yet some say, if a woman can cook a dinner or dress herself well she has culture enough.

'The mightiest and noblest of human work is given us, and we do it ill. Send a navvy to work into an artist's studio, and see what you will find there! And yet, thank God, we have this work . . . it is the one window through which we see into the great world of earnest labour. The meanest girl who dances and dresses becomes something higher when her children look up into her face and ask her questions. It is the only education we have and which they cannot take from us . . .

'They say that we complain of woman being compelled to look upon marriage as a profession; but that she is free to enter upon it or leave it as she pleases.

'Yes – and a cat set afloat in a pond is free to sit in the tub till it dies there, it is under no obligation to wet its feet; and a drowning man may catch at a straw or not, just as he likes – it is a glorious liberty! Let any man think for five minutes of what old maidenhood means to a woman – and then let him be silent. Is it easy to bear through life a name that in itself signifies defeat? To dwell, as nine out of ten unmarried must, under the finger of another woman? Is it easy to look forward to an old age without honour, without the reward of useful labour, without love? I wonder how many men there are who would give up everything that is dear in life for the sake of maintaining a high ideal purity . . .

'And then, when they have no other argument against us, they say – "Go on; but when you have made women what you wish, and her children inherit her culture, you will defeat

yourself. Man will gradually become extinct from excess of intellect, the passions which replenish, the race will die." Fools! . . .
A Hottentot sits at the roadside and feeds on a rotten bone he
has found there, and takes out his bottle of Cape-smoke and
swills at it, and grunts with satisfaction; and the cultured child
of the nineteenth century sits in his arm-chair, and sips choice
wines with the lip of a connoisseur, and tastes delicate dishes
with a delicate palate, and with a satisfaction of which the
Hottentot knows nothing. Heavy jaw and sloping forehead – all
have gone with increasing intellect; but the animal appetites are
there still – refined, discriminative, but immeasurably intensified.
Fools! Before men forgave or worshipped, while they were still
weak on their hind legs, did they not eat, and fight for wives?
When all the later additions to humanity have vanished, will not
the foundation on which they are built remain? . . .

'They ask, "What will you gain, even if man does not become
extinct? – you will have brought justice and equality on to the
earth, and sent love from it. When men and women are equals
they will love no more. Your highly-cultured women will not be
lovable, will not love.'

'Do they see nothing, understand nothing? . . . It is the hard-
headed, deep thinker who, when the wife who has thought and
worked with him goes, can find no rest, and lingers near her till
he finds sleep beside her.

'A great soul draws and is drawn with a more fierce intensity
than any small one. By every inch we grow in intellectual height
our love strikes down its roots deeper, and spreads out its arms
wider. It is for love's sake yet more than for any other that we look
for that new time . . . Then when that time comes . . . when love
is no more bought or sold, when it is not a means of making bread,
when each woman's life is filled with earnest, independent labour,
then love will come to her, a strange sudden sweetness breaking
in upon her earnest work; not sought for, but found. Then, but
not now – '

From The Story of an African Farm, *1883, by Olive Schreiner
(1855–1920), her partly autobiographical novel, published under
the name 'Ralph Iron'. It brought the South African writer, femin-*

ist and pacifist into contact with leading British free-thinkers, such as Havelock Ellis, Edward Carpenter, Karl Pearson and Eleanor Marx.

THE LIFE HISTORY OF MARY SMITH, M.A.

I – AT SCHOOL

Mary began her education at the local high school. She soon made a name for herself as a star of rare intellectual brilliance. One examination success followed another, prizes rained thick upon her, and she promised, therefore, to attain to a standard of high moral excellence.

The head mistress said at the prize-giving: 'We desire above all things so to build up the character of the young people committed to our charge, that they may, in these days of moral laxity, stand firm for all the great guiding principles of life.' (Great applause.)

From this it will be seen that the head mistress was a wise woman. Moreover, she was a diplomat of no mean order. She marked Mary out for special approval, and held her up as an example to the other students. She knew that there is no more effective way of advertising a school and increasing the number of its pupils (for the numbers of a school are, of course, a sure criterion of the excellence of its teaching) than by a continuous stream of examination successes. Mary had done admirable service as an advertising medium, and the head mistress meant her to cap it all by winning that most distinguished of all distinctions – a scholarship to the University. It was true that Mary was puny, undeveloped, overworked, and be-spectacled, but what was that in comparison with the 'kudos' she gained for the school? 'Besides, bodily health is as nothing in comparison with intellectual growth,' said the head mistress to those members of the staff who hinted at the danger of overwork.

There was a certain amount of opposition to be overcome

before a University career was finally settled upon. Mr. Smith wished his daughter to live at home and settle down 'like a sensible girl.' He visited the head mistress, with considerable trepidation, be it said, to tell her so.

'The fact of the matter is,' he said, 'Mary seems to hate her home. She is always at school on some pretext or another, and it seems to me if she goes to college, it will make her more unsettled than ever. I'm an old-fashioned man, and I think a woman's place is the home,' he added, shamefacedly.

'I quite agree with you,' said the head mistress. 'I always tell the girls that a woman's highest vocation is that of a wife and mother. But surely a woman cannot hope to be a real helpmate to a man unless she has received the best intellectual and moral training. The masculine standard in those respects is very high, you know, and we want our girls to try and attain it.'

Finally Mr. Smith, after begging the head mistress to use her influence with Mary to induce her to pay more attention to her appearance, gave his consent to the scheme.

On the last day of her last term, Mary went into the head mistress's study to say good-bye.

'Mary,' said her mentor, 'life is a great responsibility and meant for work. See that you make the best of it. Shun frivolity and have a serious purpose ever before your eyes. When you leave college, you will, I hope, take up a profession. No woman should be content to be a mere parasite upon her father. It detracts from her dignity. Women can now take their proper place in the vanguard of progress.

'You should develop into a woman of intellect, and as such make your mark in the world. Choose a career, and think well before you renounce it for matrimony. A highly gifted woman is wasted when she marries.'

Mary certainly had no intention of marrying. Boys and men did not interest her, except in so far as they were rivals to be vanquished.

She left school at the age of eighteen, and had a nervous breakdown in the holidays.

II – AT COLLEGE

Mary in due course entered into residence at St. Christabel's College. She and her fellow-students, some 150 in number, were preparing to regenerate an effete and old-fashioned civilization by the infusion of new ideals, under feminine inspiration and guidance.

To reform life, you must know life; to raise human beings to a higher standard of civic and ethical morality, you must understand them. So Mary and her companions read learned treatises, attended lectures, passed examinations, played games, fell ill from overwork, thus gaining much valuable knowledge of human nature. Altogether they gave every promise of becoming efficient citizens.

The discovered that the world was in a very unsatisfactory condition, and that women, especially those who had gained a knowledge and understanding of life by means of the higher education, must put it to rights again. Men had made a hopeless mess of things; indeed, it was hard to see why they should exist at all. The world without them would be a much pleasanter place to live in. However, their presence could be ignored in the precincts of St. Christabel's, and the students, with their attendant dons, debated the problems of life, undisturbed by masculine intrusion.

Mary studied mathematics – a subject calculated to make clear the workings of the human mind; eminently suitable, therefore, for a future efficient citizen. She knew all there was to know about dimensions, and was on the point of discovering a new one, when she had a nervous breakdown. This was a pity, because it is obvious to the meanest intelligence, that an extra dimension would have completely altered the affairs of life. As it was, her mathematical studies enabled her to reduce that most illogical of all factors, the human one, to terms of a common denominator. This simplified life so much that she felt she could face every difficulty.

She also took up science, so that she might take the scientific, viz., the right, view of things.

She joined as many of the college societies as time allowed, selecting those avowedly serious in purpose and likely, therefore, to help her to take the best line in matters of political and social import. Her ideals were high, and she meant to leave the world a better place than she found it. A mock House of Commons always sat in term-time, and Mary was the leader of the Liberal party. Questions affecting women were warmly discussed, and each party, when in power, vied with the other in passing legislation favourable to their interests.

There was not much enthusiasm or interest shown in other and more general matters which touched on the welfare of the community as a whole. It was rightly felt that men could be trusted to look after themselves, but that they must not be allowed to look after women, whom they invariably oppressed.

What Mary lacked in appearance she made up for in learning. Like one of her mathematical lines, she had length and no breadth. Her father was distressed, and told her plainly that if she didn't look out, she wouldn't get married.

'Married!' gasped Mary, 'you don't suppose I'm going to marry. Why, all my education would be wasted.'

'Wait till Mr. Wright comes along,' said Mr. Smith.

Mary flushed. Her father jarred on her sometimes.

Before going down from college for good, she gave a farewell tea-party to a few students and one or two dons. The conversation turned upon matrimony.

'I can't understand any self-respecting woman getting married,' said one student. 'The most hard-worked and ill-paid of all professions.'

'Yes,' agreed Mary. 'A man pays his housekeeper, so why shouldn't he pay his wife? She toils and slaves from morning till night, and gets nothing for it.'

'And then,' chimed in a third, 'think how a clever, well-educated woman wastes her gifts and opportunities for good work if she marries. Her life, to all intents and purposes, is over, and the community is the poorer for her loss.'

'It is only second-rate women who marry nowadays,' said a don, high-souled and serious-minded. 'We intellectual women have learnt to regulate our affections and subordinate our hearts to our heads. That is why the position of women has more dignity and importance than it had. We lead the way, others follow.'

At the end of four years, Mary came down from College laden with honours and certificates.

Her brother refused to go with her.

'I never saw such a fright as you, Mary,' he said. 'You're a learned pig.'

Mary didn't care. Why should she? He was only a man.

III – As a Politician

Mary was twenty-two at the conclusion of her residence at St. Christabel's College. Her knowledge of science and the higher mathematics proved her to be efficient; it only remained for her to assume the rôle of citizen, for which she had had so admirable and suitable a preparation.

As a preliminary, she told her father she could not live at home; it was too limited and narrow in outlook. Mr. Smith pointed out that he had no desire to interfere with what she did. He had not the smallest intention of dismissing the maids and asking her to do the housework instead; that he would like her companionship when she had any spare time; that he was quite in favour of Woman Suffrage. He would buy her as many dresses as she liked.

Mary interrupted him. 'You don't understand, father,' she said. 'Women have serious work to do in the world now. No thinking person can be interested in such banalities as clothes. Am I a doll that I should care about such things? I can't live at home – the atmosphere is so unintellectual, and Charlie (her brother) *will* bring in his friends. Young men are so dull and not in the least interested in matters of vital importance. Besides. I must be in the centre of things in order that I can devote all my energies to the great progressive movements of the day.'

Mary took rooms in a residential club in London, much frequented by the leading Feminists. She associated herself, of course, with the party of Progress and Reform, and joined all the Liberal associations she could think of. She quite understood that the will of the people must prevail. Consequently, she was a warm supporter of such legislative proposals as the Payment of Members, the State Insurance, and the Home Rule Bills, which had been greeted with the unanimous and warm approval of the whole nation. At least they ought to have been, and that is the same thing. If Demos is occasionally blind to his own interests, he must be forcibly guided along the right path by those who have the light. She was also a firm believer in the virtue of total abstinence. 'Rare, refreshing fruits' are an admirable democratic diet, provided they are not in a state of fermentation. In that condition, they are a curse and no blessing. Their sale and consumption should be prohibited. The nation must be raised to a higher moral plane.

In short, Mary stood by the party which was founded upon and lived up to that great fundamental principle of Liberalism – Government of the People, by the People, for the People. Naturally, however, she devoted most of her time and energy to hastening on that great day when she and her friends should become persons in the eyes of the law. For that consummation she worked hard. As efficient citizens, armed with the vote, they would be able to cleanse the Augean stables of a corrupt and man-governed state.

'New brooms sweep clean' was the title of an address which Mary gave, one Sunday afternoon, at a chapel P.S.A. By introducing the parable of the new wine in old bottles, she was able to give the necessary religious touch to her oratory. She pointed out that the introduction of politics into the pulpit was a sure sign of the advancement of Christian progressive thought.

The club where Mary lived was one of the headquarters of the Militant Suffragists, of whom she was one.

At a breakfast given in her honour, following on a sojourn in Holloway Gaol, after she had broken man-made laws and windows, one of the leaders of the cause made a highly eulogistic speech. 'I call upon all true women to pay their homage to Miss Mary Smith,' she said. 'She has helped to make men understand that women no longer consent to be their slaves. In a free country we too will be free and independent. Men only won their political liberty by acts of violence, and we will show them that we are as determined as they. By doing as they have done, we assert our own independence, and show that we will no longer be content to follow them in servile docility. We are not the gentle, timid, unselfish creatures it is to their advantage to represent us. We are soldiers in a sacred cause. It is war to the knife.'

Mary glowed.

IV – As Many Things

When she was twenty-four, Mary, encouraged by her former head mistress and other instructresses, made up her mind to adopt a profession.

How could she justly claim to be an efficient citizen, with its corollary, the right to be recognized as a person in the eyes of the law, unless she received money for her services? She decided to become a schoolmistress. In this way, whilst receiving a salary, she would be able, by her influence and teaching, to add fresh recruits to the army of serious-minded women ready to carry on the great fight for progress and reform.

Her father protested as usual.

'Look here, Mary,' he said. 'You profess to be working for the woman's cause. Yet, by taking up paid work, when you needn't do so, you are probably keeping another woman out of work, entirely dependent, perhaps, on what she may be able to earn. The best work is not necessarily that which has a money-wage attached. Why not go on with your unpaid work?'

'Father,' replied Mary, 'I must assert my dignity as an individual. I cannot be a parasite upon you. I must have economic independence.'

'Economic independence be hanged!' growled her father. 'Why is it more dignified to take money from an employer than from a father?'

Mary did not waste more time in futile argument. She took up a post in a London High School.

Now that she no longer lived at home, she was able to adopt a vegetarian diet. How could one be spiritual-minded and actuated by lofty ideals if one fed on such coarse and degrading diet as the flesh of slaughtered animals? Besides, men were almost invariably meat-eaters and gross feeders generally. No wonder they were so unspiritual and slow to appreciate the great work of regenerating society which highly educated women were heroically and devotedly undertaking in the face of great difficulties.

41

So Mary lived on the fruits of the earth and the products of Mr. Eustace Miles' Restaurant. She got very thin and fine-drawn – the triumph of mind over matter. She worked extremely hard in school and out. 'Women must work though men may weep,' she wittily remarked once. She drank a great deal of tea. It kept her going. 'Better wear out than rust out,' was her admirable motto, observed faithfully by herself and her pupils – the latter under compulsion. She discovered that the more you work, the more you can work. Indeed, so active was she that she found it impossible to rest.

She was a great believer in the theory of *mens sana in corpore sano*. Consequently she became a member of a eugenic society. She attached due importance to physical development, and therefore played hockey and insisted on her pupils doing the same. Moreover, this game had two other advantages. Running up and down a field violently for an hour and a quarter made her very tired, preceded and followed as it was by much hard work, and by ignoring this condition of extreme physical fatigue she felt she was subduing the flesh, that impediment to things spiritual. The other advantage lay in the fact that it was a game into which the masculine element need not intrude. Neither she nor her pupils would have dreamt, of course, of taking part in mixed hockey.

She devoted much of her time to giving lectures to ignorant mothers on how to feed and rear their children. 'Their ignorance in these matters is truly appalling,' she said.

Mary had a great friend on the staff. They shared a flat and each other's every thought. They were inseparable, and were known as Damon and Pythias. They asked nothing more of life – as, indeed, why should they? – than to live and work together for the Emancipation of Women. Did they not know how much more complete and independent life was if men, with their ineradicable selfishness, were kept out of it; and was it not their duty to preach this new gospel of freedom wherever they could?

Mary had just been made president of a eugenic society when she fell ill. 'Overwork,' said her woman doctor. 'You can't burn the candle at both ends. *Mens sana*, you know.'

V – MARY FEELS OUT OF IT

To recover her shattered health and nerves, Mary was advised to go to Switzerland for the winter sports. She meant to be on her guard against the enervating influence to morals and intellect of puerile frivolity, characteristic, so she understood, of these Swiss resorts. Her bosom friend and scholastic colleague went with her.

During the journey Mary experienced a feeling of vague discomfort, a sense of being an alien – so many men were bound for the same destination as themselves, and seemed on such friendly terms with the women – and this feeling deepened on reaching their destination. Everybody was so cheerful and animated, so obviously and whole-heartedly bent on amusement, as if life was meant for enjoyment rather than serious, strenuous work.

After lunch they went down to the rink. It was thronged with skaters, some performing alone, others in couples and in the middle, solemn people, gyrating round oranges. Many visitors were sitting in seats along the edge of the ice, basking in the warm sunshine. A band was playing a popular waltz tune.

In spite of the beauty of the surroundings, their movement, warmth and colour, Mary felt that sense of desolation and loneliness creeping over her again. She noticed a group of young men and women, laughing and chatting, as they tried, with poor success, to do some intricate figure. She wondered what it would feel like to be on such friendly terms with men, and found herself wishing that she was one of the merry, intimate party. She gave a little involuntary shake, as if to free herself from a degrading thought.

'Look at those two over there waltzing on skates,' said her friend. 'They must have spent an enormous amount of time practising to be so good at it. What a waste of energy and effort which might have been devoted to some good cause! What a mercy you and I can never drift into leading such aimless, shallow lives!'

The next day they decided to try ski-ing, and went to a slope near the hotel frequented by beginners.

So far they had spoken to nobody and nobody had spoken to them. Some of the women looked quite nice, Mary thought; but she was shy about making any advances. Her friends were all earnest professional workers like herself, and she had neither

43

the time nor inclination to mix with other sorts of women. Besides, they would certainly be frivolous-minded and interested in men and clothes.

Mary and her friend shared the usual fate of the ski-ing novice. They fell uphill and downhill with equal impartiality, and tied themselves into the most intricate of knots. Once Mary's skis came off. 'May I help you?' said a man.

'Thank you,' said Mary icily, 'I can manage by myself.'

The ultimate success of the Woman's Movement depended, she had been told, on men being made to realize that women could get on quite well without their help.

They had not attended any of the numerous dances which had taken place in the hotel during their stay. Mary suggested that they should go to one on the eve of their departure. 'Just to see what they are like,' she said, knowing in her heart of hearts she was being impelled by a feeling which she neither understood nor approved of.

They sat watching the dancers for some time. An M.C. came up and asked if they would care to dance. Mary, who had often danced 'man' at school and at college festivities, found herself saying she would. She was amazed, and so was Pythias.

A man who had arrived that day, friendless and alone, was accordingly introduced. Mary, when she felt her partner's arm round her, was overcome by a sense of shame, as if contact with him were a degradation. She was glad when the dance was over. All desire to be at one with the other inmates of the hotel vanished. They sat down, away from her friend, and Mary made up her mind to use her opportunity to sow some good seed in the frivolous mind of this empty-headed young man.

'Are you in favour of Woman Suffrage?' she asked.

'Oh – er – yes,' replied the man. Mary noticed he was looking rather wildly round the room.

'Then you agree that the country would be much better and more fairly governed with the help of women?' she insisted.

'Oh – er – yes,' answered her partner.

'We may expect more from the Liberal Government, with its high ideals, than from the Tories. Do you not think so?'

'No – that is – er – yes,' agreed the man. 'Isn't it jolly out

44

here?' he went on hurriedly. 'The sun and the snow and all that sort of thing. Are you staying long?'

'We go to-morrow,' answered Mary.

'Thank – I mean, I'm so sorry,' said her partner.

VI – AT FORTY-FIVE

Mary at the age of forty-five had been for some years head mistress of a large and flourishing high school. 'I hold in the hollow of my hand the destiny of five hundred girls,' she said, in a moment of confidence, to her great friend. The possession of power and authority seemed to her the most desirable guerdon of life, which women had only won after a prolonged and severe struggle. She wrote a pamphlet called 'Women and Power,' in which she demonstrated with great skill and eloquence that women, far from being temperamentally unsuited to the wielding of authority, were in reality far more fitted for it than men. She presented a copy to each of her pupils.

She was elected to the Town Council, and made it a matter of principle to oppose every suggestion propounded by her masculine colleagues. 'Men must be kept in their place,' she said, 'and then women have a chance of imposing their views.'

Once Mary, very subtly and with a hidden purpose, suggested that the police force should be composed of women as well as men. Why should the enforcement of law and order rest solely with males? The proposal was vetoed by the men town councillors on various trivial and prejudiced grounds. Mary withdrew her suggestion on condition that no married woman should be eligible to stand for election to any public body. The men agreed. 'They didn't want their wives,' etc., scoffed Mary. Her reason for introducing this measure was that she had discovered long ago that, reactionary though men undoubtedly were, married women were fifty times worse.

She sat on various boards and committees; indeed, her life was one long round of work in the service of her fellow-citizens, and if they were not all efficient it was not her fault.

She became a member of the Free Library Committee because the safeguarding of the morals of the young person was very dear to her heart. At her suggestion a by-law was passed prohibiting the issue of Shakespeare's plays to any person under thirty years of age.

Persistent ill-health sadly interfered with Mary's career as professional worker and efficient citizen.

'You do too much,' said her woman doctor. 'Between you and me, I am beginning to think that women can't work as hard as men. They haven't the necessary physique. Of course, I would never admit this in public, or men would hurl their usual taunt at us, "Woman's place is the home." But still, you oughtn't to be breaking up at your age.'

Mary would not admit this.

'You know perfectly well,' she replied, 'that men are nothing but slave-drivers to their women folk. If I had stayed at home I should be worse.'

'Perhaps,' said the doctor.

'Well, anyhow,' said Mary, 'I have preserved my dignity and independence, which no married woman can pretend she has done.'

A few years later she was obliged to give up her work, scholastic and civic. She lived in a flat with her great friend. Round her sofa, upon which she had to spend most of her time, she would gather a band of young women and girls, earnest, high-souled, zealous for the Woman's Cause.

'Oh, Miss Smith,' they would say, 'if only we can live lives like yours!'

Mary smiled. She had not lived in vain. She had taught others, by precept and example, that to be a professional worker and efficient citizen was the crowning achievement of a woman's career. Men could no longer claim sex-superiority.

'The Life History of Mary Smith, M.A.' by Helen Hamilton in The Freewoman, 1 and 8 August 1912. Hamilton, probably of Scottish descent but born in the Far East, wrote variously. Her play The Modern Mother Goose was published in 1916 and was followed by The Compleat Schoolmarm: A Story of Promise and Fulfilment, which was a long poem pleading for a more humane system of education. The Iconoclast (1917) was the title of a supposed free-love, propagandizing feminist journal. My Husband Still: A Working Woman's Story (1914), a forceful, implicit plea *for divorce-law reform, was based on a real-life account of a marriage.*

POOR, WEAK WOMAN

17 April [1889]   [Manchester]
I come back dead tired. As I sink into the armchair in my little
lodging the old maid lodging-house keeper says exultantly: 'See,
you are completely knocked up. You're only a woman: in spite
of your *manly* brain, you're just as much of a woman as I am.'
Poor genteel celibate! For days back you have been envying me
my energy, and peering into *Life and Labour* on my table with my
name standing out as a contributor. Still more, you have been
reading the leaders in two London papers sent me by friends
and you have been hardly able to contain yourself with silent
envy. Now you have your revenge as I roll, tipsy with fatigue,
up to bed. 'You're only a woman after all,' I hear her muttering as
she collars my bag to save me exertion, feeling herself for once a
superior. *'Poor weak woman with a man's brain,'* adds the old maid,
trying to define the exact nature of her distinguished lodger.'

From The Diary of Beatrice Webb, Vol. I: Glitter Around: Darkness Within, 1873–1892, *edited by Norman and Jeanne Mackenzie
(1982). Beatrice Webb (née Potter, 1858–1943) was one of nine daughters of Richard Potter, a wealthy and cultured railway magnate, and
Lawrencina Potter. Educated privately, she mixed in liberal circles
and developed strong social and intellectual interests.*

WOMAN'S LIBERTY AND MAN'S FEAR

Man is afraid of woman. He proves it every day. History proves it
for him – the history of politics, the history of industry, the history
of social life. An examination of woman's present position and of
man's attitude towards the woman's movement shows evidence

of fear at every turn. Yes, it is quite true. Man is afraid of woman because he has oppressed her.

It is only to be expected after all. Why should one be surprised to discover the plain truth? The Czar is afraid of his people; the master is afraid of his subject workers; the government is afraid of the mis-governed masses; and man is afraid of woman. It is ever so. Injustice and wrong thrust upon our fellows rest on so unstable a foundation that the dread of rebellion is always upon the oppressor. There is always for him the fear that the end may come, and rebellion carries with it not merely the throwing off of the yoke but alongside of it the dread of such vengeful retaliation as corresponds to the oppressor's tyranny.

So, because man has oppressed woman, he is afraid of her; because he has denied her liberty and bought her and sold her, he is afraid to face her free; because he has forced her to marriage with iron bonds of poverty, and driven her to sell her body for bread, he stands as a coward before the ages: it is a fitting curse.

There are some superficial men who are blinded by their own prejudices so far as to deny this fact. 'Afraid!' they cry – 'afraid of *women*!' and they laugh. But their laugh is still the laugh of fear. The bully and the coward always laugh bravely when the gates are barred and the keys turned upon their victims. So these men laugh believing in their ignorance that the bonds by which woman has been fettered hand and foot are too strong to be broken. But the bonds are breaking under their blinded eyes.

I do not believe that any thinking man today accepts the old dogma of masculine superiority. Those who do not think of course are many. They still believe it fondly and foolishly. It is a comfortable and pleasant doctrine for a fool. But the growing capacity of women today, their startling development, the progress they are making in every department of life, are too obvious to be mistaken. The theory is dead.

But it is amusing and enlightening to note how these very believers in the incapacity of women are the ones who most strenuously oppose the loosening of their bonds. There is such delightful masculinity in the logic! Yet these are the folk who tell women that the male sex has the monopoly of reason and of rational action.

Two children are about to run a race. Says one to the other,

'You cannot run so well as I can so I will bind your legs with a cord.' Then as the race proceeds he cries, 'You can't run – you can't run. I am cleverer and stronger than you are.' 'Unbind my legs' is the answer, 'that I may have a chance.' But the free-limbed child capers about and says, 'Unbind you? No, indeed. You have not come as far as I have. You do not know how to run. But when you catch me I will unbind your legs.'

In all essentials this little fable is analogous with the facts in the life of woman. On the ground that she is less able than man she is penalized in the struggle, and denied the opportunity which she most needs. Her demand for liberty is met by the reply that when she, with her additional burdens, has shown herself man's equal according to his standard of judgment, her claim will be considered. On the injustice and immorality of the position I will not comment. But I feel compelled to emphasize the depth of muddle-headed absurdity to which the masculine mind has fallen in its effort to justify the subjection of women.

In the industrial world man is afraid of woman. All the best-paid work is in the hands of men, and women are rigidly shut out. From all the higher posts in the lesser trades, and from all the chief trades and their subsidiary industries, women are rigorously excluded. When I was quite young I desired to be an engineer. I was almost as happy among the wonders of machinery as among flowers. The theories of impact, of momentum, of tension – the arrangements of levers, pulleys, planes and screws to make machines, were things to conjure with, with me. But as I was a woman such mechanical talent as I possessed had to be wasted. No department of engineering, theoretical or practical, was open to me. As the desire of women to practise as doctors was opposed, as the would-be woman lawyer today is thwarted, so is the would-be woman engineer, surveyor, or architect, so is the woman who desires to enter any of the better organized departments of industry.

Men shut women out of these industrial avenues, not because women are proved incapable of entering them, but because of their fear of women's entrance into what they have regarded as their preserves. All that chatter about women being incapable of doing this that or the other is so much balderdash. I apologize for using the word, but I know no other that so aptly expresses the truth. Men can never prove that women are incapable of following any given trade or profession, until women have had equal opportunity with men to follow it, and have failed. If women really were incapable the arbitrary and artificial ring-fence which men have erected, and which they so carefully preserve, would not be needed. The fact of its erection and preservation is an acknowledgement by men that they fear women's equal competition.

In such departments of economic production and exchange as women have won admittance the same coward policy is pursued. When the work is specialized women are generally given the worst work, and for this they are underpaid. Where they do the same work as men they are paid at a lower rate. It matters not what the work itself is, the principle is applied right through – from tailors to university lecturers, from prison warders to matrons of hospitals, women are robbed of a certain part of their earnings because they are women.

One can understand the employer doing this. Woman is voteless, and of the lowest social and industrial status. She is the more easily sweated and she can be used to level down the earnings of men. All this is quite satisfactory to the employer. But one cannot understand the workman giving his support to the employer's injustice. Yet this is precisely what he has done. Men teachers, men in the potting trades, in the hosiery trade, in tailoring, in printing, and in a thousand other trades, draw a jealous line between women's wages and their own. This is a grievous injustice and a lamentable mistake on the part of the male-worker. He supports a system of robbery of women-workers which by keeping their wages beneath his own immediately makes them dangerous to himself. Woman entering the labour market for wages artificially depressed because of her sex, reduces the general level of wages, undersells man, and ousts him from employment. Man has been afraid of woman's fair competition in the working world, has shut her out from the best work, and underpaid her work in all departments. He reaps the harvest he has sown.

Not only has the subjection of woman to men been harmful directly and indirectly in the economic world, but it has produced far-reaching evil effects in our social and sex-relations. There is a vital connection between woman's outlawry in industry and her pitiable position of dependence in marriage. Because man desired to keep woman under his control he has denied her the chance of economic independence, he has forced her to feed herself through him. He has done this because he was afraid that if she were free he might lose her. The cloak of marriage has been used to cover unspeakable horrors which women have suffered. Men have known this, and seen the rebellion in women's hearts, and in effect they have said, 'Unless women have no other way of livelihood we shall lose them.' The other alternative – that of removing the evil conditions against which women rebelled, and of making marriage such that they would willingly have entered it, either never occurred to men's minds or was rejected by them because of the restraint which it entailed for themselves.

Ms signed Teresa Billington, pre-February 1907. Box 404, File 6, TBC Collection, Fawcett Library. Reproduced in The Non-Violent Militant. Selected Writings of Teresa Billington-Greig, *edited by Carol McPhee and Ann Fitzgerald (1987). Teresa Billington-Greig (1877–1964) ran away from her unhappy home in Blackburn to become a pupil-teacher and then a teacher. A member of the Independent Labour Party and the Women's Social and Political Union, she went to London in 1907 as its second organizer. Her growing disillusion with what she saw as the despotism of Emmeline and Christabel Pankhurst led her to break away from the WSPU and, with Charlotte Despard, form the Women's Freedom League. However, she soon left the League and devoted the rest of her life to writing about suffrage and feminism.*

A YELLOW ASTER

When Strange set out on his honeymoon, it was with a distinct project simmering in his brain. He meditated a good three months' loiter through the byways of the Tyrol, on into Switzerland, and then home through the towns of the Netherlands, and all by routes best known to himself.

It becomes, however, a moral impossibility for a man to loiter with any comfort by the side of a new-made wife, into whose very bones and marrow the spirit of unrest has crept; and so, by intangible gradations, the loiter had developed into a tumultuous forging on.

Gwen seemed possessed by a very dignified and quite calm-seeming devil; he was a gentlemanly creature, and made no untoward fuss or excitement, but movement he must have, he dared not rest.

In spite of herself, Gwen found growing in her, from the very day of her marriage, a craving, full of subdued fierceness, to be in the very middle of the hurly-burly, no matter whether it raged in a fashionable hotel, or in the market-place of a country town. She had, besides, other uncomfortable ways. In valleys, where the sun shone and the wind rested, and where ordinary mortals were bathed in a soft entrancement of delight, she seemed to lose half her life.

On the contrary, she lived – her voice regained its timbre, her eyes shone, her mouth laughed, her hair sparkled with vitality – as soon as ever she got high on a mountain – the bleaker and harsher the better.

One day they had climbed to the top of the D'Auburg, a dour-looking mountain in the Tyrol, generally avoided of tourists, but for some reason Gwen took it into her head to ascend it.

Sne now sat glowing and tingling with radiant health, leaning up against a rock that sheltered her from the blast which was screeching across the ledge of the mountain. She looked as cool, and as beautiful and unruffled, as if she had just dropped from the clouds, instead of climbing up to them by a most villainous path. There was always a sort of exotic splendour about her, and yet she never seemed out of place.

'Are you never tired?' said her husband, as he was pouring some wine into a little silver cup.

'Never! I don't remember ever once having been tired.'

'Looked at from the carnal mind of a chaperon, that was rather a nuisance, wasn't it?'

'It was; Lady Mary suffered a good deal from it. I used to try to accommodate myself to her in this matter, and to look tired, but I never could manage it.'

52

'Have another sandwich?'

She went on in a reflective way as she ate it, –

'It is a wretched thing, generally, for a woman to be absolutely untireable. A very strong woman is docked of half the privileges of her sex. If you notice the stock, devoted husband, he has always a sickly creature of a wife to devote himself to – or one who poses as sickly – or if her body isn't sickly her brain is. You hardly ever find a woman quite sound in wind and limb and intellect, with an absolutely unselfish husband, ready to think all things for her, and to dance attendance on her to all eternity. Helplessness is such supreme flattery. I tell you, the modern man doesn't like intellect, any more than his fathers before him did, if it comes home too much to him.'

'No! Sickliness and softness of brain don't, however, appeal equally to all men.'

'I suppose not; but the things they carry in their train do. The parasitical, gracious, leaning ways, the touch of pathos and pleading, – those are the things I should look for if I were a man, they charm me infinitely. Then that lovely craving for sympathy, and that delicious feeling of insecurity they float in, which makes the touch of strong hands a Heaven-sent boon to them – those women, you see, strew incense in your path and they get it back in service. When one hears of a devoted couple, and is called on to admire with bated breath, I never can till I have dug out the reason of this devotion. I hate sticking up people on pinnacles, and then having to knock them down like a pair of nine-pins.'

'Hero worship isn't your tap evidently; but if one makes a principle of never smelling a flower or eating fruit until one has ascertained the manure used in its growth, one gets put off a lot. By the way, I haven't noticed any marked symptoms of mental or physical decay in you, and yet, God knows and can possibly score up the number of your lovers – they certainly were beyond all human computation.'

She flashed a quick, curious look at him and smiled.

'My lovers? They weren't lovers at all, they were explorers, experimental philosophers. They had the same strong yearning for me that a botanist has for a blue chrysanthemum, or a yellow aster. If a man could succeed in getting this thing he would go mad over it, and put it in the best house in his grounds for all

53

his neighbours and friends to admire; but do you think he would love it, like an ordinary sweet red rose, that he can gather, and smell, and caress, and bury his nose in, and wear near his heart? Not he!

'Do you think one of these men ever wanted to touch me,' she went on calmly, taking little sips of wine, 'or to ruffle the hair round my forehead, which is their invariable habit in novels, or to lay his hands on my bare shoulder – they do that, too, I have read – or to clasp me to his breast, the climax to these pretty little customs of theirs? Goodness! And imagine my feelings if one had! But they didn't even want to; and yet they were my slaves, to do with precisely as I liked.

'When I was in the thick of it I thought I could not live without all this, yet it was disappointing on the whole, I believe. I remember wishing, now and then, that I could flirt like other girls, and make men make palpable fools of themselves for my sake. It looks such a very delightful pastime! I have seen plain girls look positively quite beautiful when engaged in it. The undercurrent of heaps of girls' lives, upon which it seems to me all the rest is built up, is a sort of simmering, unconfessed, vague longing for the sensation of being "caught and kissed," like the little brown maid in the old rhyme; not in a general vulgar way, but in a well-bred particular way. It is a quite incomprehensible sensation to me.'

'Probably. It's natural all the same,' he said, looking at her eyes, which regarded him curiously; 'and Nature is such a vindictive, grasping beast it is as well not to run counter to her, or she will have limb for limb.'

'I wonder which limb of mine she will want?'

'Oh you, she'll trip you up in your own coils somehow! Fill you with an overpowering desire to be "caught and kissed," ' he said, with a short laugh, 'and have no one handy to do it.'

'Oh, then she must make me over again!'

She stood up and looked down over the gloomy valley. 'What is it to be natural, I wonder? I don't know.'

'Time will tell you all about it. Now, you want to be down over that precipice? Well, anyway, I am glad you are warranted sound. Come on, my yellow aster!'

They were past the precipice, far down the other side, when Gwen spoke again.

'Humphrey,' she said, with a stronger trace of emotion in her voice than he had ever detected there before, 'upon my word, I often wish for your sake I was just a good, common, frowsy red cabbage-rose.'

'Ah, do you? – Well, *"die Zeit bringt Rosen!"* '

From A Yellow Aster, *1894, by 'Iota' (Kathleen Mannington Caffyn, née Hunt, 1855?–1926). A powerful 'New Woman' novelist, Iota trained as a nurse at St Thomas's Hospital, London, before marrying a surgeon and turning to writing in Australia and Britain.*

THE GIRL OF THE PERIOD

Time was when the phrase, 'a fair young English girl,' meant the ideal of womanhood; to us, at least, of home birth and breeding. It meant a creature generous, capable, modest; something franker than a Frenchwoman, more to be trusted than an Italian, as brave as an American but more refined, as domestic as a German and more graceful. It meant a girl who could be trusted alone if need be, because of the innate purity and dignity of her nature, but who was neither bold in bearing nor masculine in mind; a girl who, when she married, would be her husband's friend and companion, but never his rival; one who would consider his interests as identical with her own, and not hold him as just so much fair game for spoil; who would make his house his true home and place of rest, not a mere passage-place for vanity and ostentation to pass through; a tender mother, an industrious housekeeper, a judicious mistress.

We prided ourselves as a nation on our women. We thought we had the pick of creation in this fair young English girl of ours, and envied no other men their own. We admired the languid grace and subtle fire of the South; the docility and childlike affectionateness of the East seemed to us sweet and simple and restful; the vivacious sparkle of the trim and sprightly Parisienne was a pleasant little excitement when we met with it in its own domain; but our allegiance never wandered from our brown-haired girls at home, and our hearts were less vagrant than our fancies. This was in the old time, and when English girls were content to be what God and nature had made them. Of late years we have changed the pattern, and have given to the world a race of women as utterly unlike the old insular ideal as if we had created another nation altogether. The Girl of the Period, and the fair young English girl of the past, have nothing in common save ancestry and their mother-tongue; and even of this last the modern version makes almost a new language, through the copious additions it has received from the current slang of the day.

The Girl of the Period is a creature who dyes her hair and paints her face, as the first articles of her personal religion – a creature whose sole idea of life is fun; whose sole aim is unbounded luxury; and whose dress is the chief object of such thought and intellect as she possesses. Her main endeavour is to outvie her neighbours in the extravagance of fashion. No matter if, in the time of crinolines, she sacrifices decency; in the time of trains, cleanliness; in the time of tied-back skirts, modesty; no matter either, if she makes herself a nuisance and an inconvenience to every one she meets; – the Girl of the Period has done away with such moral muffishness as consideration for others, or regard for counsel and rebuke. It was all very well in old-fashioned times, when fathers and mothers had some authority and were treated with respect, to be tutored and made to obey, but she is far too fast and flourishing to be stopped in mid-career by these slow old morals; and as she lives to please herself, she does not care if she displeases every one else.

Nothing is too extraordinary and nothing too exaggerated for her vitiated taste; and things which in themselves would be useful reforms if let alone become monstrosities worse than those which they have displaced so soon as she begins to manipulate and improve. If a sensible fashion lifts the gown out of the mud, she raises hers midway to her knee. If the absurd structure of wire and buckram, once called a bonnet, is modified to something that shall protect the wearer's face without putting out the eyes of her companion, she cuts hers down to four straws and a rosebud, or a tag of lace and a bunch of glass beads. If there is a reaction against an excess of Rowland's Macassar, and hair shiny and sticky with grease is thought less nice than if left clean and healthily crisp, she dries and frizzes and sticks hers out on end like certain savages in Africa, or lets it wander down her back like Madge Wildfire's, and thinks herself all the more beautiful the nearer she approaches in look to a negress or a maniac.

With purity of taste she has lost also that far more precious purity and delicacy of perception which sometimes mean more than appears on the surface. What the *demi-monde* does in its frantic efforts to excite attention, she also does in imitation. If some fashionable *dévergondée en évidence* is reported to have come out with her dress below her shoulder-blades, and a gold strap for all the sleeve thought necessary, the Girl of the Period follows suit next day; and then she wonders that men sometimes mistake her for her prototype, or that mothers of girls not quite so far gone as herself refuse her as a companion for their daughters. She has blunted the fine edges of feeling so much that she cannot understand why she should be condemned for an imitation of form which does not include imitation of fact. She cannot be made to see that modesty of appearance and virtue in deed ought to be inseparable; and that no good girl can afford to appear bad, under pain of receiving the contempt awarded to the bad.

This imitation of the *demi-monde* in dress leads to something in manner and feeling, not quite so pronounced perhaps, but far too like to be honourable to herself or satisfactory to her friends. It leads to slang, bold talk and general fastness; to the love of pleasure and indifference to duty; to the desire of money before either love or happiness; to uselessness at home, dissatisfaction with the monotony of ordinary life, horror of all useful work; in a word, to the worst forms of luxury and selfishness – to the most fatal effects arising from want of high principle and absence of tender feeling.

The Girl of the Period envies the queens of the *demi-monde* far more than she abhors them. She sees them gorgeously attired and sumptuously appointed, and she knows them to be flattered, fêted, and courted with a certain disdainful admiration of which she catches only the admiration while she ignores the disdain. They have all that for which her soul is hungering; and she never stops to reflect at what a price they have bought their gains, and what fearful moral penalties they pay for their sensuous pleasures.

She sees only the coarse gilding on the base token, and shuts her eyes to the hideous figure in the midst and the foul legend written round the edge. It is this envy of the pleasures, and indifference to the sins, of these women of the *demi-monde* which is doing such infinite mischief to the modern girl. They brush too closely by each other, if not in actual deeds, yet in aims and feelings; for the luxury which is bought by vice with the one is that thing of all in life most passionately desired by the other, though she is not yet prepared to pay quite the same price. Unfortunately, she has already paid too much – all that once gave her distinctive national character.

No one can say of the modern English girl that she is tender, loving, retiring or domestic. The old fault so often found by keen-sighted Frenchwomen, that she was so fatally *romanesque*, so prone to sacrifice appearances and social advantages for love, will never be set against the Girl of the Period. Love indeed is the last thing she thinks of, and the least of the dangers besetting her. Love in a cottage – that seductive dream which used to vex the heart and disturb the calculations of the prudent mother – is now a myth of past ages. The legal barter of herself for so much money, representing so much dash, so much luxury and pleasure – that is her idea of marriage; the only idea worth entertaining. For all seriousness of thought respecting the duties or the consequences of marriage, she has not a trace. If children come, they find but a stepmother's cold welcome from her; and if her husband thinks that he has married anything that is to belong to him – a *tacens et placens uxor* pledged to make him happy – the sooner he wakes from his hallucination and understands that he has simply married some one who will condescend to spend his money on herself, and who will shelter her indiscretions behind the shield of his name, the less severe will be his disappointment. She has married his house, his carriage, his balance at the banker's, his title; and he himself is just the inevitable condition clogging the wheel of her fortune; at best an adjunct, to be tolerated with more or less patience as may chance. For it is only the old-fashioned sort, not Girls of the Period *pur sang*, who marry for love, or put the husband before the banker. But the Girl of the Period does not marry easily. Men are afraid of her; and with reason. They may amuse themselves with her for an evening, but they do not readily take her for life. Besides, after all her efforts, she is only a poor copy of the real thing; and the real thing is far more amusing than the copy, because it is real. Men can get that whenever they like; and when they go into their mothers' drawing-rooms, with their sisters and their sisters' friends, they want something of quite a different flavour. *Toujours perdrix* is bad providing all the world over; but a continual weak imitation of *toujours perdrix* is worse.

If we must have only one kind of thing, let us have it genuine, and the queens of St. John's Wood in their unblushing honesty rather than their imitators and make-believers in Bayswater and Belgravia. For, at whatever cost of shocked self-love or pained modesty it may be, it cannot be too plainly told to the modern English girl that the net result of her present manner of life is to assimilate her as nearly as possible to a class of women whom we must not call by their proper – or improper – name. And we are willing to believe that she has still some modesty of soul left hidden under all this effrontery of fashion, and that, if she could be made to see herself as she appears to the eyes of men, she would mend her ways before too late.

It is terribly significant of the present state of things when men are free to write as they do of the women of their own nation. Every word of censure flung against them is two-edged, and wounds those who condemn as much as those who are condemned; for surely it need hardly be said that men hold nothing so dear as the honour of their women, and that no one living would willingly lower the repute of his mother or his sisters. It is only when these have placed themselves beyond the pale of masculine respect that such things could be written as are written now. When women become again what they were once they will gather round them the love and homage and chivalrous devotion which were then an Englishwoman's natural inheritance.

The marvel in the present fashion of life among women is, how it holds its ground in spite of the disapprobation of men. It used to be an old-time notion that the sexes were made for each other, and that it was only natural for them to please each other, and to set themselves out for that end. But the Girl of the Period does not please men. She pleases them as little as she elevates them; and how little she does that, the class of women she has taken as her models of itself testifies. All men whose opinion is worth having prefer the simple and genuine girl of the past, with her tender little ways and pretty bashful modesties, to this loud and rampant modernization, with her false red hair and painted skin, talking slang as glibly as a man, and by preference leading the conversation to doubtful subjects. She thinks she is piquante and exciting when she thus makes herself the bad copy of a worse original; and she will not see that though men laugh with her they do not respect her, though they flirt with her they do not marry her; she will not believe that she is not the kind of thing they want, and that she is acting against nature and her own interests when she disregards their advice and offends their taste. We do not understand how she makes out her account, viewing her life from any side; but all we can do is to wait patiently until the national madness has passed, and our women have come back again to the old English ideal, once the most beautiful, the most modest, the most essentially womanly in the world.

From The Girl of the Period and Other Social Essays, *Vol. I, 1883, by E. Lynn Linton. Daughter of a clergyman and grand-daughter of the Bishop of Carlisle, Lynn Linton (as she was known) supported herself by her writing. Married and separated from the noted artist and engraver William James Linton, her anti-feminism proved a commercial success. She contributed regularly to the* Saturday Review, *in which this article first appeared, and her novel, 'the book of my whole career',* The Autobiography of Christopher Kirkland, *is still a highly regarded three-volume example of Victorian fiction.*

LIVE ALONE FOR A WHILE

But, once in a way, it is as well to renounce the purely objective life of every day in favour of this other one. Ordinarily, you are scarcely on speaking terms with your real self; you catch hurried glimpses of it, darting before you, out of reach of touch and realization, in the groves and alleys of commonplace concerns, among the brush and underwood of crowding 'things to do,' and you are barely acquaintances. But live alone for awhile, with no special pressing occupation, and how different it is. You have time to think over things that puzzled you, time to look into the conclusions you have had to jump at, leisure to unravel all the tangles that have pained you, opportunity to disinter the reason of your feelings for this and that. It is very good for man or woman to live alone, calmly and quietly, for a period, of whiles; to let their restlessness, their dissatisfaction, and their cares drop from them, 'like the needles shaken from out the gusty pine.'

A voice 'from the intense, clear, star-sown vault of heaven' told Matthew Arnold that he 'who finds himself loses his misery;' and if you are alone with Nature, it is not unreasonable to hope that you may find yourself. Never can you so absolutely return to Nature with a friend or 'with a party' – you must be alone. That burr civilization, and those other burrs of custom and habit, are bad enough to shake off; and if you have some one with you – some other who is also slave to them – it makes it harder: for that other person represents custom, habit, propriety, and civilized uses to you; and, in fact, you have taken the world's opinion with you into the wilderness.

It is better to imitate Nebuchadnezzar – if you must imitate any one, and some people certainly must – and go out to grass for six weeks at least by yourself. Give your whims a loose rein, follow the promptings of that queer live soul in you which always retains its affinity to simpleness and green-growing things, and be prepared to be thought very odd when you come back.

You will have acquired a calm smile, an ability to suffer fools gladly, which will stand you in good stead. For, though with slight comment, loneliness is permitted to a man, it seems the opportunity for immense chaff to a woman. A public resents fiercely the conclusion that a woman, a fairly light-hearted young woman more especially, is happy alone and from choice. A preference of Nature to human nature, of green trees to people, and of her own reflections to their witless comments, is an oddity, a whimsical

61

eccentricity which may be smiled upon, but which requires solid demonstration and justification before it be accepted and believed in.

'Well, but why *did* you go alone?' people will say, having heard all my high-falutin arguments; and they say it with an air of 'Come now, you'll tell me, I know!' And I gaze at their indulgent, smiling eyes, and their self-satisfied faces, and I dare not tell them that I do it from sheer bald preference. I couldn't have the heart to wound and shock them so, and I say, what is perhaps also true, that I am driven to it, for nobody cares to come to the places I care to go to.

From A Girl in the Karpathians, *1891, by Ménie Muriel Dowie.*

THE FIRST FOREIGN WOMAN

Monday, 20th [1907]

We had the devil's own ride yesterday. It was a bright morning with a bitter wind, and I determined to start. So after prolonged farewells I set off with a Druze zaptieh, name of Yusef, and we plodded through the mud and the stones gradually rising into the hills. All went well for the first three hours or so, except that it was so cold that I rode in a sweater (Molly's, bless her for it!) a Norfolk jacket and a fur coat; then we began to get into snow and it was more abominable than words can say. The mules fell down in snow drifts, the horses reared and bucked, and if I had been on a sidesaddle we should have been down half a dozen times, but on this beloved saddle one can sit straight, and close. So we plunged on, the wind increasing and sleet beginning to fall, till at last we came out on to a world entirely white. The last hour I walked and led my horse for he broke through the deep snow at every step. Also I was warmer. By the time we reached Saleh, our destination, it was sleeting hard. The village was a mass of snow drift and half frozen mud and pond. There wasn't a dry spot. So I went up to the house of the Sheikh, Muhammad ibn

Nassar, and there I found a party of his nephews who took me into the Makad, which is the reception room, and lighted a fire in an iron stove and made me tea. The Makad was a good sized room with closely shuttered windows, by reason of there being no glass, felt mats on the floor and a low divan all round on which carpets were spread for me. Rather a fine place as Makads go. As I sat drinking my tea and conversing with the nephews – who were delightful intelligent young men – in came the Sheikh, a tall, very old man, and offered me every hospitality he could in the most charming way. Some interest surrounds me, for I am the first foreign woman who has ever been in these parts. Sheikh Muhammad insisted that I should spend the night in his house, and I gladly agreed, for indeed even for a lover of tents, it was not a promising evening. All the family (males) came in one after another, he has six sons and more nephews than I ever saw, and I established myself on the divan, all the Druzes sitting round in rows, and answered all their questions about foreign parts, especially Japan, for they are thrilled over the war, and explained to them how we lived. They asked particularly after Lord Salisbury and were much saddened to hear he was dead. They knew Chamberlain by name – the real triumph of eloquence was when I explained to them the fiscal question, and they all became Free Traders on the spot.

From The Letters of Gertrude Bell, *Vol. I, selected and edited by Lady Bell, DBE (1927). Gertrude Bell (1868–1926) was the only daughter of a wealthy Durham iron magnate, whose mother died when she was three. After studying at Oxford, Bell travelled in Europe and the Near East, visiting her stepmother's family, who were diplomats. She taught herself Persian and Arabic and travelled widely in Asia Minor, pursuing her interest in archaeology. During the First World War she worked in the Intelligence Service in Cairo. She was a champion of Arab independence after the war and worked to bring stability to Iraq. Before she died she was involved in the foundation of the national museum in Baghdad.*

1879–91: IN THE DESERT

That spring the invention of ladies' bicycles was to demonstrate her superiority to stupid prejudice. In the *Illustrated London News* were to be seen pictures of wild women of the usual unprepossessing pioneer type riding about Epping Forest, and I at once decided to buy a bicycle. Aunts, cousins and friends were horrified . . . never has the word 'indelicate' been bandied about with more righteous conviction. But my mother said this was perfect nonsense. 'When we are dead,' she would reply to her objectors, 'she won't be able to keep horses, and I can think of nothing more sensible than her buying a bicycle.' And buy one I did – with bad paces too, for pneumatic tyres were not yet invented; I also took lessons at a place called Cycledom, and the scene of my first unaided attempts was, O wonder! the gravel sweep in the front of Lambeth Palace, where I even had the honour of giving instruction to the Dean of Windsor. (Needless to say this was during a brief period of favour with the Archbishop.)

Strange to say one then looked upon this very useful and sometimes pleasant way of getting from one place to another as a form of sport, and though for many a long day to come no 'nice' women rode bicycles, I pursued my solitary course with enthusiasm. By degrees, as we know, the thing caught on, and one day, about eighteen months later, when I met Mrs R., the arch-prude of the neighbourhood, wobbling along the high road, and beheld her fall off her machine at my feet to explain that she had taken to it in order to avoid having out the horses on Sunday, it was clear that the indelicacy ghost had been finally laid.

From The Memoirs of Ethel Smyth, *abridged and introduced by Ronald Crichton (1987). Smyth (1858–1944), composer and suffragette, was a strong feminist in the male-dominated world of music. She studied at Leipzig Conservatory and in 1891 her Mass in D was performed at the Albert Hall; in 1909 the opera that was to make her famous,* The Wreckers, *was first performed in England. She became an active member of the suffragette movement and her*

March of the Women *(1911) – the theme of which came from the overture of her opera* The Boatswain's Mate, *with words by Cicely Hamilton – became a campaigning song for the movement. When she was imprisoned for throwing stones at a Cabinet Minister's office, Smyth conducted her fellow-suffragettes in this work, waving a toothbrush from her cell window in Holloway. Smyth was also a prodigious writer and her mostly autobiographical books include* Female Pipings in Eden *(1933). She was created a* DBE *in 1922.*

IF . . .

If, after four or five generations of freer choice and wider life, woman still persists in confining her steps to the narrow grooves where they have hitherto been compelled to walk; if she claims no life of her own, if she has no interests outside her home, if love, marriage and maternity is still her all in all; if she is still, in spite of equal education, of emulation and respect, the inferior of man in brain capacity and mental independence; if she still evinces a marked preference for disagreeable and monotonous forms of labour, for which she is paid at the lowest possible rate; if she still attaches higher value to the lifting of a top hat than to the liberty to direct her own life; if she is still untouched by public spirit, still unable to produce an art and a literature that is individual and sincere; if she is still servile, imitative, pliant – then, when those four or five generations have passed, the male half of humanity will have a perfect right to declare that woman is what he has always believed and desired her to be, that she is the chattel, the domestic animal, the matron or the mistress, that her subjection is a subjection enjoined by natural law, that her inferiority to himself is an ordained and inevitable inferiority. Then he will have that right, but not till then.

From Marriage as a Trade, *1909, by Cicely Hamilton. Hamilton (Cicely Mary Hammill, 1872–1952) was an actress, playwright, novelist and suffragist. Her first successful play,* Diana of

Dobsons *(1908), dealt with sweated industries;* Marriage as a Trade *was followed by a fictional account of the financial degradation of marriage,* Just to Get Married *(1911). Her later works,* William, an Englishman *(1919) and* Theodore Savage *(1922), reflected her horror and pessimism at war.*

A SEVENTH WAVE

'Women have been cramped into a small space so long that they cannot expand all at once when they *are* let out; there must be a great deal of stretching and growing, and when they are not on their guard, they will often find themselves falling into the old attitude, as newborn babes are apt to resume the ante-natal position. She will have the perception, the inclination; but the power – unless she is exceptional, the power will only be for her daughter's daughter.'

'Then she must suffer and do no good?'

'She must suffer, yes; but I don't know about the rest. She may be a seventh wave, you know!'

'What is a seventh wave?'

'It is a superstition of the fisher-folks. They say that when the tide is coming in it pauses always, and remains stationary between every seventh wave, waiting for the next, and unable to rise any higher till it comes to carry it on; and it has always seemed to me that the tide of human progress is raised at intervals to higher levels at a bound in some such way. The seventh waves of humanity are men and women who, by the impulse of some one action which comes naturally to them but is new to the race, gather strength to come up to the last halting place of the tide, and to carry it on with them ever so far beyond.' He stopped abruptly, and brushed his hand over his forehead. 'Now that I have said that,' he added, 'it seems as old as the cathedral there, and as familiar, yet the moment before I spoke it appeared to have only just occurred to me. If it is an ill-digested reminiscence and you come across the original in some book, I am afraid you will lose your faith in me for ever; but I pray you of your charity make due allowance. I must go.'

From The Heavenly Twins, *1893, by 'Sarah Grand' (Frances Elizabeth McFall, née Clarke, 1854–1943). A novelist and feminist, Grand was born in County Down, Ireland. The Beth Book, published in 1897, drew on her experiences of life with her alcoholic father, and on her marriage to a doctor who worked for an institution where prostitutes with venereal disease were incarcerated. Grand lived in the Far East for a time and on her return started publishing fiction and articles in magazines. Her first successful novel,* Ideala, *was published in 1888, and* The Heavenly Twins, *which dealt with sexual double standards, became an immediate best-seller. She was a member of the Women Writers Suffrage League, a campaigning lecturer and, after the First World War, Mayoress of Bath.*

CHAPTER TWO

THE GETTING
OF WISDOM

The New Woman had to battle to get an education appropriate
to her desired independence.

The struggle stretched a long way back. In 1739 an anony-
mous writer, 'Sophia: A Person of Quality', had written in her
work *Woman Not Inferior to Man*:

> It is a very great absurdity to argue that learning is useless
> to women, because forsooth they have no share in public
> offices, [for] why is learning useless to us? Because we have
> no share in public offices? And why have we no share in
> public offices? Because we have no learning.

And Mary Wollstonecraft, in *A Vindication of the Rights of Women*
(1792), recognized that without educational equality there could
be no sexual equality.

It was this connection between access to learning for women
and their economic, social and sexual equality – and thus their
independence – that made the debate about women's education in
the nineteenth and early twentieth centuries such an urgent one;
and one that still resonates at the end of the twentieth century.

With a very few exceptions, women at the end of the
nineteenth century were educated to fit their station in life:
middle-class women to wifehood, economic dependence and
intellectual subservience to their husbands; working-class women
to domestic drudgery.

The demand for increased educational opportunities for women challenged these assumptions and, its opponents realized, would set women on the path towards further demands for independence and for opportunities beyond the domestic. What were women to be educated for, if not for wifedom, motherhood and as an ornament to society, in the case of upper- and middle-class women? If women were to be educated like men, they would claim the same career opportunities and access to the public sphere, and then the whole basis of the Victorian family would be destroyed, society would deteriorate, and women themselves would be the losers.

The arguments were cast in different guises. Either women, for reasons of mental or physical weakness, were not strong enough to be educated (the excessive use of the brain would lead to damage to their constitutions, and might even render women unfit for motherhood); or education would be wasted on women who were destined for a life of wifely and maternal duties. Moreover, education would breed a race of malcontents – unwomanly women, unstoppable in their demands for men's privileges. For implicit in this argument was the recognition that once the gates of educational opportunity had been stormed, other citadels would fall; man's 'natural' authority in the home was in jeopardy and women would demand entry to 'male' professions, and equal recognition and payment for these careers.

The gains were hard won. In the 1840s members of the Governesses' Benevolent Society founded Queen's College in London to offer qualifications to governesses – that most frequent of occupations for middle-class girls required to earn their living – and to introduce professional standards, and hence better pay. When Cheltenham Ladies' College was founded in 1853, its intention was to fit a girl 'for those responsible duties which devolve on her as a wife, mother, mistress and friend, the natural companion and helpmeet for man'; and even then the name 'college' frightened people, its second principal, Dorothea Beale, explained. 'It was said that girls would be turned into boys if they attended a college.'

Largely at the insistence of Emily Davies (who was to found Girton College, Cambridge), the Taunton Commission, set up in 1864, included girls' schools in its report on education. The findings were devastating, revealing abysmally low standards in most girls' schools, but of course its remit did not include those many middle-class girls still educated at home by governesses of varying competence and education themselves. The report was an impetus to the creation of new schools for girls, with higher educational standards, turning out pupils who would be able to hold their own in competition with boys in national exams.

The 1870 Education Act provided for the education of working-class children at elementary level, but the only way that a working-class girl could hope for higher education was by winning a scholarship to a maintained school. The 1907 Act required such schools to keep one-third of its places free, but even then the family had to provide uniform and books, and many families decided that in these circumstances their slender resources were required for the education of sons. But if the provision of education could be seen as becoming more generous for girls by the beginning of the twentieth century, its content was often still determined by narrow considerations.

There was little encouragement, either, for women at the older universities. Women were limited to 750 places at Oxford and 500 at Cambridge and were not allowed to take degrees. It was not until 1923 that women students had the right to attend lectures – until then, each individual lecturer had to be approached for permission. Women were finally allowed to take degrees at Oxford in 1920, but not until 1947 was the same right granted at Cambridge.

MY SCHOOL

I should like to describe my school, as I remember it. It was in a narrow street opposite a soap factory and surrounded on three sides by high tenement buildings, and the playground was between the backs of these. Mothers could look out to see the children playing. The school looked as though it had been a wealthy gentleman's house in days gone by. Fancy iron railings ran in front of a small courtyard. The building was two stories high with an attic above where the caretaker lived. There was a window on either side of the double front door through which you entered into the small hall. Against one wall were large hot-water pipes; opposite was the door of the teachers' room.

At the end of the hall was the infants' school, which took in both boys and girls. There were three classes: first, second and babies. Children were accepted in special circumstances at the age of two-and-a-half. If the mother had a large family or another baby was expected, then the child went to school. These children were not trained and many poor mites had to be cleaned up by the teacher. If the child had an elder sister in the school, then she would be called to clean up the child. Sometimes these babies were so tired by lunch-time that they fell asleep where they sat, much to the relief of the long-suffering teacher, I expect.

At the other end of the passage were the cloakroom and a washroom in which were a few basins with cold-water taps over them. A door led from the washroom to the playground. The playground was small, and at one end it was covered by a glass roof; we played there when it rained. At the end of the part with the glass roof were half-a-dozen toilets, which were always frozen up in winter. The playground was a playground, and nothing more. There were no outdoor games played there other than those we invented. We played 'touch' and skipping and we chased around pretending to be bus-horses.

Throughout my years at that school, I always kept to the same classroom, teacher and desk. The room held thirty-six desks; with two girls at each desk, seventy-two girls must have been in the one class. The desks did not open and the seats were attached. Each had an inkwell at either end, filled each day by the ink monitor. We were each given a pen with a nib which had to last a week. Books, too, were given out for each subject and collected and put in a cupboard when the lesson finished. We learned spelling, writing, reading, history, geography, arithmetic and nature study. My one and only prize while at school was for nature study. No one was more surprised than I when I received this prize. I still remember the name of the book. It was *Captain Curly's Boy*. Each year we had a pot-plant competition. Each child who wished could have a geranium or a fuchsia. I always took a fuchsia. The delicate flower of it always delighted me and I longed to win the prize. Alas, I am afraid I always killed it with kindness. Long before it was time to return it each year, it was dead.

We would drone our tables out loud until we knew them by heart, and to this day, if I cannot remember six fives, or seven nines, I repeat the table through until I come to it. The tables were lessons never forgotten. My teacher was Mrs Hamlyn. She was tall, thin and terrifying. If we misbehaved she would bring us out to the front of the class, stand behind us, fold our arms over our chest, and lean over us. Then, pushing our sleeves up, she slapped us as hard as she could until our arms burned with the sting. We had a punishment book, kept by the Governess (Headmistress). If you were really naughty, you were sent to the Governess for the cane and to have your name put in red ink in the punishment book. This went against you when you left school, as each of us was given our 'character' (reference) when we left school. Without a good 'character' you could not get a job, as it was always asked for when applying for one. I still have my 'character'. It is one of my treasures, of which I am rather proud.

My Governess – Miss Meikle – was quite old and always dressed in black. She wore a tight bodice with long, tight sleeves drawn into a band at the wrist, and a long, very full skirt which just showed the toes of her black boots. I think she quite liked me, maybe because she had known my mother. Children have a way of knowing who approves or who disapproves. Anyway, I always felt happy in her presence. (I feel I have rambled a bit, but I put these thoughts down as they come to me, for maybe in five minutes' time I shall have forgotten them.)

Back to my classroom. In winter there was a very large coal fire lit before we came into class. In front of it was a large, iron fire-guard. The fire was lovely to look at but didn't seem to warm the classroom. My seat at the back of the class was always cold. I had so many chilblains on my fingers that I sometimes could not hold the pen. Not being able to afford gloves for us, my mother sewed up the legs of worn-out socks and threaded them through with elastic to keep them on. This was quite all right for going to school, but one cannot write with sewn-up socks on one's hands; and so, once at school, I had to go cold.

Most of us girls were very poorly shod, some coming to school with no boots or stockings at all. Those of us who did have them were lucky. Even so, most boots were made with cardboard soles which wore out very quickly, especially in wet weather.

Nobody carried a handkerchief. Pieces of rag did in most cases, but where these were not available sleeves came in most useful. My mother always sewed the hems of her pieces of rag, and mine was always pinned up to my dress to stop me losing it.

Our teachers must have been heroines, for we were for the most part an ignorant and uncouth lot. They persevered, nevertheless, and, much to their credit, turned out some very good girls, who went on to sit for scholarships and, in quite a few cases, made good and were a credit to the school.

We had no homework, therefore no satchels were needed. We had no school milk and no school dinners. If a child was very poor, she could apply for a dinner ticket which entitled her to a free dinner at a coffee-shop. Not many applied for dinner tickets, for even the poor of the community were proud. The children went home for dinner, sometimes to a couple of slices of bread, cut thick to fill them up.

As we grew older, we were sent for one half-day a week to a central school for a course of either housewifery, laundry or cooking. We could not choose the course, it was chosen for us. At the laundry we were taught how to wash clothes, iron with a flat iron, goffer with a goffering iron, to starch and to smooth with a smoothing iron. All these processes are now things of the past, and I doubt very much if the young will have any idea of what I am talking about. If we did the housewifery course, we were taught to sweep, dust, polish, make beds and bath a life-size doll. We had great fun on this course, for it was held in a house set aside for the purpose, and with only one teacher in charge we were quick to take advantage when she went to inspect some other part of the house. We jumped on the bed, threw pillows, drowned the doll and swept dirt under the mats. This was the highlight of the week, the one lesson that we never minded going to.

I do not remember our ever having an Open Day; nor was there any Parent–Teacher Association. Parents were not consulted except in the case where a girl was found to have vermin on her. The school nurse came to inspect our heads regularly. We were marched a few at a time into the teachers' room; there the nurse looked through our hair, using a comb which she dipped in a bowl of carbolic. If your hair was found to contain nits, then you were given a card to take home. If the head had vermin, then you were given a card which warned that if this was not clean by the nurse's next visit you would be sent to the cleansing station, where all your hair was cut very short. This was a disgrace, for all who saw you with your hair cut this way knew you were dirty, and shamed you until the hair grew long again. Many a girl suffered in this way; no one who has not experienced it can understand the misery this practice entailed.

In my school there was no provision for accidents or illness. I remember once swallowing a pin and nearly choking, as it had lodged in my throat. I choked and spluttered so much that I interrupted the lesson. My teacher was told by another girl what had happened. She was nonplussed, as was the Governess. Not knowing what to do they sent me home, still with the pin lodged in my throat. Another girl was sent with me. Luckily, my mother was in when we reached home. She promptly put her fingers in my mouth, making me vomit. Needless to say the pin dislodged itself, but not without some scratching of my throat. This done, Mother sent me back to school again so that I did not miss my lesson.

When I was older I attended the central school full time. It was situated in the Jewish quarter in Stepney. On Fridays we had what was called 'double session'. Usually we had two hours for lunch break, but on Fridays we had only an hour. On all other days we left school at four o'clock but on Friday we left at two-thirty. This enabled the Jewish children among us to get home, have a meal and prepare for their Sabbath, which started at sunset on Friday evening and spread over Saturday. On my way home from school I used to make myself a nice bit of sweet-money, for if I walked slowly along, Jewish women would ask me to light their gas, or put a match to their fire or bank it up with coal. In fact any small job that needed to be done, I did. If a Christian could not be found, then the job went undone, for the Jews in that area observed their religious rites most strictly. The table was laid with a clean, white

74

cloth upon which stood candles especially kept for the Sabbath. I was paid one halfpenny for each job done and welcomed the chance to earn some sweet-money so easily.

From My Part of the River, *1974, by Grace Foakes. Foakes was born in 1901 in a tenement in the East End of London, 'the place to which outcasts and refugees came'. Her books,* My Part of the River, Behind High Walls: A London Childhood *and* Cousin Reuben *told her recollections of the East End and her life there.*

ON MATTERS OF SEX

The girls were thrown thus upon the Book of Books for their contraband knowledge, since it was the only frankly outspoken piece of literature allowed within the College walls: the classics studied were rigidly expurgated; the school library was kept so dull that no one over the age of ten much cared to borrow a volume from it. And, by fair means or unfair, it was necessary to obtain information on matters of sex; for girls most of whom were well across the threshold of womanhood, the subject had an invincible fascination.

Such knowledge as they possessed was a strange jumble, picked up at random: in one direction they were well primed; in another, supremely ignorant. Thus, though they received lectures on what was called 'Physiology', and for these were required to commit to memory the name of every bone and artery in the body, yet all that related to a woman's special organs and chief natural function was studiously ignored. The subject being thus chastely shrouded in mystery, they were thrown back on guesswork and speculation – with the quaintest results. The fancies woven by quite big girls, for instance, round the physical feat of bringing a child into the world, would have supplied material for a volume of fairy-tales. On many a summer evening at this time, in a nook of the garden, heads of all shades might have been seen pressed as close together as a cluster of settled bees; and like the humming of bees, too, were the busy whisperings and subdued buzzes of laughter that accompanied this hot discussion of the 'how' – as a living answer to which, each of them would probably some day walk the world. Innumerable theories were afloat, one more fantastic than another; and the wilder the conjecture, the greater was the respect and applause it gained.

On the other hand, of less profitable information they had amassed a goodly store. Girls who came from up-country could tell a lively tale of the artless habits of the blacks; others, who were at home in mining towns, described the doings in Chinese camps – those unavoidable concomitants of gold-grubbing settlements; rhymes circulated that would have staggered a back-blocker; while the governesses were without exception, young and old, kindly and unkindly, laid under such flamboyant suspicions as the poor ladies had, for certain, never heard breathed – since their own impudent schooldays.

This dabbling in the illicit – it had little in common with the opener grime of the ordinary schoolboy – did not even widen the outlook of these girls. For it was something to hush up and keep hidden away, to have qualms, even among themselves, without knowing; and, like all knowledge that fungus-like shrinks from the sun, it was stunted and unlovely. Their minds were warped by it, their vision was distorted: viewed through its lens, the most natural human relations appeared unnatural. Thus, not the prim-mest patterns of family life could hope for mercy in their eyes; over the family, too, man, as read by these young rigorists, was held to leave his serpent's trail of desire.

For out of it all rose the vague, crude picture of woman as the prey of man. Man was animal, a composite of lust and cruelty, with no aim but that of brutally taking his pleasure: something monstrous, yet to be adored; annihilating, yet to be sought after; something to flee and, at the same time, to entice, with every art at one's disposal.

From The Getting of Wisdom, *1910, by 'Henry Handel Richardson' (Ethel Florence Lindsay Richardson, 1870–1946), novelist and short story writer. Richardson was born in Melbourne, Australia of British parents who went to Victoria during the gold rush of the 1850s. She was educated at the Presbyterian Ladies' College in Melbourne and*

The Getting of Wisdom reflects that experience. She studied music at Leipzig Conservatory, but after her marriage to J.G. Robertson in 1895, and his appointment as Professor of German at the University of London, Richardson became a reclusive writer with an interest in spiritualism. Maurice Guest *(1908) was based on her Leipzig years, and* Ultima Thule *(1929) made her an international reputation. She was nominated for the Nobel Prize for Literature in 1922.*

THE FACTS OF LIFE

At a quite early age, I exercised my embryonic reasoning powers to elucidate some of the facts of life, about which no one had been willing to enlighten me. If hens laid eggs, then it was logical to suppose that puppies and even babies came from inside their mothers. And the idea that you had to be married in order to have children did not seem reasonable in face of the fact that dogs and cats evidently had no need of any ceremony. This was borne out by reading stories in which fallen women were mentioned, and their attempts to conceal their shameful maternity. It soon became obvious that the arrival of the offspring was not due to chance, but to some definite and conscious act of intimacy. Why such intimacy should ever occur, when the penalties were so frightful, puzzled me until I hit upon the explanation that it must in itself be highly pleasurable. This led straight to an understanding of what was meant by physical passion in contrast to spiritual love. Physical passion was of course extremely discreditable, but I suspected that, since it was part of the system on which the rest of creation worked, it was probably very difficult to confine it to the wedding-ring principle. Having arrived unaided at these conclusions, I considered that I had solved the entire sexual question, and at that time thought very little more about it. My one care was to spare my mother the embarrassment of enlightening me with her own construction of these unpalatable facts, and myself the embarrassment of admitting that I 'knew.' As a matter of fact, she attempted no enlightenment until I was eighteen, and was then easily persuaded that there was not anything I wanted to know. She was, however, a little hurt that I wouldn't talk about it, nor allow her to correct any undesirable impressions I might have received.

I was eager to leave school when the time came, for by then there had settled in Adelaide a red-headed little firebrand of a woman who was not only an excellent painter, fresh from Paris, but a most inspiring teacher. She had opened a studio in the city, and I should think was the only person in South Australia to employ a nude model. She had about twenty pupils – mostly older women, and none from amongst my mother's circle of friends, but I was absolutely determined to study with her. The piano lessons had by now been abandoned, and my mother was persuaded that it would be right for me to cultivate my talent for art, provided it was in moderation. So, in spite of her dislike of the nude model (who after all was only a little girl of fourteen) I was allowed to go to Rose MacPherson's classes on two days a week.

Going up the stairs to that studio were the happiest moments of my life. All sorts of new aesthetic sensibilities began sprouting in my spirit like mushrooms.

I was taught to paint by tone-values, to study degrees of light and shade, and to make a direct attack upon the canvas. I found this method still in vogue in the first art school I subsequently attended in London. It is not the method which I now follow, and I could wish that I had had an architectural rather than a photographic sense developed in those early lessons. It would have saved a lot of time.

All the same, Rose MacPherson's knowledge, integrity, and dynamic enthusiasm did wonders in setting all my machinery in motion. And what else is a teacher for?

After my mother's death, I found a pathetic entry in her diary, deploring the undue influence of Miss MacPherson who was convinced that I would one day escape to Europe in order to study. 'You know, Mrs. Bowen, you won't be able to keep her,' she had said, and to my poor mother this must have sounded like the knell of doom. She lived entirely for us children. Even her activities as secretary to the Mother's Union were but an extension of her own parenthood. And she was a simple person whom it would have been easy to make happy if one had not become such a prickly young egotist. Brother Tom was still at school, and anyway he had the prerogatives of his sex. Boys did leave home. Girls didn't. So my mother and I got in trouble together and were both quite unhappy for some months, whilst I went chasing sententiously after alien gods which I probably called Beauty and Freedom!

From Drawn from Life, *1941, by Stella Bowen. Born in Adelaide, South Australia in 1895, Bowen came to England in 1914 and studied art under Walter Sickert at the Westminster School of Art. She lived with the writer Ford Madox Ford in England, the South of France and Paris, and had a daughter, Julia. After they separated, Bowen began to paint, and during the Second World War was appointed official artist by the Australian War Memorial Board.*

A PIONEER IN EDUCATION

Coming into the school at the age of sixteen I saw its glaring faults and absurdities. The whole seemed to me an elaborate machine for doing the minimum of useful things with the maximum of fuss. I didn't see then, as I saw later, that Miss Buss was faced by a herculean task. The endless anxieties she caused her pupils were as nothing to her own big anxiety. She was a pioneer, and almost single-handed, in getting some kind of systematic education for girls. She had no school to copy, no precedent of any kind. Her private school had been so successful that she found herself before long with five hundred girls – all to be taught something and to be trained along Victorian lines of good behaviour.

To be taught something – but what? Negatively the problem was easy. All the hitherto satisfactory ideals of accomplishments and 'finishing' must be wiped out, but what was to take their place? While the education of boys had been gradually shaped from ancient times, engaging the attention of philosophers, that of girls had as a rule no other aim beyond making them pleasing to men. This idea was to Miss Buss anathema, and she failed to see all its great possibilities when really well done. To be deeply pleasing to a husband, and widely pleasing to other men, seems to me as good an ideal as a woman can have. But instead of facing squarely the real needs of future wives and mothers, as the vast majority of girls were to be, Miss Buss seized the tempting instrument at her hand – the stimulus to mental ambition afforded by outside examinations. By this means the curriculum was ready-made. And thus, for better or worse, the education of girls became a feeble imitation of what the boys were doing, for the public examinations made no distinction of sex, and no woman's voice was heard at the examination boards.

A more serious problem than the curriculum was the discipline. The girls came day by day from a great variety of homes, and never before had there been so many at work together. Here the example of the boys' Public schools was no help. Three essentials of their system were entirely lacking: games, effective punishment, and respectable learning.

I don't think it ever occurred to Miss Buss that games are far more than games, that they provide a vent for high spirits, develop natural obedience, and prevent mental over-strain. True, we had only a tiny yard of open space, nothing to call a playground, but there was a big gymnasium where games could have been freely played. All we did in it was Swedish exercises – bouncing balls or balancing poles – and marching round to music. Were they afraid that if we played free games we might start a riot? Even our short breathing-space of quarter of an hour in the middle of a long morning's work gave us no freedom except to talk. We filed down into a basement room, bought a bun or a biscuit at a table as we passed, and then stood in *rows* till the time was up. I used to recall with a pang the jolly games of rounders in the grassy garden of my private school, whence we returned to work all hot and recreated.

Punishment as the boys knew it was impossible. Caning was out of the question, and detention was almost equally so. The bulk of the girls came from considerable distances, and the double journey for an afternoon school had to be ruled out. Consequently the lessons had to be over by half-past one, to allow time for getting home for dinner. But parents had complained that the girls had not enough to do during the afternoon and evening. Therefore, since hobbies were considered frivolous, the curse of homework was started. A detention would involve stopping at school for dinner, and an imposition would add to the already over-burdened homework, so neither of these was widely practicable.

Reproof, therefore, was the only form of punishment available, and it is hardly to be wondered at that Miss Buss had brought it to a fine art. It ranged from the mild disgrace of 'signing' to the third degree in the private room. Very rarely, I believe, expulsion was used. The knowledge that there was always a waiting list of pupils gave Miss Buss absolute power, and this must always be dangerous for a woman. Now by nature she was generous and kind-hearted, and did most sincerely long for the loyal co-operation of her pupils in making the school a success. To this end she delivered every week a moral lecture, and would frequently enlist our cheerful compliance with the innumerable rules. 'Multiply the results' was her great slogan for deciding whether a rule was necessary or not. She would point out that one girl running downstairs might not be dangerous, but what if five hundred did? One shoe-bag untidily hung doesn't matter, but five hundred look bad. One girl talking makes no disturbance, but five hundred do. The fallacy of this argument never struck her. Or did it? and that's why she repeated it so often? I think that her sleep must often have been broken by the nightmare of five hundred girls all running amok at once.

Underlying all this iron discipline must have been the subconscious fear that the assistant teachers could not carry on if there were much freedom for questioning and discussion in class. Hard as it is to realize to-day, a well-educated and cultured woman-teacher was extremely rare. It was in this direction that Miss Buss made her greatest mistake. Instead of searching far and wide for the best, she almost invariably chose women who had been through the school and could be relied on to follow her methods; no doubt from a subconscious fear that those methods might be called in question by some lively and original member of the staff. After all, fresh ideas are always upsetting.

Not quite so easy to understand was the objection to the teachers having any interests outside their work. Now it is obvious that no teacher, and no parent, can inspire children if he thinks too much about them; he must have some wider outside interest about which they must be left guessing. But for

Miss Buss the school, the scheme, the orderly plan – this was the one absorbing thought.

From A London Girl of the Eighties, *1936, by M. Vivian Hughes. Educated at the North London Collegiate School and Homerton College, Cambridge, Hughes was a teacher for much of her life, eventually becoming a school inspector.*

ALL THOSE OPPORTUNITIES

To S.C.C.S.   CAPE TOWN, *18th Feb* [1912]
I went to see Bill [W.P.'s eldest son] take his degree at the City Hall yesterday. When I saw the great crowd of girls in their caps and gowns sitting among the boys I was suddenly astonished to find myself crying. Lady Innes sat next to me but with her back turned partly to me. She had asked me to motor out to lunch with her at Kenilworth. When she got up, I found her face was all red and swollen. She hurried out. When we were in the motor I found she'd been crying as I had been at the sight of the girls. It was so grand to see them – all those opportunities we'd never had, that they have! – all the girls sitting among the boys their equals! – such a strange mingling of feeling that bore one quite off one's feet! And as Jessie Innes said when we were driving in the motor 'I felt I ought to have girls! Oh, where are my eight girls that I ought to have had to carry on!' I never saw Jessie Innes shed a tear before in my life! When we got home Innes asked why her eyes were so red. Jessie told him – he looked at us in astonishment, and said, 'Whatever *were* you crying for?' I said, 'Because we were so glad.' He said, 'Will you cry also when you get the vote?' I said, 'Of course, with joy!' And the curious thing was there came a wateryness about Jim's eyes! I suppose caught from us. I have never been more moved in my life, than by the sight of those girls. The first *little gleam* of the realization of the ideal that haunts us – and which *we* shall never see fully realized.

Olive Schreiner to her husband, Samuel Cron Cronwright Schreiner, from The Letters of Olive Schreiner, 1876–1920, *edited by S.C. Cronwright Schreiner (1926).*

COLLEGE [1882–5]

My last term at school was greatly disturbed by anxiety as to what was to happen to me next. The Head had inspired in me an intense desire to go to Girton College and I particularly wanted to study Economics. I was determined to qualify myself to earn my own living, not at all relishing the idea of living as a dependent at home, with a strong mother quite competent to run the household without help. I did not quite see how my independence was to be accomplished, but I have never looked very far ahead in my life, taking opportunities as they came. My mother saw no necessity for me to go to college and wished me to live as a 'daughter at home.' In this my father, though personally indifferent, supported her. I was given to understand that there would be no money to pay for a university course.

My hopes went up and down. Miss Jones told me that a benefactor of the school had promised a scholarship to the girl in my year whom the headmistress should select, and that she had selected me. But when I told my mother, she dashed my hopes by saying that the scholarship would by no means cover the annual cost, and it was out of the question that any more should be spent on me. As the fees at Notting Hill had been only £15 a year, I did not think my four years' schooling had been very expensive; but clearly, if there was not enough money, that settled it. By an extraordinary piece of good luck, my godmother, Mrs. Nichols, of Holmwood Park, Dorking, whom I ever after thought of as my fairy godmother, at this time paid my mother one of her rare visits and heard about my dilemma. Without any hesitation, she undertook to make up the balance of my expenses, and in the Michaelmas Term 1882 I entered Girton College. I was eighteen, but still very unevenly educated, and exceedingly undeveloped in mind and character. At a students' supper-party, when I, in turn with other freshers, was asked what tripos I was taking, and replied 'Moral Sciences,' a third-year student cried, 'What! That babe?'

I arrived at an unfortunate time, because there had been no students taking that tripos lately and the Tutor had therefore gone down, and I (with one other morals student) was left without any expert advice as to my course. Miss Bernard, who was still Mistress in my first year, had a talk with me, but she knew nothing whatever about the subjects and I was too ignorant to discover this. When my Little-Go had been polished off, she examined the lecture list and remarked that Dr. Venn and Dr. James Ward were very distinguished lecturers and I would probably find them interesting. Dr. Venn was lecturing on 'The Logic of Chance' and Dr. Ward was giving his highly original and difficult course on Psychology.

I faithfully attended these classes as recommended; of Dr. Venn's I think I understood nothing whatever, whereas of Dr. Ward's I may have understood one sentence in ten. My philosophical vocabulary was still so childish that I used to take notes phonetically, and I can remember puzzling over the question as to what on earth 'discreet' points could be. Dr. Ward became aware of the chaotic state of my mind and once startled me horribly by opening his lecture with the remark: 'Miss Sickert, you won't understand a word of what I am going to say to-day.' And I didn't. But I rather wish now that I had had the nerve to get up and go out.

I look back with amazement at my serenity under these circumstances. I ought, after a few weeks, to have felt exasperated at being offered only such indigestible food, and to have made a row about it. I expect I should have secured some helpful advice if I had done this. But I was still in the receptive mood of the good girl who takes what is given her. It was such a miracle to be at college at all and I was far too shy to hold up the class for explanations which the others appeared not to require. The idea of waylaying these great men with questions, even if I could have formulated them, never occurred to me. When at school, I had worked largely alone and had worried out my difficulties without the proper equipment of books of reference. There were

84

no encyclopaedias either at home or at school and only very inadequate little dictionaries, though my father possessed a magnificent Stiehler atlas.

I read some elementary books on Psychology in the college library and understood them readily enough, but I could not bridge the gulf between them and Dr. Ward's highly original expositions. Bain and Sully's accounts of our notions of Time and Space did not go beyond my childish conceptions, while Herbert Spencer's jargon amused me for a time but never seemed to get to the core of my difficulties. As for the Logic of Chance – it required a far better mathematical grasp than I had, and, moreover, it was not necessary for the tripos that I should master it. Still, faint but pursuing, I was not unhappy at my work; I always hoped I should understand some day, and I was cheered by occasional gleams.

On the other hand, the social life of the college was to me so intoxicating that it was more than enough for me. I was too excited to eat or sleep properly. To begin with, I now had a study as well as a bedroom to myself. My mother had brought me to Girton on the first day and we were shown round by an old student. The building was still in its infancy, and the only public room was the dining-hall; but I was impressed by it and by the long corridors, the 'gyps' wings,' the wide stone stairs with their shallow rises. When the door of my study was opened and I saw my own fire, my own desk, my own easy chair and reading-lamp – nay, even my own kettle – I was speechless with delight. Imagine my dismay when my mother turned to me with open arms and tears in her eyes, saying, 'You can come home again with me, Nell, if you like!' It was horrible. That which had enraptured me had struck her as so unutterably dismal that she was prepared to rescue me at all costs. I hardly knew how decently to disguise my real feelings. I could not help thinking how differently I should have answered if she had said as much ten years before.

To have a study of my own and to be told that, if I chose to put 'Engaged' on my door, no one would so much as knock was in itself so great a privilege as to hinder me from sleep. I did not know till then how much I had suffered from the incessant interruptions of my home life. I could have worked quite easily in a mere noise. I never found it at all difficult to do prep. in a crowded schoolroom. What disturbed my mind were the claims

85

my mother made on my attention, her appeals to my emotions and her resentment at my interest in matters outside the family circle.

Here I found the college societies very tempting. I joined debating, literary and philosophical societies, choral society and fire-brigade, and was, later, conductor of the choral and an officer of the fire-brigade. Before long, I joined the Cambridge University Musical Society Choir, and, under the fiery conductorship of Dr. Stanford, enjoyed the weekly practice.

Since I have alluded to the parsimony of the public towards the higher education of women, I should like to record the deplorable fact that rich women in England have but rarely helped substantially to endow women's colleges, in the same way as they and rich men have endowed men's colleges. Whereas they will leave many thousands to the churches, to hospitals, to soldiers and sailors, and to dogs' homes, they rarely make large bequests to women's colleges. Searching in my mind for a reason, I think that one powerful reason may be that rich women have inherited, not made their wealth. Even now it is almost impossible for a woman herself to make a quarter of a million. So the kind of women who inherit great wealth, who are, anyway, much fewer than the men, are unlikely to understand the struggle of the poorly endowed girl for a training which will give her some chance with trained men, or to care about the consequences of this struggle on girls, on women and on society in general. For people seem unable to grasp that it is a serious social mistake to impoverish the lives of one half of the population.

At the beginning of a term my mother used to buy my railway ticket and give me £1 for petty cash. I had to render an exact account of that before I could have any more, and I never spent more than £3 in a term. Out of this, I had to pay for books and stationery and postage, subscriptions to college societies and small luxuries like tea (college tea was deadly), biscuits, or flowers. I could not afford to pay for cabs or concerts and it was very difficult to screw out what I actually required for books. But I had generous friends both then and later.

Our college rules were imposed partly from without. One of these was the insistence upon a chaperon for all women-students attending lectures in Trinity. We might go un-chaperoned to lectures in the Divinity Schools, but not in Trinity, and I was told that it was the wife of the Master, not Dr. Thompson himself, who insisted on this. It was an unfortunate rule for me. In my first year, I was the only Girton student attending Dr. Ward's lectures, and my chaperon was an incurably unpunctual person; a decayed gentlewoman with the poorest sort of twittering manners. I was expected not to go in alone to the lecture, but to wait in the porch of Trinity Chapel, to be the butt and mockery of a certain type of undergraduate, until my silly guardian chose to turn up, out of breath and apologetic. I would not go in without her, for fear of getting her into trouble, for I think her small fee was of importance to her. At last it was reported that Mrs. Thompson, having made observations from the Master's Lodge, had given out her ukase that 'the young ladies had shown themselves so ladylike and so businesslike that they might be trusted in future to attend lectures without chaperons.'

There can be no doubt that all this prudery on the part of authority retarded the growth of respect and comradeship in the male undergraduates. If our own authorities guyed us, I used to think rather bitterly, what chance did they give us of establishing franker and more dignified relations with our male fellow-students? One result of these conventions was that it was difficult for us to understand each other and I preferred the society of dons to that of undergraduates.

The rules about men visitors had absurd results. We might receive them in the public 'reception room' (a dismal little hole about twelve feet square) or in our studies, provided we left the door open and did not sit down. An extremely loquacious young acquaintance of mine once kept me standing by my fire, with the door open, for two hours, after which I told him that I was too exhausted to endure more; a good example of my social helplessness. We were expected to see our male visitors out of the house, but not to go as far as the gate of the grounds with them. This jig-saw puzzle of proprieties led a few students into elaborate plotting, just for the fun of the thing; but I did not find that sort of thing amusing.

One ridiculous incident occurred when I was returning with two friends in a cab from an evening party. It was a bitterly cold night and snowing. Our miserable horse could scarcely get up the 'hill' beyond Magdalene and frequently stopped. I remonstrated with the driver for flogging him and he replied, 'He's not exhausted, he's just sick of it.' However, we declared that we wouldn't sit behind him and I said we would walk it. But my companions explained that we were not allowed to walk out to Girton so late, unchaperoned. Finally, we decided that we would walk, but we would take the cab as a chaperone, and so the procession at last reached college, for the horse did not refuse to walk when lightened of his load. I wish I could remember our conversation with the driver who walked beside us. But I daresay I didn't say very much, for I was very young and mortified.

It seems queer to me that none of the authorities appreciated the effect of all this mincing prudery on the undergraduates of both sexes. Into the old monastic life of the university had been introduced women. Not 'Woman,' the legendary snare and lure of the devil, but real individual women, with qualities and capacities and ambitions and difficulties quite unconnected with sex. The marriage of Fellows was still a comparatively new thing, and perambulators in the quads were still matters of comment. We felt acutely that we were on trial, on sufferance even, and while this made us circumspect and docile in an exaggerated degree, I cannot deny that it perpetuated and strengthened in some of us the revolt against the indignities to which women were submitted merely on account of their sex.

We had but recently been admitted as of right to the degree examinations. All the honours won by women before 1882 had been by grace of individual examiners, who corrected their papers and placed them from a sense of fairness. But, in my time and for years after we were not allowed to receive the degree for which we had qualified by residence and examination. The unwillingness to admit that women could be on the same footing as men was illustrated by the fact that when the class-lists were read in the Senate House, the men and the women were segregated in them; so that a woman was read out not as 'tenth Wrangler,' but as 'equal to tenth Wrangler' or 'between ninth and tenth Wrangler.' This led to the curious result that, in Philippa Fawcett's year, a woman was declared to have done what it was impossible for any man to do. It was a dramatic moment when, having cheered the senior Wrangler and heard the lists of the men, down to the 'wooden spoon,' we heard the Vice-Chancellor (was it the Vice-Chancellor?) say impressively: 'Women': (Pause) 'Above Senior Wrangler' . . . but the tornado of applause drowned the name of the woman who had won this impossible honour. Everyone knew what it was. I will say that the men cheered magnificently, and if they could have caught the woman they would have chaired her. Needless to say, Miss Fawcett remained *perdue*.

Of course we were told that one step at a time was necessary, and our college songs celebrated what we had won, not what was still to be won. Nevertheless, the injustice of the situation did not improve the relations between men and women undergraduates, and I resented the fact that when men misbehaved, women were made to suffer for it. When there was an anti-women riot of men, graduates as well as undergraduates, carrying an effigy of a woman upside down through the streets and threatening to batter the gates of Newnham (gates which were a memorial to Miss Clough), it was the women who were gated, not the men. I have heard a middle-aged don who witnessed the scene describe it as 'capital fun.' Now, modern women undergraduates have shown that they can enjoy a rag as much as men and, if that happens to be your temperament, perhaps there is not much harm in occasionally indulging it, in moderation. What is intolerable is the pretension that men are to be allowed to rag women, but the ragged women must remain perfect ladies.

I still wonder whether a more robust attitude on the part of Authority would not have hastened the development of the young and have prevented some of the more deplorable events of the suffrage agitation. If we had defied these demonstrations and gone about as usual, I'm not sure that the young women would not have proved themselves capable of dealing in their own way with the young men, and we should have at least avoided the inference that when we say, 'Boys will be boys,' what we actually mean is, 'Boys will be cads.' As a matter of fact, there are but few real cads among Cambridge undergraduates (though a mob of them may become very silly and very dangerous, as I was to experience many years later). The decent feeling of the great majority would have been enlisted by a more frank liberation of women undergraduates. It is not possible to establish sound relations between men and women students on a theory that boys must be cads, but girls must remain young ladies. I seem to note a far deeper respect for the human rights of women since the suffrage agitation and war-work of many kinds released them from the necessity of being ladylike. Manners may be free and easy; they are the better for that.

One of a woman's heaviest handicaps is the common tendency to view any failure or dereliction on the part of a woman as due, not to her individual idiosyncracy, but to her sex; any merit or success on the other hand, being set down to her being 'an exceptional woman.' I would not deny that it was sometimes stimulating to know that one had to make good for one's whole sex. But it was also sometimes very intimidating and the cause of much anxiety and self-depreciation in women not of heroic build.

Moreover, one was made to feel that not to make a mistake was more important than getting something done or making a plucky try. It has been often and truly said that he who is not prepared to make a fool of himself will make nothing of worth. In my youth it was considered dreadful for a woman to make a fool of herself, except, of course, in the consecrated ways of womanhood. Along the paths of fashion and custom, the sillier she was, the more she was praised for true femininity; but the pack was still in full cry for any 'hyena in petticoats' who ventured to champion her own sex.

From I Have Been Young, *1935, by Helena Swanwick (née Sickert), suffrage worker and pacifist. The daughter of the artist and cartoonist, Oscar Sickert, she was born in Munich in 1864. She read Moral Sciences at Girton and became a lecturer in psychology at Westfield College, London. In 1888 she married Frederick Swanwick and moved to Manchester, where he lectured and was later Professor of Mathematics at Owens College. Swanwick worked as a lecturer and journalist and was active in working men's clubs, the Co-operative Guild and the Women's Trade Union Council. She joined the North of England Suffrage Society in 1900 and was editor of the suffragist paper* The Common Cause *from 1909, resigning after disagreements in 1912. When war broke out in 1914 Swanwick was a vociferous critic and became British President of the Women's International*

League for Peace. After the war she was adviser to the Labour Party on international affairs and was involved in the activities of the League of Nations.

WRITING HOME

My dear mother

I sent you a postcard did you get it. I told you I got here all right and liked it very much. I could not write a long letter before I had no time and we are only alowed to write letters two evenings a week Tuesday and Friday. When we have done our lessons for next day we say please may I write now and Miss Chapman says have you done everything and if we say we have she says yes and if you sit at Miss Days table Miss Day says it. And sometimes we haven't but we say so. I sit up by Miss Chapman and she can see everything I do and at tea and dinner and breakfast I sit beside Mrs Gurley. Another girl in my class sits opposite and one sits beside me and we would rather sit somewhere else. I dont care for Mrs Gurley much she is very fat and never smiles and never listens to what you say unless she scolds you and I think Miss Chapman is afraid of her to. Miss Day is not afraid of anybody. I am in the first class. I am in the College and under that is the school. Only very little girls are in the school they go to bed at half past eight and do their lessons in the dining hall. I do mine in the study and go to bed with the big girls. They wear dresses down to the ground. Lilith Gordon is a girl in my class she is in my room to she is only as old as me and she wears stays and has a beautiful figgure. All the girls wear stays. Please send me some I have no waste. A governess sleeps in our room and she has no teeth. She takes them out every night and puts them in water when the light is out. Lilith Gordon and the other girl say goodnight to her after she has taken them off then she cant talk propperly and we want to hear her. I think she knows for she is very cross. I don't learn latin yet till I go into the second class my sums are very hard. For supper there is only bread and butter and water if we don't have cake and jam of our own. Please send me some strawberry jam and another cake. Tell Sarah there are three servants to wait at dinner they have white aprons and a cap on their heads. They say will you take beef miss

> I remain
> > your loving daughter
> > Laura.

Dear Pin

I am very busy I will write you a letter. You would not like being here I think you should always stop at home you will never get as far as long division. Mrs Gurley is an awful old beast all the girls call her that. You WOULD be frightened of her. In the afternoon after school we walk two and two and you ask a girl to walk with you and if you dont you have to walk with Miss Chapman. Miss Chapman and Miss Day walks behind and they watch to see you dont laugh at boys. Some girls write letters to them and say they will meet them up behind a tree in the corner of the garden a paling is lose and the boys put letters in. I think boys are silly but Maria Morell says they are tip top that means awfully jolly. She writes a letter to boys every week she takes it to church and drops it coming out and he picks it up and puts an answer through the fence. We put our letters on the mantlepiece in the dining hall and Mrs Gurley or Miss Chapman read the adress to see we dont write to boys. They are shut up she cant read the inside. I hope you dont cry so much at school no one cries. Now Miss Chapman says it is time to stop

> I remain
> > your afectionate sister
> > Laura.

P.S. I took the red lineing out of my hat.

From The Getting of Wisdom, *1910, by Henry Handel Richardson.*

HOME ARTS

In recent years there has been a widespread movement to bring the education of our girls into relation with their work as home-makers. The old 'blue-stocking' type, who prided herself on not knowing how to sew and mend, and who thought cooking menial, and beneath her, no longer appeals to anyone. The ideal is developing, and we are learning to regard with pity anyone, girl or woman, who is helpless in a home. But at the same time we no longer share the conception of a woman's whole duty held by our grandmothers. We do not applaud the mother or daughter who spends long hours in the kitchen, or who revels in turning the whole house upside down and inside out in that most bewildering and least methodical of all human inconveniences – the spring cleaning. We have come to see that method and system are better than rule of thumb and guesswork, that housekeeping is as much a science as an art, and that in it, as in all other departments of life, it is brain that tells. We want our girls to grow up into sensible, methodical, practical women, able to direct intelligently and sympathetically the manifold activities of the home – ready themselves to lend a hand if the call come – and imbued with a deep sense of the worth and dignity of all true work, whether it be scrubbing a floor or construing a crabbed Greek chorus.

With this change of ideal there has entered into many of our schools an effort to equip girls for such work. The action of the Board of Education has done much to encourage this aim. But prejudice dies hard, and in too many schools the ideal is still purely intellectual in the strictly limited and scholastic sense, and cooking and domestic economy generally are looked down upon as all right for 'poor dears' or 'duffers,' but a waste of time for a really clever girl.

From Home Arts, *1911, by Margaret A. Gilliland.*

HOME MANAGEMENT

Work *should be the end and aim of education*, for work is the source of all true felicity – it is the *secret of happiness in life*. (RUSKIN)

Begin by asking why all girls and boys have to attend school from five to fourteen years of age. Then lead on to the subjects taught in the girls' school, and in a pleasant, chatty style get the girls to name their favourite lessons, and tell why they are so. (The teacher will find that even girls of this tender age manifest keen appreciation of those subjects that will help them most when they leave school.) Then lead them to think which is the most important subject for girls to learn – a subject that every girl can even now take a great interest in – a subject that, when she is older, may become all-important to her, namely, the management of a home.

How proud a girl is of her *doll's* house! How delightful it will be for these girls to have, some day, a *real* house of their *very own* to manage! Do not be content until the eyes of every child in the class sparkle with enthusiasm. Contrast various types of homes – some so comfortable; some, alas! just the reverse. What makes the difference? Not money – for a poor home may be a very happy one – but the disposition of the people and *the way the homes are managed*.

Nobody can manage a home well unless she feels in her heart what a splendid work it is she is doing. The cleverest *men* in the world may make good, wise laws, and strive with all their might to make the nation happy and prosperous; but unless *woman's* work is well done they cannot succeed, for mismanaged homes can never make a happy nation. It is not only good *law-makers* that are needed, but good *home-makers*. In no walk of life is there more need for unselfishness; there is no more self-denying, no more heroic, no more truly lovable person than a good mother. From morning to night, week in, week out, she thinks for others, and looks after their comfort. To the mother in the home, to sisters and daughters, has been given the *most important* and *noblest work in the world* – that of home-making.

Lead the girls to think what makes a happy home, and how it may be recognized. From a happy home goes forth, morning by morning, a happy, healthy, well-cared for father, who, because he has such a comfortable home, is never tempted to spend his evenings in the public-house or club. A happy home means happy children also – healthy-bodied, clear-minded, good-mannered, light-hearted, and fond of fun.

Home management needs not only a woman's loving heart and willing hands, but a *clever brain*. It is not true to say that *any one* can manage a home. The best home manager is the one who begins, when quite a little girl, to fit herself for the work. Ask the girls which of them would like to begin now; to have lessons in school that they can at once carry out in their own homes, and surprise and gladden father and mother. Then when the time comes – and speak of this in a matter-of-fact sort of way – that the girls have homes of their own, what happy, comfortable homes they will be – a credit to themselves, a credit to their town, and a credit to the nation!

Enthusiasm having thus been aroused, the teacher may proceed with the lessons, giving the subject of each beforehand, so as to lead the children to think about and talk over the matter with their mothers. The teacher who gives the lessons in a tactful, sympathetic way creates a bond of union between herself and the parents, and brings out the dullest children in the class in a most wonderful manner. (The writer recalls with pleasure the case of a poor girl, the very personification of dullness, who became a perfect enthusiast in the art of furniture-polishing, and who, after seeing the effect of the polish on the school piano, could with difficulty be restrained from cleaning and polishing every other wooden article in the school.)

I. Need for Method and Forethought

Much discomfort is caused in very many homes through lack of method, and consequent waste of time. It is *wrong* for mothers and those at home to have housework going on in the evening, when fathers and elder brothers and sisters return after a hard day's toil, and naturally expect peace and comfort. Dwell at much length on this point; lead the children to think of the great number of fathers and elder brothers who are practically *driven* outside, to seek at public-houses, clubs, or music halls the comfort that should be theirs at home. A good housewife is never happier than when she has all the members of her family around her.

Show the school time-table. Lead the girls to imagine what a *school* would be like without one. It is just as necessary to have a working time-table for the *home*, and it is an excellent plan for the young, inexperienced home manager to write one out. Tell the girls that later on they shall make a time-table in their note-books – a good-sized exercise-book, used not only for the Home Management lessons of the first year's course, but for those of the second and third years' courses also. This book should become the property of each girl on leaving school.

No girl has the least chance of becoming a good home mana-ger unless she is orderly and methodical in her work. There must be no rushing about at random, no sitting down and wondering what to do next. To 'run a house' smoothly, the work must be carefully planned beforehand, and carried out, so far as possible, as planned. 'Order is Heaven's first law,' and it must be the home manager's too. If she would avoid hopeless muddle, her rule must be, 'Clear as you go.' There must be one place, and no other, for everything in the house, but more especially in her kitchen.

From Home Management, *1910, by Wilena Hitching.*

CHAPTER THREE

WORKING LIVES

'Within these few years,' wrote the reformer Maria Grey, in 1889:

> a vast and sweeping change has taken place, of unprece-
> dented rapidity, causing a reaction from this doctrine of
> idleness and dependence as essential to ladyhood toward
> the opposite extreme, of work and independence as essential
> to honourable womanhood; work meaning paid work, and
> independence meaning life apart from the home life and
> free from the duties and constraining order of home.

The perception of the 'redundancy' of middle-class women's
lives was a natural outcome of the impetus for the reform of
women's education, with the ambition and wider horizons that
education instilled and which led to incursions into the male-
dominated workplace. Yet at the beginning of the twentieth
century only 29 per cent of the workforce comprised women
and only 10 per cent of married women worked. On the whole,
middle-class women did not work outside the home – certainly
not after marriage – and the concept of the man earning a 'family
wage' supposed that they would not do so.

For the young, unmarried woman, employment opportunities
gradually increased towards the last quarter of the nineteenth
century, with horizons expanding beyond domestic work and
governessing, and new jobs on offer in the professional world,
in teaching and nursing. Commerce and the retail industries –
once the preserve of the male clerk or assistant – became increasingly open to women; and the introduction of the typewriter into
offices provided them with job opportunities beyond the dreams

97

of their male counterparts (albeit less highly paid).

For most working-class women at the turn of the century the concept of idleness must have seemed a bitter joke. Often confined to a narrow range of domestic or factory work before marriage, their work after marriage was equally hard, in difficult conditions. With inadequate wages coming in, and many mouths to feed, women were often forced by financial necessity to seek whatever employment they could get to supplement their daily overwork in the home. Women's wages were in general about half those of men, and their invasion of the workplace was therefore often resented by men, who saw them as undercutting wages and thereby threatening their jobs.

While working-class girls had to help, and often take responsibility, in the home from as young as five years old, and by thirteen were earning a living – or at least contributing to the family budget – middle-class women were often depicted as too delicate for work. Many novels of the period portrayed the poignancy of women venturing into the harsh world of employment, in danger of either defeat and ill-health or a regrettable loss of womanliness implicit in success; though it was pointed out that it was usually the better-paid jobs that were regarded as unsuitable for women. Many working-class women did not venture out into the market place either, but that was because, confined at home with the responsibilities of young children, they were forced into the great army of 'sweated labour' – assembling, dressmaking, tailoring, for a few essential pennies for hours of hard toil in their own homes.

INTERRUPTIONS

I should have a study in the house and carry out my projects of earning my living. [My mother] went so far as to furnish my father's studio as my study. But I soon found that if I sat up there to work, she spent her time in weeping downstairs. So I brought my work down to her sitting-room and did the best I could amidst the incessant interruptions which constituted her life.

Visitors ebbed and flowed in her rooms and I was not able to ignore them.

I stress the importance of this incessant interruption, which is the common lot of girls and women far more than of boys and men, because it seems to me of vital importance in the estimation of women's capacity for mental work. It is universally conceded that a man must have some consideration if he is to produce, but in regard to women this is still a rare concession. Of course there are some people who say frankly that it is quite enough if one half of humanity has a chance of doing intellectual work and it makes for good economy if the other half – which is in any case handicapped by sex and its responsibilities – is dedicated to ancillary offices alone. With such people it is not a question whether a woman *could* under the same conditions as a man do intellectual work of value; they think that whatever value it might have is more than compensated for by the withdrawal of many women from the services which the more intellectually valuable man requires.

This view is one which is perhaps taken by most women as well as by most men; because, clearly, the number of women (as of men) who are keenly driven to use their brains to the limit, and are prepared for the drastic effort this requires, are few, and very subject to the lure not only of idleness but of routine drudgery; and it would be absurd to expect men in the mass to object to women's voluntary sacrifices of their minds. Women who don't want to use their minds, or who have deliberately committed mental suttee for domestic reasons, are naturally prone to jealousy and even derision of their fellow-women who have refused the sacrifice.

From I Have Been Young, *1935, by Helena Swanwick.*

MY MOTHER'S AWFULLY CLEVER . . .

That Lilith and she undressed for bed together had also some-thing to do with their intimacy: this half-hour when one's hair

99

was unbound and replaited, and fat and thin arms wielded the brush, was the time of all others for confidences. The governess who occupied the fourth bed did not come upstairs till ten o'clock; the publican's daughter, a lazy girl, was usually half asleep before the other two had their clothes off.

It was in the course of one of these confidential chats that Laura did a very foolish thing. In a moment of weakness, she gratuitously gave away the secret that Mother supported her family by the work of her hands.

The two girls were sitting on the side of Lilith's bed. Laura had a day of mishaps behind her – that partly, no doubt, accounted for her self-indulgence. But, in addition, her companion had just told her, unasked, that she thought her 'very pretty'. It was not in Laura's nature to let this pass: she was never at ease under an obligation; she had to pay the coin back in kind.

'Embroidery? What sort? However does she do it?' – Lilith's interest was on tiptoe at once – a false and slimy interest, the victim afterwards told herself.

'Oh, my mother's awfully clever. It's just lovely, too, what she does – all in silk – and ever so many different colours. She made a piano-cover once, and got fifty pounds for it.'

'How perfectly splendid!'

'But that was only a lucky chance ... that she got that to do. She mostly does children's dresses and cloaks and things like that.'

'But she's not a dressmaker, is she?'

'A dressmaker? I should think not indeed! They're sent up, all ready to work, from the biggest shops in town.'

'I say! – she must be clever.'

'She is; she can do anything. She makes the patterns up all out of her own head.' – And filled with pride in Mother's accomplishments and Lilith's appreciation of them, Laura fell asleep that night without a qualm.

It was the next evening. Several of the boarders who had finished preparing their lessons were loitering in the dining-hall, Laura and Lilith among them. In the group was a girl called Lucy, young but very saucy; for she lived at Toorak, and came of one of the best families in Melbourne. She was not as old as Laura by two years, but was already feared and respected for the fine scorn of her opinions.

Lilith Gordon had bragged: 'My uncle's promised me a gold watch and chain when I pass matric.'

Lucy of Toorak laughed: her nose came down, and her mouth went up at the corners. 'Do you think you ever will?'

'G. o. k. and He won't tell. But I'll probably get the watch all the same.'

'Where does your uncle hang out?'

'Brisbane.'

'Sure he can afford to buy it?'

'Of course he can.'

'What is he?'

Lilith was unlucky enough to hesitate, ever so slightly. 'Oh, he's got plenty of money,' she asserted.

'She doesn't like to say what he is!'

'I don't care whether I say it or not.'

'A butcher, p'raps, or an undertaker?'

'A butcher! He's got the biggest newspaper in Brisbane!'

'A newspaper! Great Scott! Her uncle keeps a newspaper!'

There was a burst of laughter from those standing round.

Lilith was scarlet now. 'It's nothing to be ashamed of,' she said angrily.

But Lucy of Toorak could not recover from her amusement. 'An uncle who keeps a newspaper! A newspaper! Well, I'm glad none of *my* uncles are so rummy. – I say, does he leave it at front doors himself in the morning?'

Laura had at first looked passively on, well pleased to see another than herself the butt of young Lucy's wit. But at this stage of her existence she was too intent on currying favour, to side with any but the stronger party. And so she joined in the boisterous mirth Lilith's admission and Lucy's reception of it excited, and flung her gibes with the rest.

She was pulled up short by a hissing in her ear. 'If you say one word more, I'll tell about the embroidery!'

Laura went pale with fright: she had been in good spirits that day, and had quite forgotten her silly confidence of the night before. Now, the jeer that was on the tip of her tongue hung fire. She could not all at once obliterate her smile – that would have been noticeable; but it grew weaker, stiffer and more unnatural, then gradually faded away, leaving her with a very solemn little face.

From this night on, Lilith Gordon represented a powder-mine, which might explode at any minute. – And she herself had laid the train!

From the outset, Laura had been accepted, socially, by even the most exclusive, as one of themselves; and this, in spite of her niggardly allowance, her ridiculous clothes. For the child had race in her: in a well-set head, in good hands and feet and ears. Her nose, too, had a very pronounced droop, which could stand only for blue blood, or a Hebraic ancestor – and Jews were not received as boarders in the school. Now, loud as money made itself in this young community, effectual as it was in cloaking shortcomings, it did not go all the way: inherited instincts and traditions were not so easily subdued. Just some of the wealthiest too, were aware that their antecedents would not stand a close scrutiny; and thus a mighty respect was engendered in them for those who had nothing to fear. Moreover, directly you got away from the vastly rich, class distinctions were observed with an exactitude such as can only obtain in an exceedingly mixed society. The three professions alone were sacrosanct. The calling of architect, for example, or of civil engineer, was, if a fortune had not been accumulated, utterly without prestige; trade, any connection with trade – the merest bowing acquaintance with buying and selling – was a taint that nothing could remove; and those girls who were related to shopkeepers, or, more awful still, to publicans, would rather have bitten their tongues off than have owned to the disgrace.

Yet Laura knew very well that good birth and an aristocratic appearance would not avail her, did the damaging fact leak out that Mother worked for her living. Work in itself was bad enough – how greatly to be envied were those whose fathers did nothing more active than live on their money! But the additional circumstance of Mother being a woman made things ten times worse: ladies did not work; someone always left them enough to live on, and if he didn't, well, then he, too, shared the ignominy. So Laura went in fear and trembling lest the truth should come to light – in that case, she would be a pariah indeed – went in hourly dread of Lilith betraying her. Nothing, however, happened – at least as far as she could discover – and she sought to propitiate Lilith in every possible way. For the time being, though, anxiety turned her into a porcupine, ready to erect her quills at a touch. She was ever on the look-out for an allusion to her mother's position, and for the slight that was bound to accompany it.

From The Getting of Wisdom, *1910, by Henry Handel Richardson.*

RURAL EMPLOYMENT

WORCESTERSHIRE

FIELDWORK. – Within the memory of people still alive women worked habitually in the fields in many parts of England. Now it is only in few and far apart districts that women are to be found who, as part of their daily routine, perform certain duties about the fields and farms of their own neighbourhood.

In the North West of Worcester and the contiguous parts of Herefordshire lies a tract where no great change has taken place in the work of women for the last fifty years, and where the young wife of to-day living 'under a farmer' takes her share in the work of the farm almost as much as a matter of course as did her grandmother. Four parishes were visited, situated in the North Western arm of Worcestershire, spreading over many square miles of land and containing, at the census of 1901, a population of 663 persons. Of these 140 were male householders, of whom 23 farmed over 20 acres, 39 were small holders and 58 agricultural labourers; while the remaining 20 included the squires, clergy, school teachers, gamekeepers, etc. There were also some women householders. The countryside is fruitful and extremely picturesque. No glacial period can have sent its rollers to flatten out this landscape. High ridge and deep valley are broken up with indescribable irregularity into a thousand hills and valleys watered by rushing streams. Even the different fields have each their well marked natural features and varieties. There are old-fashioned orchards where apples, plums and damsons grow together upon trees set in no rigid lines, and drop, when ripe, into rich meadow grass. There are gardens, hayfields and arable lands; and there are also hop-yards with their thousands of poles upright as a regiment of soldiers. Through the pleasant country the habitations lie scattered, here a hamlet bordering the highway, there a pair of cottages, then a single homestead buried in a crevice of the hillside and approached by a lane knee-deep in mire which entraps the stranger, while the native follows some scarce visible track through the long grass of meadow or orchard. The houses, too, are picturesque. Old timbered cottages, in the walls of which rough-cast lath-and-plaster has been replaced by mellow red brick generally contain three or four rooms. Within, the rooms are often whitewashed; hams and strings of onions hang from the oak beams of the kitchen ceiling; the great open fireplaces are filled with blazing logs, and behind them run deep baking ovens. The red brick floors are uncovered, the furniture plain and simple, and there is an absence of useless litter that, together with the warm colouring, helps to give an impression of genuine comfort. The comfort, however, is too often rather apparent than real. So damp are the walls that where they have been papered the paper is generally peeling off; the bricks that pave the living room are often broken, and generally so porous that a bucketful of water poured upon them vanishes at once. Needless to say, rheumatism is prevalent, and although the disease is usually attributed to cider drinking, the dampness of these dwellings appears to provide a sufficient cause. Many of the men employed by farmers live rent free or nearly rent free in a cottage with garden or 'pig-run' *i.e.*, orchard, belonging to their employer; but it is a condition of so living – and there is usually no alternative – that the wife shall perform certain services for the farmer, such as tying a certain acreage of hops and helping in the hayfield at the busiest times. The monopoly of cottages by the farmers is a hardship to the labourer, who is rendered liable to be turned out at a week's notice, and who but for this circumstance would be in a very independent position, since labour appears by no means overabundant, and unemployed farm hands few. Rents for tenants who do not live 'under a farmer' range up to £8 a year.

Agriculture is the only industry of importance, and the main branches, here, are stock raising, hop growing, and fruit growing. Ancient freehold small holdings are numerous, but diminishing;

the owners tend to sell, and most of the holdings are mortgaged.

Men employed as regular farm hands earn, broadly speaking, 12/– to 14/– per week, and are allowed in summer three quarts of cider per day. Little harvest money is given. An able-bodied day labourer earns 2/6 to 3/– per day, with cider.

Nearly all the cottages keep pigs or poultry, and it is estimated that they can make £2 to £3 a year by the sale of fruit. There is no market for vegetables but the gardens supply a large part of the food consumed at home.

About thirty women, known to be workers, were visited, most of whom were wives of labourers. Probably a chief share in the work of the homestead falls upon the wife, who also usually bakes her own bread and walks to the nearest town, some five miles distant, for her weekly marketing. Many women work three or four ten-hour days a week (from eight till six, or till dark) for the farmer, and a few go out to work every day in the week. Public opinion approves of wage earning by married women; and the woman who abstains from working in the fields is taunted – even if she has young children – with being lazy. Various inhabitants of the district assert that the houses and children of the women who go out to work are better kept than those of the women who stay at home; and appearances on the whole confirmed the assertion. The work of women is, nevertheless, tending to decrease, and probably no pressure is put upon the mother of young children, even when living 'under the farmer,' to go to work.

A woman who works for a farmer as a condition of occupying his cottage is paid 10d., or in some cases 1/– for her day's work, and is usually allowed one pint of cider if she cares to fetch it, which as a rule she does not. A woman whose work is not contributory to her rent receives 1/– per day. Piece work rates – which vary somewhat – yield different totals of course, according to the skill and speed of different workers. Employers and workers alike declare that the women are not pressed. They can take their children with them to the fields, and one farmer said that if his women took an hour or two off to go and look after their babies no complaint would be made.

By their own account they frequently stop to rest. In an orchard, one day, where they were 'apple picking' several women were found in a picturesque group warming themselves around a

105

large bonfire that they had lighted, and appeared in no hurry to resume their work.

Except farm servants, whose duties are of course, of a different kind, no women are employed regularly the whole year round. Those who desire regular work can have it for five to nine months of the year; and during those months the most energetic often work almost daily, filling the places of others less willing to do so.

The following processes are those in which women are principally employed:

GROUND DRESSING, i.e., picking up bits of stick or stone from the fields, begins towards March.

HOP TYING is the fastening of wires up which the young shoots of the hop are trained. The fastening of each wire requires the worker to go three times round each pole. It is delicate work – some of the women said 'fiddly' and tiresome – and the smaller hands of women are considered better adapted for it than those of men. The work is generally paid for by the piece, at 5/– an acre. Some women can earn 1/4 a day at it, but an unaccustomed and unskilled worker coming fresh to the district and bound to the farmer may be unable to make 6d. a day.

HAY MAKING often entails lengthened hours of work. As a set-off, however, tea is given by some employers; and in some cases a bonus is also given at the conclusion of the hay harvest, which brings the rate of pay up to 1/3 per day. Some women are asserted to have earned 1/6.

ROOT SINGLING is often performed by a man and his wife together.

HOP PICKING employs not only nearly all the women and children of the district – including women who do no other field work – but also large numbers of people from Dudley and the Black Country, as well as from Bewdley and Kidderminster. The two populations seldom hold much intercourse, natives and visitors working, as a rule, in different 'yards.' Whole families, parents, children and even babies go together into the hopfields where the very young can be of help. Each family has a 'vat' and the rate of pay varies according to the size of the hops. In some seasons eight bushels must be picked for 1/–, in others, only, perhaps, five.

FRUIT PICKING generally means, for women, the picking up of

fallen fruit. Occasionally, however, women mount ladders into the trees and gather damsons, and for doing so their pay will exceed 1/– per day. One woman said she made 1/6 on piece rates.

The picking up of fallen fruit is paid in some cases by the piece, in some, by time. One old lady declared herself able to make 2/– a day by some knack of gathering up the apples into her apron; she seldom, however, got employed at the work. Some women, especially, of course, those who are rheumatic, find the continuous stooping tiring. Apple picking is passing to some extent into the hands of men, although men are less skilful and more highly paid. Farmers probably prefer to employ their regular farm hands when these happen not to be fully occupied.

MANGEL AND SWEDE PULLING occupies the women in November. A worker said she was paid 10/– the acre for getting up the roots. The Annual Report of the Hereford Diocesan Social Service Committee states the usual rate to be 1½d. per 100 yards.

POTATO SORTING AND SACK MENDING affords employment on some farms for wet days, under shelter in the farm buildings.

THRESHING by machine often makes work for a woman who sits at the top of the machine to cut the binding round the sheaves.

From Married Women's Work, 1916, by Clementina Black (1855?– 1923), a social reformer who worked from the 1880s to improve the lot of women employed in industry and manufacture. An active suffragist, she also wrote novels, translations, biographies and plays for children.

WHAT IT MEANS TO BE A LADY JOURNALIST

As an increasing number of girls look with envious eye on the lady journalist every day, it is well that there should be a good understanding of what it means to be a lady journalist.

It means, in the first place, that you must be a great deal more than a writer of Pitman's shorthand. Nothing could be more erroneous than the idea that a reporter is a mere machine, whose duty is to take down notes and translate them in much the same way as a phonograph 'takes' and repeats a song. Even if that were the true definition of a reporter, it could never accurately define the lady journalist. Women are certainly not employed in journalism to do merely mechanical work of that kind. As a rule, they are engaged to do original work, which men could not do so well, or which they could not do, perhaps, at all. Imagine a man at a society ball, describing the thousand and one marvels of the Duchess of So-and-so's gown, or the wonderful shape of the Honourable Lady Blank's new hat. It is Fashion, no doubt, which created the lady journalist. It must have been some blundering man's description of a dress which first suggested to an editor that he should engage a woman on his staff. At any rate, some sensible editor made this daring departure some years ago, and women have been on editors' staffs ever since.

It is to be presumed, therefore, that the majority of lady journalists find their work congenial. And there is no doubt that, on the whole, it is so. It must not be imagined that the lady journalist does exactly the same kind of work as the mere man. The first thorough lady journalist has yet to come. However one may long for the equality of the sexes, there is something repugnant to a man's ideas in the picture of a woman on the track of a murder, or reporting a police case, or writing an account of a football match. It must be distinctly understood that woman's work in journalism is essentially the feminine side. It need not be narrow. There are plenty of better things in the world than inquests and police-courts and football matches.

As none can speak with such authority on the subject of journalism for women as those who have had experience of the work, it will be well to let some of these decide the question for us. Mr. Stead, perhaps the most brilliant of living journalists, and certainly the most famous, has given his opinion in very emphatic language. Writing in THE YOUNG WOMAN more than seven years ago, Mr. Stead warned women who desired to enter the ranks of journalism that they must not presume upon their sex, and imagine that because they were women all sorts of special treatment would be meted out to them.

'After the false kindness and undue consideration on the part of some editors, which, after all, at the beginning, may be excused for the sake of encouraging the timid to do their best, the chief foe that women have to contend with in journalism is their own conventionality, and the fantastic notion that a lady cannot be expected to do this, that, or the other disagreeable bit of work. That such and such a duty is not the thing to ask from a lady, that a lady must not be scolded when she does wrong, or that a lady ought not to stay up late, or go about late – all that is fiddlesticks and nonsense, as our good old nurses used to say. Ladies with such notions had better stay at home in their drawing-rooms and boudoirs. The great, rough, real, workaday world is no place for them. Until it is the recognized thing that the women on a staff may be admonished as freely as their male comrades, the latter will have an unfair advantage in the profession. It is the sharp edge of the employer's reproof that keeps the apprentice up to his work. To spare the rod, metaphorically, is to spoil the child, and women can bear spoiling quite as little as any child. But many women take it as their right. If a woman cannot be admonished as roundly as a man, she had better keep outside a newspaper office. The drive is too great to permit of periphrastic circumlocution in giving orders, in making criticisms, or in finding fault.'

That, in Mr. Stead's view – and nobody knows better – is what it means to be a lady journalist. 'If a girl means to be a journalist,' Mr. Stead explains further, 'she ought to be a journalist out and out, and not try to be a journalist up to nine o'clock and Miss Nancy after nine. I don't want her to be unladylike. The woman who is mannish, and forward, and generally aggressive, simply throws away her chances, and competes voluntarily at a disadvantage. For no editor in his senses wants either mannish women or womanish men on his staff. What he does want is a staff that will do whatever work turns up without making scenes, or consulting clocks, or standing upon its conventional dignities. A girl who has proper self-respect can go about her business at all hours in English-speaking countries without serious risk of safety or of reputation.'

The girl who would be a journalist must begin with this idea firmly rooted in her head. Though, as already hinted, there are certain natural restrictions, the lady journalist must, generally speaking, be prepared to do anything at any time – and do it, let it be understood, *at once*. 'Time is money' is true of no profession more than of journalism, and the woman who wishes to succeed in newspaper work must be ready to respond to any demand, yea or nay, without asking for a day to consider it. That is one of the severest strains upon the woman-writer – the liability to be called upon at a moment's notice to undertake an engagement which she has not expected, and which may demand a long journey or constant attention for many hours. Let us take the opinion of another – a lady:–

'If a woman cannot do night work, and regular night work, the prizes of Fleet Street are not for her,' says Janet E. Hogarth. 'I do not say that she may not make a living, but she will have to content herself with a kind of journalism far enough removed from literature, with the chatty article, or the women's papers, and the hundred and one scrappy periodicals which have so successfully hit off the taste of the rising generation.' That is not a pleasant outlook for a woman; yet Miss Hogarth asserts that it is what awaits the woman journalist who is not prepared to take her stand side by side with a man. She wishes that those girls who look eagerly to journalism as a means of livelihood knew 'a little more of the position and prospects of the average woman journalist, of the desperate struggle to make both ends meet, of the necessity of accepting the most hum-drum and distasteful tasks, of the trials of the interviewer, and the endless subterfuges of the society reporter.'

As to the actual daily work of the lady journalist, let still another speak:–

'The lady journalist,' says this lady, 'in preparing her fashion article, must go the round of some of the shops, note-book in hand, and learn from the principals of these establishments what is to be worn; she must also have access to some of the Court dressmakers, and hear what the prevailing fashions are to be. The lady journalist must attend fashionable weddings, and describe the dresses. She must see the trousseau of the bride, and describe that. The description of dresses at balls, operas, races, cricket matches, and other functions of the London season is a considerable part of the work of a lady journalist who makes fashions her speciality; to be able to write this she must, of course, go about to the various entertainments, and learn to know the celebrities of the day by sight. She must attend funerals and interview undertakers.

All sorts and conditions of men, or more often women, will the lady journalist have to interview; she may be sent to a duchess and a lady chiropodist on the same morning; the popular novelist, the fashionable poetess, the favourite actress, the latest public singer, and all the lesser lights of the literary, theatrical, musical, and fashionable world are game she must pursue at her editor's bidding. Sometimes she has to act as dramatic or musical critic, and after a hard day's work may have to go to a concert or the first night of a new piece, and write an account of it before she goes to bed on her return. Sometimes she is sent to private views at the picture galleries as art critic, sometimes merely to describe the dresses of the celebrities present, sometimes to write a chatty article on the pictures and the visitors.'

And so on, and so on. The lady journalist, says this authority, must be a Jack-of-all-trades. Women may add to their incomes by casual work of a pleasant kind, but to be a journalist proper a woman must be prepared to face situations of which she may never have dreamed, and endure hardships of which she may never have thought in connection with newspapers. Still, on a first-class newspaper, and especially on the magazines, there are frequently good openings for clever women who wield an easy pen; and the woman who will work hard and take up her place side by side with a mere man may win distinction in journalism as in anything else.

From The Young Woman, *Vol. VIII, October 1899–September 1900. Started as a companion to* The Young Man, The Young Woman *was a mildly pro-feminist monthly journal published between 1892 and 1915.*

WASH DAY [c. 1900]

Monday was always wash-day. After sending us off to school, Mother would collect all the dirty washing and sort it into groups. First came the sheets and pillow-slips, then the shirts and towels, petticoats, dresses, teacloths and handkerchiefs and – last of all – the coarse aprons and stockings and my father's socks. A zinc bath was placed on the kitchen table, the copper was lit and heated with wood picked up from the foreshore. When the water was hot it was baled out into buckets with a small bowl with a wooden handle – Mother called this the 'copper bowl'. Enough water was carried in buckets until the bath was half full. She added a handful of soda to soften the water and then the washing commenced.

My mother, a coarse apron made from a sack round her and a square of mackintosh pinned over her chest, rubbed each piece with 'Sunlight' soap, giving an extra rub to the very dirty parts. Not being very tall, she had to stand on a wooden box so that she could reach the rubbing board. After the whites were washed, they were put into the copper to boil together with more soda. They were continually stirred with the copper-stick and kept boiling for half an hour. The whole place smelt of boiling washing and steam. After this, they were lifted out on to the wrong side of the copper's wooden lid and left to drain, for the water had to be saved ready for the next boil. The washing was then put through the wringer to extract the rest of the water. The wringing had to be left until the rest of the washing was done as, having only one bath, she could not rinse the clothes until it was empty. Mother struggled to the sink with the bath of dirty washing water and emptied it. Then it was filled with cold water and placed under the wringer. The washing was rinsed once and put through the wooden rollers. If the weather was fine, it would be hung out to dry.

Everyone had a double washing line. From our small window in the kitchen we looked on to a blank wall. At intervals along this wall, standing like sentinels, were tall barge oars. On each oar, one below the other, were pulleys. There were about six pulleys fixed on to each oar, and into the pulleys went the washing lines. These stretched the width of the yard to the pulleys fixed to each balcony, one below the other. The women leaned over the balconies to peg each piece of washing on to the line. Then they pulled the line along through the pulley and pegged on the next piece, repeating this until the first piece of washing was at the end of the oar. Line after line of washing from the ground floor to the top met your gaze when you looked out of the window on Mondays.

If it was a wet day, then the washing had to be dried in the kitchen. For this purpose, Father fixed a batten of wood at each end of the kitchen wall just below the ceiling. He put hooks into the battens and threaded a long length of line through the hooks so that there were lines across the length of the kitchen. On to these went the washing. The ceiling was not very high and most of the time the washing was dangling on our heads. The place was damp and smelly, with steam running down windows and walls. Sometimes in bad weather the washing took two or three days to dry. At length it was taken down, folded and mangled and put back on the lines again to air. Nothing was ironed unless it was absolutely necessary, when a heavy flat-iron was placed in the oven to heat or on its end in front of the fire.

On each packet of 'Sunlight' soap there were the words 'Why does a woman look older sooner than a man?' It went on to explain the merits of the soap, but it was small wonder that women *did* look old at forty. This one day alone was truly an exhausting one, for not only was the washing done but the children had to be cared for, the meals prepared and a thousand and one other things done before the day was over.

From My Part of the River, *1974, by Grace Foakes.*

THE SWEATING SCANDAL

Girl as bookkeeper required by West-end stores, excellent opening for beginner; good writer and typist essential; salary to start 4/–, Apply, HERBERT & Co. 102 Great Portland Street, near Oxford Circus, W.

The above advertisement was brought to me by a little group of girls at our Hackney meeting! 'What are we to do,' they said, 'when such wages are offered to us? It costs a girl perhaps £15 to get her training and then she is asked to work for 4s. a week.'

One of them told me that she was out of employment, but

that she would be ashamed to accept such a wage for skilled work. 'But what are we to do?' they said with heart searching pathos, 'people think we can live on almost nothing, what are we to do?'

Then they said that some Hackney ladies had started a little sewing guild to keep some of them going. 'We don't know what we'll be paid. Perhaps they can't pay us very much. Perhaps we're slow as it's not our regular trade. But the ladies do patronize us so.' 'They oughtn't to patronize us so, ought they, when we're working for our money?' one of them said and looked up at me with her pretty wistful face.

'What are we to do?' they said again. I could only answer: 'My dears *something* must be done.'

Lying on the table when I came on to the platform was a woman's letter:

Being in need, not having had a substantial meal since August 23rd, I asked for temporary aid. On October 6th, a woman called and after asking me fifteen questions and noting the replies on a form and getting eight of my testimonials reaching back over 24 years, and getting good personal character for me from my late employers, she offered me employment as a charwoman.

I went to her house and was instantly set to work turning out bedrooms, etc.

Beginning on Monday, I worked all through the week from 9 till 3, and on Friday till 6 having one light meal, dinner only given to me. On Saturday I came away still without payment and leaving the house spotlessly clean. I have been in good service. On Monday I was paid 4s. 6d. for the seven days work. The woman who used to do the work that I did was paid 2s. a day, and she had a husband in regular employment. I am a widow.

When I complained she said we 'ought to be glad to take anything.' Of course being sent from the committee she made her own case good with them, and had me under her thumb to do exactly as she liked with.

And this is charity!

114

At G.B. Kent and Sons, Brush Factory in Victoria Park Rd., women and girls are employed just now on a War Office order of brushes for our soldiers.

I have seen the brushes that they are making, oval shaped brushes with brownish black bristles. The bristles are supplied to the workers all roughly tumbled together, lying this way and that, and the women have to pick out from the mass a certain quantity of them, pat and push this into a neat little bundle, twist wire round the bundle, push it into a hole in the wooden brush back and fasten off with wire behind: 163 little bundles must they make and wire and fix into 163 holes for one penny.

Working very quickly they can make two brushes in an hour and the brushes are paid for at the rate of 1s. 2d. a dozen, which works out at a little over 2¼d. an hour.

The women and girls work in the factory from 8 a.m. to 6 p.m. and take more brushes home with them to do at night because they cannot live on what they can earn after being in the factory ten hours each day.

One, who had worked five years at the trade and was considered extraordinarily quick, earned 11s. 1d. one week. Three shillings worth of this was done after she left the factory. She stayed up working each night till ten o'clock. She had earned more than any of the others. Another had earned 7s. 5d., 1s. 3d. of it at home, another 6s. 9d., 1s. of it at home.

Their fingers, especially the last ones, were sore and disfigured with the wire, some of them grown all swollen and stiff so that they will never be able to straighten them out any more. Some of them had sore eyes, a common thing they said, from working so many hours, especially with dark coloured bristles. Two of the girls, who had worked four-and-a-half years at the trade, had specially bad eyes.

They told me that these same soldiers' brushes when given out by Kent and Sons to women to make in their own homes, are paid for at the rate of 1s. ½d. a dozen instead of 1s. 2d.

When the bristles are put in by machinery, these same brushes are paid for at 9d. a dozen. The women who do it earn a little more than the others, but the machines are very hard to work. There is a treadle to press with the foot and a heavy weight to lift, not many women can be got to do it.

115

The women employed at japanning the brushes in the same factory earn but 6s. or 7s. a week; as girls they begin at 4s.

Here is sweating indeed, and sweating seems almost universal amongst women employed in War Office contracts.

The Army contractors are making huge sums of money out of the War. When will the Government see to it that this exploitation of the women who are piling up the profits of these contractors is made to cease? When will the people of the country unite to insist that this shall be? Women, even without the vote that we need so much, we can unite in leading this demand!

The newspapers have chronicled in much detail, the visits of Queen Mary to the workrooms established in connection with the fund called by her name, and these same chronicles have told the world of the work that is being done. The excuse most frequently given for the underpayment of women in the Queen's Workrooms, *for every one admits that a maximum wage of 6d. is underpayment* is that the employment is only intended to be temporary and the women are being trained.

But what is being done to secure that the employment shall be only temporarily needed, what other work is being provided for the women? Alas, the Nation is providing none. The War, Lord Kitchener tells us, is likely to be a long one. The Central Unemployed Body for London tells us that the tale of workless women in London is being augmented by 4,000 every week. What prospect is there of any but relief work being found for those thousands? Alas, at present none.

As for the training, the chronicles of the Queen's progress have revealed to all what it consists of, chiefly the making of well to do people's old clothes into garments for the poor. The triumph of one workroom was the manufacture of a pair of little boy's trousers out of a woman's blouse. 'Some must waste and others must work,' is the motto of such efforts.

But the main point is that a woman cannot learn to earn a living from such teaching. For factory work the main essential is speed, not cogitation as to how to turn one garment into another, but how to fashion many and many gross of garments from many and many bales of stuff.

Another excuse made by those who defend the sweated rates paid to women in Queen Mary's workrooms is that half a loaf is better than no bread. But why should no bread or half the bread that is necessary, be the choice of the daughters of the richest country in the world?

Men and women who use this pitiful half loaf argument, or who hear it without a protest, are you content that masses of women and children should be having far less than enough to eat, whilst as yet there is plenty of food in the country for us all? Even if a scarcity should come upon us, would you not rather we should share alike?

Women, those of you who are organizing workrooms, do not shelter yourselves behind the sweating practised by other people. Do not bolster up the sweating scandal – pluck out the beam from thine own eye!

From The Woman's Dreadnought, *24 October 1914.*

A FARMER'S MAID [c. 1890]

I 'ad one friend as I were particular fond of, called for some reason as I never did know, 'Shady'. Shady's adventures at service 'ould fil a book on their own. They lived close to us, and we'd allus bin friends, so she were nearly like my sister. She went to service when she were about thirteen, to a lonely, outlaying fen farm in a place called Blackbushe. The house were a mile or more from the road, and there were no other house near by. A big open farm yard were all around it on three sides, and at the back door, it opened straight into the main drain, about twelve feet wide and ten feet deep with sides like the wall of a house. There were no escape there. Her duties were as follows.

She were woke up at 6 a.m. every morning by the horsekeeper, who had walked several mile to work already, and used a clothes prop to rattle on her window to rouse her. She had to get up straight away and light the scullery fire in the big, awkward old range, that she had to clean and black-lead afore it got too hot. Then she put the kettle on to get tea made for 6.30 a.m. for the horsekeeper, who baited his horses first, come in for his breakfast

117

at 6.30, and went out and yoked his horses so as to be away to work in the fields by seven o'clock. While the kettle boiled, she started to scrub the bare tiles o' the kitchen floor. This were a terrible job. There were no hot water, and the kitchen were so big there seemed nearly a acre of it to scrub – and when you'd finished that, there'd be the dairy, just as big and the scullery as well. Skirts were long an' got in the way as you knelt to scrub, and whatever you done you cou'n't help getting 'em wet. In the winter you'd only have the light o' candles to do it by, and the kitchen 'ould be so cold the water 'ould freeze afore you could mop it up properly.

At 6.30 the horsekeeper come in for his tea, and as soon as he'd gone Shady had to start getting breakfast for the family. When they'd had theirs, she could have hers, which was only bread and butter, and the tea left in the pot by the family. If there were little children in the house, she'd be expected to have them with her and give them their breakfast while she had her own. After breakfast she washed up, including all the milk utensils and so on from the dairy, and then started the housework. Very often another woman from the farm 'ould be employed to help with this and to do the washing, while the missus done the cooking and housekeeping duties. On churning days Shady had to get up extra early to make time to fit the churning in. There were no time off at all during the day, and after supper she had to wash up all the things and prepare for next morning. This meant cleaning all the family's boots and shoes, and getting things ready for break-fast next morning. Farmers cured their own bacon and hams, so she would be given the bacon taken from a side 'in cut', but the custom was to have fried potatoes for breakfast with the bacon. These were supposed to be the 'taters left over from supper, but there were never enough left, so one of her evening jobs was allus to peel and boil a big saucepan of potatoes to fry next morning. As I'm said afore, she was allowed only bread and butter for her own breakfast.

Then if she had any time before it was bed time, she had to sit by herself in the cold dark kitchen in front of a dying fire that she wern't allowed to make up, except in lambing time. In lambing time it were took for granted that any lambs as were weakly 'ould be looked after in the kitchen, and while the season lasted the old shepherd 'ould come in and set in the kitchen while he waited for his ewes to lamb. I'm 'eard Shady say 'ow she dreaded this. The Shepherd there were a dirty, nasty, vulgar old man as no decent girl were safe with; but at the best o' times he wern't very pleasant to have to sit with, stinking o' the sheep, belching and blowing off, and every now and then getting up and straddling over to make water in the kitchen sink. The only other choice she 'ad were to go to bed, once she were sure she wou'n't be needed again, but that di'n't offer such pleasant prospects, either. Maids' rooms were allus at the very top, at the back on the north side o' the house. There were nothing in them but a bed with a hard old flock mattress, a table by the side of it, and the tin trunk the girl had brought her clothes in. It was icy cold in winter, and Shady wern't the only one o' my friends an' acquaintances by a long way as told me they slept in all their clothes to keep warm at all.

Though 'the woman' done the washing for the family, she di'n't do Shady's. She wern't allowed to do it herself, but 'ad to send it home to her mother once a week by the carrier. This took most o' Shady's 'afternoon off', because she had to walk up to the high road and meet the carrier's cart, often hanging about an hour or more waiting for him, to get her dirty washing exchanged for clean. Sometimes her mother 'ould walk the five or six mile with the clean washing, just to see her for a few minutes afore walking it all the other way. On the first time she did this, she found Shady on her knees scrubbing the kitchen floor. Shady got up to greet her, and her mother lifted her skirt and said 'Let's 'ev a look at yer britches.' As the poor mother expected, they were wet through with cold water and black as a soot bag with the constant kneeling and scrubbing and blackleading. It were a sort o' test to the experienced mother's eye o' what sort of a 'place' she were forced to leave her daughter in. I don't know which of 'em 'ould suffer most, the mother or the daughter. But there were no help for it, and every girl as left home were one mouth less to feed. If she behaved herself and stuck it out a whole year, there did come a day when she'd draw her years wages, which stood then at £5.

From Fenland Chronicle: Recollections of William Henry and

Kate Mary Edwards, collected and edited by their daughter, *Sybil Marshall (1967)*.

MEMORIES OF SEVENTY YEARS' MIDWIFERY
[*c.* 1890]

When my husband was promoted to the position of under-guard, we had to leave Brondesbury and come to Cricklewood to live. Then it was I gave up washing and took up nursing. My husband's wages had now risen to £1 3s. a week, and he had an allotment. I got a nice little flat for 7/– a week, so that I did not live a life of drudgery, but had to do something to help. The chance of nursing came to me through one of the members of our Management Committee, who advised his master to come for me when his wife was ill, saying, 'She is not a nurse but I am sure she will do, and be kind to your wife.' I did what I could and satisfied both patient and doctor, who recommended me to others of his patients. My first maternity case came to me in an unexpected manner. One of our Guild members was expecting her confinement and could not find a nurse. So at last I got a crippled girl I knew to stay in my house while I went into the Guild member's house, and acted as maternity nurse for a fortnight. I did not intend to take up maternity nursing, but after I had started, other Guild members came to me to attend them. I began to like the work, and the doctors were so satisfied with me that I determined to keep on. Then several doctors advised me to go in for midwifery, but I could not go into hospital for training. The fees were a bar to me. I found that the cheapest training I could get would cost anything from £30 to £50, and then I should have to be away from home for three months. This was quite impossible for my husband's health needed all the care I could bestow on it to keep him anything like fit for work part of his time. I had no money, only as I earned it week by week, and it was impossible to save. So I had to content myself with being a maternity nurse, but I always hoped I should ultimately become a midwife. I read and asked questions of the doctors and in this way knew a great deal about the theory of midwifery, and I was gaining experience in the practical part. There were three doctors who were very good to me and were willing to lend me books or to teach me anything. I was taught to deliver with forceps, which midwives are not taught in hospitals. I went to several post-mortems with a doctor. One was the case of a young girl who was pregnant and had poisoned herself. The doctor opened the womb and let me see the dear little baby lying so snugly in its mother, and gave me a lot of information that was real knowledge to me, showing me things in the human body which were both interesting and instructive.

Quite a large number of young married people came to live in Cricklewood, and I had sometimes as many as a hundred cases in a year. The doctors left so much to me and did so little for their fees, that people asked me to take their cases without a doctor. I did not care to do so at first, so I asked a doctor (who, when he thought my husband had not many days to live, had promised him to help me) if he thought I should be right to take cases without a doctor. He told me I was quite all right, and that if at any time I came across a case that I was not sure was quite straightforward, he would come to my assistance. I was very pleased with his offer and did many cases on my own responsibility, and both patients and doctors were satisfied, but I was not. I was called a midwife, but I felt I should have liked a hospital training, and as I earned more money I began to save to get the training I longed for. I scraped and saved, twisted and turned clothes about, even went as far as to turn an overcoat for my husband. I managed to save £30, and got the necessary papers which had to be signed by a doctor. When I went to him, he positively refused to sign it. He said it would be a wicked waste of money, that I knew more than the hospital would teach me, that I could not be spared from the neighbourhood for three months, and advised me to give up the idea. I gave up the idea. I had gone without the necessaries of life to save the £30, and I felt that if I was to get no benefit from the expenditure on training I might keep and use it for something else. I don't think I should have taken his advice if I had known that the Midwives' Act was coming along. The doctors trained me and sent me up for examination in midwifery. But alas! I failed, as about 130 did at the same examination. The written examination took place at 9 p.m., in a closely packed room. We had two hours to answer the questions, and a fortnight later an oral examination. It was just five minutes past 10 p.m. when I went into the examiners' room; at ten minutes past I came out with a slip of paper to give the Secretary with the word 'failed' written on it. I was told I could pay another fee and go through another exam., but I refused to do so. I was always a little nervous when writing or answering questions, and when I had to do both in a room full of doctors, I felt I should not make a better job of another exam. When the Midwives' Act became law, I was recommended for a certificate as a *bona fide* midwife. I have never let anyone see my certificate.

By Mrs Layton of Bethnal Green, from Life as We Have Known It, *edited by Margaret Llewelyn Davies (1931).*

WOMEN WHO WORK

The time was when no woman worked unless dire necessity made her. In that case, if she were one of the class designated 'ladies,' she cross-stitched impossible flowers in wool for private sale amongst her friends, or she essayed to teach the 'young idea how to shoot.' In either case, days of unsatisfactory drudgery with small pay were the result, because adequate training was absent even in the case of the governess, who administered 'rule of thumb' as freely as did the cook. Happily, things are now changed, and there are a variety of occupations open to women who have the laudable desire to work.

Typewriting appears to have 'caught on' with young girls more quickly than any other form of modern occupation. Probably that is because their fingers are nimble for the work, it is sedentary in character, does not take very long to learn, and serves as an equipment for a variety of posts. The fair typist, her fingers dancing quickly over the tiny ivory keys, is to be seen in the merchant's office, in the editor's sanctum, in the classic seclusion of the author's study, and amongst the Blue Books in Government offices. The click, click of her machine is not unmusical, either, when one gets used to it; at least, it will bear comparison with the monotonous playing of scales and five-finger exercises, or with the unmusical rendering of musical pieces, and besides, it has the advantage of being useful.

In London, the headquarters of women who typewrite are in and around Chancery Lane. There, throngs of girls are to be seen each morning hurrying along to the offices of the typewriting firms where they are employed, or to the school where they go for instruction. And although the pay is never high, the competition to obtain a typewriter's post is always keen. In spite of the labour of deciphering and copying manuscript much corrected and often well-nigh illegible, the fair typists show no falling off in numbers, and continue, in fact, to hold the field against the male competitor whose fingers nature did not intend, it would appear, for work requiring a touch so delicate as that needed by an expert typist.

In addition to all this, the fair typewriter has actually figured in the region of romance. I read quite a charming love-story the other day, in which the heroine was a fair, brown-eyed girl of gentle birth acting as secretary and typist to a middle-aged man, in whom the romantic element was not extinct. He desired to make his fair amanuensis his wife, but being a cautious lover he devised a novel plan for finding out the state of her feelings. Summoning her to the typewriter, he dictated a letter offering his hand and heart to a fair unknown. He watched the face of his secretary very keenly as she clicked on the paper his words of love. When the pretty lips quivered and something very like tears gathered in the brown eyes, the good man was content. The letter was completed, handed to the gentleman for direction, and the typist took her solitary walk home, thinking of the happiness awaiting the woman who had obtained the affections of such a good and kind man as she knew her employer to be. A few hours later, and behold the typewritten love-letter arrived addressed to herself. Sequel – they lived happily ever afterwards, and on the wedding-day a spray of orange blossom adorned the keyboard of the typewriter.

But to turn to a vocation of a totally different character, we question if there is any class of woman worker more universally honoured than the hospital nurse. We all know her, with her bright, serene-looking face and Quaker-like attire. The sight of her suggests to our imagination hours of patient watching, tender, soothing ways, and an endurance truly wonderful. The 'bus conductor stops promptly when he sees her coming, the collector takes her ticket with a subdued and respectful air, and even 'cabby' forgets to wrangle for an extra sixpence when she is his 'fare.' I know of at least one authentic case where a tradesman made a spontaneous discount upon learning that the goods were for a hospital nurse.

She well deserves the general consideration which the public accord her. There is a stern reality about her life. It means plenty of brain, muscle, and nerve, as well as a kind heart and a patient spirit. Hours are long, anxiety ceaseless, and experiences harrowing in hospital work, yet it attracts women of gentle birth, who hitherto have known only ease in life. Many young girls aspire to the vocation from ideas of sentiment, and because, perhaps, they fancy the nurse's costume to be becoming. Such give up in disgust at the end of the first week's probation. 'Can you lift a heavy man, lying helpless in bed?' was the very practical question which I once heard a hospital matron address to a frail girl who desired to be received as a sick-nurse. The idea seemed absurd, but a physician to whom I repeated the incident said that a girl who looked very unmuscular might yet have a storage of nerve force which would enable her to follow a hospital career. But though the work is arduous it becomes fascinating, and it is also an employment for which women seem 'to the manner born.' Little mites in sash and pinafore nurse 'dolly' through the measles with assiduous care, and every woman, trained or untrained, tends the sick couch some time or another in the course of her life.

The intuition of the poet discovered woman's vocation in this respect before Florence Nightingale and her brave pioneers tended the wounded on the battlefield. Longfellow's *Evangeline* entered the 'chambers of sickness' to moisten the 'feverish lip' and the 'aching brow'; and Scott has, for all time, condoned the little frivolities of woman by hailing her as the 'ministering angel' when 'pain and sickness wring the brow.'

124

The hospital nurse occupies, too, an unique position – she is positively without a male competitor.

Let us turn now to a woman worker whom some would, perhaps, scarcely admit to the ranks of labour. Yet her duties are arduous though she may never soil her hands – I mean the lady companion. In bygone times it was enough for her to be of gentle birth, with a smattering of polite accomplishments and a docile spirit. A capacity to fawn and flatter was also not amiss. She was expected to be an eminently useful person in matters of small and genteel import. One might almost call her the living embodiment of that useful receptacle in leather, furnished with scissors, thimble, bodkin, and toothpick, which, twenty years ago, young ladies received as presents on their birthdays, and which was termed the 'Ladies' Companion.'

When magazines specially intended for feminine readers appeared timorously in the market, they frequently bore some such title as the 'Ladies' Companion,' or the 'Ladies' Companion and Journal of Fashion.' However, a truce to these small gentilities – the lady companion of to-day has to be a very brisk and up-to-date sort of person. She must know how to attend a clearance sale and 'bag' the best bargains, and be equal to securing a good cook on the shortest possible notice, and to getting the 'better' of a house agent in the matter of houses or apartments. Cook's agents might envy her knowledge of continental routes, and a professor of languages her linguistic acquirements. In short, it is her duty to be eyes, hands, and brain for her mistress. The old waiting gentlewoman of the past has merged into the lady help of to-day, a person useful and domestic; but the companion proper is an individual of infinite resource – a woman with a head on her shoulders.

You may see her at a seaside resort leisurely sitting on the beach as she reads aloud to her lady the latest novel. Very winsome and innocent she looks, but there is a reserve power beneath that calm exterior which will be found equal to most emergencies. Watch at the railway station on the morning when her mistress resumes her travels, and you will see the reserve force in full working order. Landladies, carmen, porters, and small boys fly to right and to left, as, clinging to the rugs and the poodle, the lady companion delivers her commands. Well, we need not pursue her career further, but truly she is one of the women who work.

Literature is a field in which women have been very conspicuous workers during the last half of the century. Into journalism they have come at a hop, skip, and a jump, and by their ready wit, light, facile pen, and indomitable pluck have made themselves necessary adjuncts to every editorial staff. But fiction appears to have been the woman writer's first love, and in it she holds her own with remarkable ability. It is to Jane Austen we owe the first impulse towards the natural method in fiction. While Wordsworth was showing that the commonest things of daily life were not beneath the poet's eye, Jane Austen was painting the ordinary life around her as she contrasted *Sense and Sensibility*, and attacked *Pride and Prejudice*. After her death, Scott wrote of her in his diary: 'That young lady had a talent for describing the involvements, feelings, and characters of ordinary life, which is to me the most wonderful I ever met with. The big bow-wow I can do myself like anyone going, but the exquisite touch which renders commonplace things and characters interesting from the truth of the description and the sentiment is denied me.' Since the days of Jane Austen, the lady novelist has increased and abounded. At first she sought the public favour under masculine disguise, like George Eliot, George Sand, or Charlotte Brontë as Currer Bell. But the author of *Jane Eyre* repented of her *nom-de-plume* when her honours were persistently given to the male creature, and it was necessary for her to take a journey to London – for her a wonderful expedition – to convince her own publishers that she was a 'she.'

The woman fiction writer of to-day has developed very largely into a novelist with a purpose. Some would have us suppose that this is not 'high art,' but it is too knotty a question for discussion here. The fair novelist is a fearless critic of both social and religious problems, reaching respectively the high-water mark in *An African Farm* and *Robert Elsmere*. Between these two extremes she has played up and down the gamut, extracting not a few discordant sounds. But she means well, and thinks she has a mission to fulfil, so we leave her to finish her tunes in her own way, and presently the grating sounds will cease and the better note of tuneful melody will be struck.

Mr. Walter Besant tells us that the young girl of the period shows a disposition to make literature her calling with a persistency which is almost alarming. The secretary of the Authors' Society is inundated with packages from the country containing the verse and fiction of young ladies in their teens who are wishful to earn money and consider the pursuit of literature to be the best means to that end. It matters little to them that they scarcely know the meaning of 'life,' they essay to depict it all the same. When an 'unfeeling' editor or publisher declines 'with thanks,' the fair scribblers take refuge in the comforting thought that their merits are unappreciated from want of ability on the part of the popes of the press to rightly discern. They forget that writers are born, not made, and that the literary gift comes unsought, like the artist's eye and the musician's ear. I heard a young lady announce the other day in the most nonchalant manner possible that she was intending to give up the profession in which she was successfully engaged, because she intended to 'adopt' literature. The inborn literary instinct can be fostered and trained, but it needs no adoption. It is home-born.

The artist of the pencil and brush is a more modern development, as a serious worker, than her sister of the quill, and she has not yet reached the same degree of recognition. Still the doors of the Royal Academy are closed against her, even the painter of the 'Roll Call' not being able to write the magic R.A. after her name. Yet the lady artist is to be met everywhere. We see her busily plying her brush in the public galleries, amongst the statues in the British Museum, and in the woods and lanes of rural regions. She sketches, too, for the fashion papers, paints Christmas cards, and illustrates books. In attire she is not infrequently a disciple of Oscar Wilde – that is to say, the aesthetic element predominates. A loosely made green serge with a Vandyke collar of lace is a favourite costume, and one cannot by the utmost power of the imagination conceive the lady artist in a smart tailor-made gown. It takes many years of patient industry to gain recognition in this field of work. The number of lady exhibitors in the Academy increases, but there are, I believe, only some six or eight women who can claim rank as creative artists. Below these are innumerable painters of landscapes, heads, and copyists of the work of others. In this sphere the woman worker has not displayed the creative and dramatic power which marks the production of the woman novelist. The vocation is one which seems eminently fitted to women, and one which no one disputes the propriety of their following. This is not the case in other departments of work, for there is a strong disposition to turn a searching eye on all that woman essays to do. She may wear out her eyes over the eternal 'gusset and seam' at starvation wages, but if she seeks new ways, untrodden heretofore by feminine feet, criticism is fierce and strong. It would take a long list indeed to set forth all the ways in which women earn their bread, and so rapid is the onward march of the toilers that each week one hears of some new occupation for women. Steady and sure is the advance of the women who work, and their success and recognition brings with it a sense of dignity which was absent in the 'good old times,' when no woman worked for money unless she was obliged. Not long ago I talked in a Night Shelter with an old woman, coarse and hard of feature, who spent her days in turning over rubbish heaps and dustbins to look for saleable pieces of paper. Do you think she thought her occupation mean or unimportant? Certainly not. When I inquired how she earned her living, she informed me with dignity that she was a 'paper merchant.' Surely this is a sign of the times.

By Marion Leslie in The Young Woman, *Vol. III, October 1894–September 1895.*

'LIBERTY' AND 'INDEPENDENCE'

'Stitch! stitch! stitch!' I stood in the doorway of a fifth-floor back-room in a Camberwell lodging-house, listening to a modern edition of 'The Song of the Shirt,' sung to the accompaniment of the sewing-machine. The scenery was similar to that painted by Thomas Hood half a century ago. The woman and the unwomanly rags, the crust of bread, the table, the straw, and the broken chair, all were there. The singer of the song sat at the machine, her head bent over the work which her hands were guiding, while her feet pushed the treadle up and down. I looked on until my brain grew weary with the monotony of her movements and the grating noise of the unlubricated wheel.

'How much do you earn a day at that work?' I asked.

'Eighteenpence, Miss,' was the answer.

'And you pay for your lodging, food and clothes, all with that eighteenpence?'

'Yes, Miss.'

'But is there no other work you can do – nothing that is less wearing on body and brain?'

'Nothing, Miss. Some other girls that write a good hand get work in the City at £1 a week, and some that are quick at figures earn almost as much in the shops; but I can only sew. I bought my machine on time, and it's not paid for yet. Excuse me, but I must be on with my work.'

Stitch! stitch! stitch! The noise commenced again.

'Stop!' I cried. 'I have it. I will help you. Can you do housework?'

'Why, yes, Miss, I suppose so,' she answered, with wondering eyes.

'Then fix yourself up a little and come with me. I will give you a place as housemaid in my home. What you don't know, you will soon learn. You shall have a nice clean bedroom, with plenty to eat, print dresses in the morning, black stuff in the afternoon, with white caps and aprons, and collars and cuffs. I will buy them for you as we go along. We will pay you £16 a year to commence. Come, why don't you get your things on? We will settle up the back rent and return the sewing-machine to the instalment people.'

The girl had risen from her chair and, to my astonishment, confronted me angrily, her cheeks aflame and her eyes blazing.

'Did you come only to insult me?' she demanded, stamping her feet. 'I go out to service! I wear caps and aprons, those badges of slavery! No, thank you. I prefer to keep my liberty and be independent.'

What was she talking about? Her liberty, her independence? I was bewildered, and could scarcely believe my ears. I had been so interested in this girl, and for the past two months had vainly tried to think of a plan whereby I could help her. I knew she was poor and proud, and would not take a penny from me unless she felt she had earned it. I had finally decided to give her a comfortable situation in my own home, and this was the way she received my suggestion. She had deemed my offer an insult. So this was the outcome of my maiden effort in the missionary line! She had asked for bread, and I, according to her way of thinking, had proffered her a stone. Disconsolate and disappointed, I left her, and in my bitterness was half resolved to steel my heart for ever against the woes of my own sex, and never again venture outside the legitimate paths of journalism.

However, my cynical resolution was not carried out, for the following day I was seized with a womanly curiosity to learn something more about this wonderful 'liberty' the sewing girl seemed to value so highly; and, with that in view, I passed considerable time among the working women of London, trying to gain a clue to the meaning of their war-cry, 'Independence.' Everywhere I heard that word. It sounded above the clickety-clack of the type-writer while the fingers flew over the keys; the noisily-turning factory-wheels failed to drown it; I heard it over the clink of the barmaid's glasses; it mingled with the ring of the telephone-bell, the whirr of the cash-machine, and the refrain of the chorus-girl. The telegraph-operator murmured the word as she took down the letters of the various messages, the schoolmistress whispered it as she gave out the morrow's lesson in arithmetic, the female book-keeper uttered it while she added up the long column of figures. Even the little sub-editress, earning a salary of £1 a week for stealing copy from the daily journals, seemed imbued with that so-called 'spirit of independence.' 'Give me my liberty and independence!' That was the burden of their song. Some of them belonged to 'The Independent Young Ladies' League,' some to a 'Liberty Club,' others to 'The Society for Promoting the Equality of Classes,' and the rest were members of various societies and orders with similar names, while all prated of liberty and freedom like Young America just let loose.

Their ideas seemed to be vague and wandering, and the majority of them were hardly able to give a proper definition of the word they used so glibly. They were not a cheerful lot of girls by any means. Indeed, their solitary happiness was apparently in the belief that they were independent. Some of them were what are generally termed 'ladies by birth,' others were ladies by education. Each individual girl rejoiced in the appellation 'young lady,' whether she were a visiting governess or a clerk in a tobacco shop. They worked early and late at their professions and trades, and their salaries varied from 6s. to 30s. a week. They supported themselves, and often had several younger brothers and sisters dependent upon them. Week after week, month after month, and year after year, they had toiled with little advancement or encouragement. Most of them belonged to the commonplace order, neither clever nor stupid, only ordinary, everyday young women, working for their living.

Many were hungry, some were badly clothed, few had comfortable beds or clean lodgings. A number of them had porridge for breakfast and watercress for supper, with no midday meal. One young woman assured me that boiled rice was her perpetual diet, and that, while it was filling, it became tiresome in the long run. But, despite these numerous inconveniences, they were all 'independent' girls, every one of them. Several times I broached the subject of domestic service as a possible release from their troubles, but they laughed me to scorn and flaunted the flag of liberty in my face. What! go to service? Not they! Why, they could only have one night off each week, and no followers. Besides, who could wear caps and aprons without despising herself?

I began to wonder if there really could be anything terrible connected with domestic service which should make these poor girls so shrink from it. For myself, I knew little or nothing about housework, but the belief that there was nothing incompatible between gentility and domestic work had always been a hobby of mine. Why could not a refined English girl wash dishes, make beds, and roast a leg of mutton just as well as a member of the lower classes? Wherein would she demean herself by doing this work and receiving wages for the same?

But there were the caps and aprons. Could an educated girl wear them without diminishing her self-respect? Why was not a housemaid's cap just as respectable as that worn by a 'lady nurse'? For my own part, I had always insisted that no Paris milliner could manufacture any headgear more becoming to the majority of women than the white ruffled cap of the domestic servant employed by members of the upper classes. A pretty maid, to my mind, was much prettier with a cap than without

131

one, while the face of an ugly girl was also improved by it. But these 'slavery badges,' I was told, were not the only bugbears of the servant-girl.

I had a curiosity to find out just what these trials were, and to discover why this service was looked upon with so much contumely. As a mistress, however kind and considerate I might be, it was impossible for me to get a perfect understanding of the inner working of the household machinery. There was only one way to get at the root of the matter, and that was to go out to service myself.

I arrived at this decision one morning in the latter part of August, and I no sooner decided than I began to make preparations for my campaign. I first purchased some goods for a print dress, which I had made up in the prevailing style for housemaids, together with a black serge gown for afternoon wear. Then I bought three linen aprons for morning, and as many fine muslin ones for dress-up occasions. They were prettily trimmed with embroidery, and the ruffled epaulettes were a joy to behold. Cuffs and collars and caps with long streamers completed my outfit. Then I hired a room in Camberwell for 2s. 6d. a week, where I might have letters addressed, and arrangements were made with a titled friend to give me a reference as to respectability and honesty.

Until all these details were settled, I gave little thought as to how I should get the situation I desired, nor the difficulties I should be likely to encounter. I had a nineteenth-century woman's confidence in my ability to accomplish whatever I should set out to do, and the remembrance of my first and only attempt at sweeping a floor (which left me with blistered hands) did not in the least daunt my spirit. I should never have been tempted to call myself a domesticated woman, and my experiences in household duties, so far as the actual work might be concerned, was very limited; yet I prided myself upon my abilities in the 'knowing how' line. If I had never washed dishes, I knew how they ought to be done; and I was thoroughly convinced that dish-washing, sweeping, dusting, making beds, and 'turning out' rooms, could be reduced – or, rather, elevated – to a science. I felt sure that in all kinds of work there were hard methods and easy ones. By going out to service I should discover which was which, and then

132

I should be able to write a series of articles on 'Housework Made Easy,' thus benefiting womankind in general and servant-girls in particular.

In order to inform myself as to just where my valuable services were required, I picked up the morning paper and looked among the 'Situations Vacant.'

> WANTED. – Housemaid where Parlourmaid is kept; must be neat, of good appearance, tall, and thoroughly capable, with at least twelve months' character.

It was evident that I would not suit that advertiser, for I was not tall, neither was I possessed of a twelve-months' character. I proceeded down the column, and to my utter dismay I found that length of body, as well as length of character, was considered indispensable in a housemaid or parlourmaid. There were several places open to 'generals,' but most of them were required to look after the babies, besides doing the other work, and I felt unequal to the task. Cooks were in great demand, but they also must needs have long characters.

Still, I did not lose heart, but bearing in mind the motto of the Americans, 'Trust in the Lord and advertise,' I wrote out an advertisement and took it to a newspaper office in Fleet Street. As I handed it to the receiving clerk, I observed that a puzzled look overspread his features. My notice was apparently something of a novelty to him, for, after re-reading it, he took it across the room to another clerk, who, when he had read it, smiled, and said, 'It's all right. Put it in.' The next morning – August 23rd – there appeared in the columns of 'Situations Wanted' the following:–

> As Housemaid, Parlourmaid, or House-Parlourmaid. – A refined and educated young woman obliged to earn her living, and unable to find other employment, wants situation as above. Expects only such treatment as is given to servants. Will wear caps and aprons, but would not wish to share bed with another. Thoroughly reliable and competent. References; town or country. Wages, £14. – Address —— .

From Campaigns of Curiosity: Journalistic Adventures of an American Girl in London, *1894, by Elizabeth L. Banks. An essayist*

133

and journalist who was born in New Jersey, Banks came to England in 1893 and pursued a journalistic career in London, exposing snobbery, supporting the suffragist cause, and turning her various experiences into copy for lively books and articles.

DOMESTIC STUDIES IN 2000 AD

Eliza Fanshawe, K.C., sat back in her chair at her chambers in the Temple in deep abstraction. Mr. Evelyn Fanshawe, whom she had rescued in the days of her first professional success from the sweated labour of a curacy, and who had so loyally looked after her household and children for upwards of fifteen years, had 'made a scene' that morning. He had found secreted among various legal documents a passionate effusion from a well-known minor poet, who rented on her guarantee an elegant little flat in the suburbs. And to the eminent K.C. there had at that very moment been forwarded from her club a letter from an obscure don at Oxford threatening instant communication with Evelyn.

To Eliza Fanshawe all this seemed highly unreasonable. Her income of £15,000 a year would amply provide for all the gentlemen if only Mr. Fanshawe continued the admirable system of domestic economy to which she had trained him from youth, and which had given scope, so far, to pay the minor poet's debts and to take the don for an occasional trip to France. She was tired of the old-fashioned phraseology in which both her lovers asserted crude male claims to exclusive possession fortified by no economic sanction. Her home was comfortable, and she was honestly grateful to Mr. Fanshawe for long years of services rendered. She telephoned wirelessly to Mr. Fanshawe, who in five minutes aeroplaned neatly on to the roof of the building and came down in the lift. Waving him to a chair she explained the situation. 'I am sure,' she concluded, 'that you will co-operate with me to get rid of these blackmailers. Into my relations with them you need not inquire. You have a charming house, social circle, and family, together with the use of several aeroplanes, waterplanes, and other modern conveniences. You can of course get a divorce but I shall only allow you alimony with the well-known condition *"Dum castus et solus vixerit,"* and you *know* you won't like that. You are too *passé* now to pick up anyone else with my earning power or chance of being in the Cabinet with all the opportunities of successful investment which that position confers. You can do what you like. The female committee of the Bar Council would undoubtedly sympathize with me, and most of your men friends would think you a fool. Just think it over, and consider especially how the children would miss you for the large part of the year when they would be under my roof.'

Mr. Fanshawe sobbed for five minutes without stopping. He gurgled the usual exclamations about deception, ingratitude, and infidelity. Eliza let him have his cry out and then tried to soothe him. She reminded him of the temptations incidental to long spells of brainwork unrelieved by leisure or amusement . . . 'Better this,' she said, 'than that I should ruin your happiness by gambling or drugs in which other brainworkers seek relief when they want diversion.' 'Let me go,' Mr. Fanshawe exclaimed, and rose to call his aeroplane. 'I will do all I can to forget the past – *but you must never see those horrid men again.*' And as he disappeared Eliza fell back into her chair and heaved a sigh of relief, inwardly cursing the antiquated prejudices of the other sex which she had to appease in order to avoid the temporary disorganization of her home.

By E.S.P. Haynes in The Egoist, *1897.*

ALL IN THE DAY'S WORK

MRS. BOLT

A glorious summer morning. Five sonorous strokes from the Town-hall clock. The stone-flagged streets of a factory town in North-East Lancashire already show signs of life. From the electric tram depôt one car after another comes forth to carry its human burdens to their daily toil. Here and there a man may be seen carrying a long pole, having a kind of mop made of thin wires at one end. Up and down the long streets he goes, stopping here and there, in some streets at nearly every house, and applying his mop to the bedroom window-pane. A rattling hail-storm of sound results, calculated to wake the dead. Mrs. Bolt lives in the middle of one of these long streets, and on this summer morning is fast asleep when the 'knocker-up' applies his instrument to her window-pane. Morning already! It's only a minute since she came to bed!

But there is no time to lie; for there's a lot to do between now and six o'clock, when she is due at the factory doors.

'Fred,' says she, nudging with her elbow the sleeping man at her side, who had opened his eyes drowsily at the familiar noise on the window-pane, and then had turned over with a grunt:– 'Fred, ger up! It's time to be off.' Another grunt from Fred.

Meanwhile she is dressing. Before going downstairs she gives her husband another admonition, accompanied by a shake. But he knows from long experience that she is not really in earnest yet. So he settles down for another forty winks, after she has bustled out of the room. She goes down the narrow, crooked stairs, leading into the back kitchen, which is about two yards wide and three yards long, in which is the set-pan (a boiler for washing clothes), the mangle, and the sink, which is of stone, like the flagged floor and the little back yard. On the slop-stone is a gas-ring, on which Mrs. Bolt places the little enamel kettle. She then washes her face in the back kitchen, but she does not take out her curling-pins. What's the good of bothering with your hair to go to the factory? She then goes into the front room, about four and a half yards square, which opens directly on to the street. It is Friday, the weekly 'siding-up' day; so she blackleads the bars of the grate, which is of the kitchen-range type, a large oven for bread-baking on one side and a boiler on the other. Next she lays the fire, ready to light at tea-time. By the time she has done this it is nearly half-past five, and after making 'a sup o' tay,' she goes upstairs. Fred is summoned again from the land of slumber, and five minutes later follows her downstairs; yawning sleepily, as he, too, swills his face at the slop-stone. A gill pot of tea, 'sugared and milked,' is ready for him by the time he has donned jacket, cap, and the woollen scarf which he wears winter and summer alike.

They stand – there's of course no time to sit – drinking the tea, blowing it till it cools. Then she pins her factory shawl under her chin, and takes up two other shawls which lie ready on a chair. She hands one to her husband, as they both go upstairs and into the back bedroom, over the scullery. In the bed in this room lie their two children. The five-year-old lies with arms stretched out above his head, smiling as he dreams. The two-year-old has kicked off every bit of clothing and his curly hair is damp with moisture. He opens his eyes as his mother picks him up hastily and wraps him in the shawl, but is asleep again in a moment. The elder boy is used to this morning visitation, and does not wake as his father wraps him in the other shawl and follows his mother downstairs. As they pass through the front room the man picks up a square tin containing the food for their breakfast, and two tin cans in which to make their breakfast tea; and Mrs. Bolt takes a bundle which contains the children's clothing. Her husband locks the door, and they hurry along the street, which now resounds with the clatter of clogs and is alive with old men and women, young men and maidens, boys and girls. Doors open and shut, and out they come, as though drawn by some invisible Pied Piper. Mr. and Mrs. Bolt meet many with similar burdens, on their way to the electric cars. On the opposite side of the main road is a street the exact replica of the one in which they live. They enter a door without knocking, and lay their burdens at each end of the sofa. Mrs. Earnshaw, who 'minds' their children, is up, and of course, expecting them, but there is no time to waste in words.

In this town the finishing stage only of cotton manufacturing is done, so all the factories are 'weaving sheds' and nearly all the operatives, men and women alike, are cotton weavers; there is almost no other industry in the town.

Mr. and Mrs. Bolt work at the same factory, and both are paid at the same rate. Both 'mind' four looms, and therefore are doing exactly the same work. The factory is five minutes' walk along the main road, and down a side street, and on this particular morning they arrive just in time, as the last whistle blows. The engine has already started, and as they enter the factory a deafening roar, comparable to no other noise on earth, greets their ears, but noise is not one of their grievances.

Mrs. Bolt's looms are on one side of the factory and her husband's on the other. She threads her way through closely-packed looms, by a passage-way wide enough for one person only, and as one weaver after another takes his position and pushes the 'knocker-on' which sends the flying shuttles from one end of the loom to the other, the shooting, banging, clacking sound of the regular impact of metal on metal is added to the prevailing roar. Mrs. Bolt's shuttles are soon adding their quota of sound, and the lengths of sheeting in her looms begin their day's growth under her watchful eye. The machine needs continuous feeding, and Mrs. Bolt's job is to replace, ever and always, the cops of cotton inside the shuttles. A cop lasts about three minutes, so Mrs. Bolt has not much idle time in keeping her four looms supplied.

Breakfast-time, eight o'clock. The whistle blows. Each weaver releases the 'knocker-on' on each loom, the steam goes off, and a heavenly peace descends. Mrs. Bolt joins others who are going to the copper boiler, for boiling water for breakfast, for which each operative pays a penny a week. She fills her own and her husband's can, in which she has already placed the tea and sugar, and carries them back to her looms, where she finds her husband awaiting her. They sit on turned-up weft-cans, and eat their breakfast of bread and butter, between the slices of which are fried ham and eggs. Mr. Bolt announces that he has had a 'smash' (an entanglement in the threads of the warp) and that it has taken a full hour to 'get it reet.' She listens intelligently, while he describes at length the exact kind of 'smash' it was, but her only comment is, 'An' a'll bet tha swore some!' She knows exactly what sort of experience he has had. An hour's patient piecing of broken ends, between the intervals of keeping his other three looms at work – because, of course, it would not do to have all the looms standing: the wage stops when the loom stops.

'A see tha' wants thy weights shiftin',' says Mr. Bolt, presently, noticing that one of his wife's warps is working towards its end.

'Ay,' she answers, 'tha mun shift 'em afore tha' goos.'

When a warp is first put on a loom it is heavily weighted down. As the warp is woven, the weight is reduced. The weights are usually fifty-six pounds each.

Mrs. Bolt is fortunate in having her husband at hand to adjust hers when needed: otherwise she would have to do it herself. How hot it is! The roof is half glass, because a good light is essential to the production of flawless cloth; and it is whitewashed to reduce the heat. But to-day's sun is fierce, and the temperature mounts higher and higher as the morning waxes older. The sleeves of Mrs. Bolt's cotton blouse are already rolled up. She unfastens the neck, and wishes she could take it off altogether. Beads of perspiration stand out on her forehead, and ever and anon run down the sides of her face, and, between the momentary intervals of her cop-filling, she wipes it with her apron. It is impossible, even to the noise-inured weavers, to hear themselves speak in a weaving shed; but they have invented a kind of finger-and-mouth action, and Mrs. Bolt uses this language to convey to her neighbours her commentary on the heat.

The half-past twelve whistle blows at last. Mr. and Mrs. Bolt are at home by a quarter to one, being a little later to-day owing to Friday being pay-day, and their having to stop to get their wages before leaving the factory. The five-year-old meets them at the end of the street, and goes with them to dinner; but there is no time to bother with the baby, who dines with Mrs. Earnshaw. Nor is there time for a tablecloth and an elaborate set-out for dinner. The kettle is put on the gas-ring again. Mrs. Bolt wipes the oilcloth, which covers the square deal table in the middle of the room, with the dishcloth; and brings out bread, butter, knives, forks, and spoons, and the milk which the milkman has left in the jug on the window-sill outside; and then goes to the 'eating-shop' at the end of the street, and brings sixpennyworth of hot potato pie, two twopenny custards, and a pennyworth of pickled cabbage. Her husband, meanwhile, is having a look at the *Cotton Factory Times*, which has been pushed under the door during the morning. Some more tea is made and poured into the gill-pots. Whilst they are dining Mr. Bolt gives his wife his wages, except what he keeps for his own special manly needs. He cannot manage to minister to these on less than four shillings a week. If, as this week, his wages happen to be twenty-six shillings, he keeps six shillings and gives his wife a pound: if, as sometimes happens, his wages are only a pound, he keeps four shillings and gives her sixteen shillings. The only unalterable condition is that he must have a minimum of four shillings for his own pocket. As he gives her the money he tells her of what a man told him at the club last night – that a lady lecturer had publicly stated that in Lancashire all the women work, and at the week-end turn up their wages to their husbands! So he suggests that Mrs. Bolt shall turn up hers to him instead of the other way about!

'Tha' can have it all, owd lad, if tha'll do th' buyin' in,' she answers. But she makes no attempt to act on her words. Her own wages this week are only a pound, because for four or five days she had in bad warps, and could not get on, owing to continual 'floats' and 'smashes.'

They leave the boy with Mrs. Earnshaw on the way back, and Mrs. Bolt has a look at her baby while her husband waits for her at the end of the street.

The afternoon waxes hotter, till the temperature of the weaving-shed is up to a hundred. Four hours without intermission Mrs. Bolt stands at her post, eyes and hands mechanically performing their never-varying tasks. At last the releasing whistle blows, and Mr. and Mrs. Bolt draw in the fresh air with relief as they trudge home again. Their white faces and drooping movements show marks of the day's toil. Mrs. Bolt calls for her boys on the way home, and by the time she gets there her husband has put the kettle on the gas-ring, and has brought out the gill-pots and the sugar, and is now resting, and having a look at the evening paper, which he has bought on the way home. She puts a match to the fire. It's hot, but the childer'll have to be bathed, and can't be bathed without hot water. Then she gets out bread from the pan in the scullery, and the butter out of the cupboard in the corner of the living-room, and the milk from the open shelf in the scullery (the latter is the only receptacle provided for food in the houses in this town), and then makes the tea, and fetches the chips and fried fish from the little shop never very far from the Lancashire factory home. Tea over, she clears the table, and asks her husband to keep an eye on the children, whilst she, with a large carpet-bag and a basket, sallies forth to the co-operative shop in the main street, where the cars runs. She joins a shopful of women all bent like herself on buying enough butter, bacon, cheese, flour, eggs, tea, cocoa, soap, potatoes, and numerous other articles, to last a week, and finds that she has 'made a hole in half-a-sovereign.' Returning home with her load, she finds 't' Union man' waiting. Eightpence satisfies him – fourpence each for trade-union benefits.

Her next job is to blacklead and polish the grate in the living-room, before it gets too hot with the fire. The fender, with the brass top, and the brass fire-irons, and dogs, and brass 'side-pieces,' are dragged out from under the sofa, where they repose from Sunday night till Friday night, and are polished ready for to-morrow, and placed on the sofa 'out o' t' road.' It is nearly half-past seven now, and Mr. Bolt, who up till now has been sitting on a chair in the open doorway, where it's cool, reading the cricket news, proceeds to wash himself, and to change into his 'second best,' preparatory to spending the evening at the Working Men's Club and Institute.

Now here comes the rent-man, and hard on his heels the Death Insurance man. Mrs. Bolt declares that her hand is never out of her pocket!

At last the grate and fire-irons are shining enough to satisfy her critical taste, and she is glad to leave such a 'hot shop,' and to go upstairs to make the beds.

Coming down, she debates with herself as to the advisability of bathing the children, or first swilling the flags. The children both being happily at play outside, she decides on the flags. She cleans the outside of the window; then fetches bucket after bucket of water from the tap over the slop-stone and brushes and swills her own patch of street. She treats the back window and the back yard in the same way. She decides to do 'the front' whilst she is about it, gets more water, a stout cloth, a scrubbing-brush, and a donkey-stone, and performs the sacred rite to which homage is faithfully paid every week by the women of Lancashire. The stone window-sill first. A wash with the cloth. A rub with the stone. A scrub with the brush. Another wash. A thorough wiping with the wrung-out cloth. Another rub with the stone. Then a very careful wiping with the cloth. The result, when dry, is a resplendent windowsill of spotless white or deep cream, according to the colour of the stone. The door-cheeks receive the same attention, also the flags of stone which skirt the wall alongside the whole length of the house. Finally, the doorstep. That finished, and Mrs. Bolt's front is as nice as everybody else's.

It is after eight o'clock, and two-year-old is becoming fractious. The panful of water has been ready some time, and he is soon in and out of the zinc bath which occupies the hearth. He is sleepy, and 'drops off' before his brother's bath is finished. By a quarter to nine they are both in bed and asleep, and Mrs. Bolt is free to wash up the day's dirty pots. She is wiping the cupboard shelves, which are covered with oilcloth, before putting the pots away, when somebody knocks at the door.

The lady explains that she is working for the Weavers' Association. They want to get their women members to come to the meetings and to take more interest in it: to help to govern it, instead of leaving it all to the men. Won't Mrs. Bolt come to the meetings?

Mrs. Bolt is tired, and inclined to feel the least bit cross. She did so want to 'break the back' of tomorrow's work, and now here's this tiresome woman to bother with! She explains that she hasn't time to come to meetings, or to 'take any interest in anything.'

'Not an evening a fortnight?' suggests the visitor, persuasively.

'Well,' answered Mrs. Bolt, 'I'll tell you what this week's been like, and then you'll know what every other's like. I put my washing out, and pay eighteen-pence a week for it. But it comes back to me 'rough-dry,' and I have to mangle and iron it. Every night there's washing-up and bed-making, and the children to wash. Monday night the clothes come back, and if I can't finish the ironing that night it has to be finished on Tuesday night. Tuesday's baking night. Mr. Bolt can't abide shop bread. I make brown and white, and tea-cakes, and a bit o' currant bread (it's tasty for t' factory), and some pies and cakes. Often I'm too tired to clean up after t' baking, and then that has to be done on Wednesday night. Wednesday and Thursday I have to clean upstairs, and Friday I've to do as much as I can downstairs, and finish on Saturday afternoon. Sunday's the only day in the week when we have a "proper" dinner. That takes me all morning, and after washing up and tidying up a bit, it's half-past three before I've any time to myself. Could you do any better?'

The visitor is nonplussed. 'I suppose you couldn't pay for a little help?' she suggests, tentatively.

'Nay, that I cannot,' answers Mrs. Bolt. 'I pay seven shillings to have my two children minded, and then there's the washing.

Rent, five shillings; "Death-man," sixpence; "Sick-man," sixpence; "Union," eightpence; gas; coal; milkman; "knocker-up"; "going-off" club; besides food and clothes! Then we've had all our good furniture to buy since we were wed. Mr. Bolt turned up all his wages (nobbut pocket-money) to his mother till six months before we were wed; and I turned mine up to my mother (nobbut "spence" – a penny in the shilling) reet up to the week before; so you see we hadn't had a chance to save much for furniture. We've paid for t' sideboard' (glancing with pride to the walnut sideboard with bevelled glass back which occupies one side of the room) 'and t' suite' (of carriage rep); 'for t' mangle and sewing machine: and for t' ornaments' (three large gorgeous vases which occupy the places of honour on the sideboard) 'and they cost nearly three pounds; and now we're paying for t' bedroom suite. It cost ten pounds; and the sideboard cost ten; so you see all that's taken a bit of paying. And I'm like my mother I believe in putting a little bit away for a rainy day, every week, no matter what I have coming in. I can tell you, I've got enough to do it all on both us wages. How could I pay it all if I paid away my own wage in help?'

'It almost looks as if you'd be as well to stop at home,' suggested the visitor.

Mrs. Bolt laughed.

'Stop at home!' she exclaimed, 'and live on a pound a week! The only expense which wouldn't be going on just the same would be the money for the children and for the washing. In a poor week I can more than double that at the factory, and what I get makes all the difference between having summat decent to eat and wear and going short. You like summat tasty to eat when you're working in a factory all day, and you can't get it, even for the man, out of a pound a week. I fair dread having another little 'un, for you can't put three children out, and I should be forced to stop at home then. And that means nursing other folks' childer, and washing other folks' clothes – besides doing all your own. I know what that sort of life is. My mother did it, and the house was always messed up wi' babbies and wet clothes. I'd rather go to t' factory, by half!'

The visitor left.

Mrs. Bolt resumed her work, first sweeping the stone floor,

then scrubbing round the oilcloth surround. After to-morrow's dinner the square of matting and the hearth-rug (now reposing in the scullery after being shaken last night) will be laid down, the fire-irons will assume their week-end office, and there'll only be the dusting to do; the washing-up and bed-making, and the scullery to 'side' and clean. With good luck she'll manage to get washed and dressed, and her curling-pins out, and the children rigged up by tea-time, and perhaps even the stocking-mending may get pushed in: and then after tea she'll be free to enjoy her weekly treat – a promenade round the shops and the market and a finish up of the week's 'buying-in.'

When she has finished the floor she goes to the little eating-shop for some potted meat for breakfast, as she is too tired to cook anything to-night. When she comes back, her husband has arrived, and they have a bite of the meat and bread for supper, Mrs. Bolt eating hers as she cuts up the food and packs their breakfast-tin. She makes some cocoa, and sits down to drink it, falling asleep before she has finished it, and having to be roused by her husband. One more job! The little clothes and shawls to place ready for morning, and then bed.

Mrs. Bolt sleeps without rocking.

Judged by the standard of use to the State, which is of more value, Mrs. Bolt or her husband? He takes part in the productive work of the world – so does she. He is of no further value, except to provide other producers to take his place when he falls out of line. And he cannot perform that duty to his country without Mrs. Bolt's help. But her duty to her country does not end with her productive work, nor with the production of future citizens. In addition she keeps clean a decent home, and cares for her children during all the hours when she is out of the factory.

Has that work no national value?

Apparently not, since Mr. Bolt is consulted and has a voice in the making of the conditions which govern his own and his wife's life; and Mrs. Bolt is not consulted at all, and is classed with children, paupers, and lunatics when law-making is the order of the day. No wonder the greatest needs of her life – opportunity for human development and release from domestic slavery – are not even recognized as necessary!

They never will be till women help to make the conditions of life.

By *Ada Nield Chew* in The Englishwoman, *Vol. XV, 1912. A suffragist and trade unionist, Chew was one of thirteen children of a farmer-turned-brickworker, William Nield, and his wife, Jane Hammond. In 1884, while she was working as a tailoress, she wrote a series of letters in the local newspaper under the pseudonym 'A Crewe Factory Girl', which showed her writing skills, and later when she was appointed an organizer for the Independent Labour Party she turned out to be a fine speaker too. In 1897 she married a fellow-ILP organizer, George Chew. After the birth of her only daughter, she started to work as an organizer for the Women's Trade Union League. But it was not until 1912, when the National Union of Women's Suffrage Societies changed its policy and sought links with the Labour Party and trade unions, that Chew – who had until then opposed the call for women's suffrage, believing that only full adult suffrage would benefit the working classes – became active in the movement. Her sketches of working-class life began to appear in the local press and in The Common Cause, the suffragist paper; she organized activity in the Rossendale Valley; spoke at meetings and wrote propaganda. After the war, Chew, who had lost her job on the outbreak of hostilities, turned to commerce and, committed to a firm belief in women's economic independence, started a successful mail-order business.*

CHAPTER FOUR

A NEW MAP
OF MARRIAGE

Throughout the nineteenth century women's rights within marriage were becoming slowly and partially established. The Infant Custody Act of 1839 gave mothers for the first time the right to custody of children under seven, providing that the Lord Chancellor was convinced that the woman concerned was of good character. The Matrimonial Causes Act of 1857 allowed divorce through the courts, rather than the prohibitively expensive and protracted business of a private Act of Parliament – though whereas a husband had only to prove his wife's adultery, his own sin had to be compounded by incest, bigamy, desertion or cruelty as well. The second Married Women's Property Act of 1882 gave married women the same rights over property as unmarried women, and in 1886 the Married Women (Maintenance in Case of Desertion) Act enabled women to sue for maintenance without going to the workhouse first. In the same year, the Contagious Diseases Act, which had allowed for the forcible examination and imprisonment of any woman in an army garrison or naval port thought to be a prostitute, was repealed.

In addition, family sizes were declining. In 1871 there were over 295 legitimate live births per 1,000 women aged fifteen to twenty-four, but by 1911 this had dropped to 173.5, and the average family had 3.04 children – though many working-class families still ran into double figures.

Marriage was still regarded as the destiny – and the desideratum – of most women. They were educated for it, conditioned to seek fulfilment in the roles of helpmeet and mother, and the alternatives were presented as chilling indeed. But there were many women who could not fulfil their 'natural destiny'. At the turn of the century the unequal ratio between the sexes meant that there were over one million more women than men, women destined to remain 'superfluous' or 'redundant', in the language of the time; women whom the novelist George Gissing compared to 'an odd glove' – useless without a partner and condemned to face a lonely and marginal existence, living with their parents or in the homes of a male relative.

But more women were beginning to question this state of affairs – and even some of those who 'could' marry chose not to. In 1888, when the *Daily Telegraph* published a series of articles by the novelist Mona Caird, called 'Is Marriage a Failure?', which argued that the freedom of both sexes was restricted by the institution of marriage when it was based on the economic dependence of the wife, she received over 27,000 letters, and most readers agreed with her. Many women were clearly becoming increasingly critical not only of economic dependence but also of the sexual double standards in marriage. They recognized the opportunities that could exist beyond the sphere of home-making and child-rearing, and were demanding more equality of treatment and a new kind of esteem within marriage.

If, for most spinsters:

> the plain unvarnished truth is that work open to women is not sufficient in amount or sufficiently well-paid to enable them to live in a condition of ordinary comfort or dignity

as Ethel Snowden wrote in 1913, the same could be said of almost all working-class women of the period. The 'family wage', however low, meant that wages paid to women were barely sufficient to sustain independent life. And for married women that same wage was usually inadequate to support a large family, forcing them to supplement the family income by finding whatever part-time, badly paid work they could, on top of hard, primitive domestic work and often almost annual childbirth and its accompaniment, infant mortality.

In questions of love, as opposed to – though often present

147

within – marriage, the advanced campaigners and proselytizers may have been less successful, and the re-definitions less clear. Legislation was unable to intervene to regulate personal relationships between men and women, 'free love' was not necessarily pain-free and, with some notable exceptions, the gulf between principle and practice seems to have been wide. Women's writing often bears witness to passions that went unacknowledged, expectations that remained unfulfilled, a new sort of loneliness, and a feeling that, in those instances where she continued to seek him, the New Woman still awaited her New Man.

I AM YOURS FOR EVER

[47 Redcliffe Road, Fulham]
Saturday Night. May 18th [19th] 1917

My darling,

Do not imagine, because you find these lines in your private book that I have been trespassing. You know I have not – and where else shall I leave a love letter? For I long to write you a love letter tonight. You are all about me – I seem to breathe you – hear you – feel you in me and out of me – What am I doing here? You are away – I have seen you in the train, at the station, driving up, sitting in the lamplight, talking, greeting people – washing your hands – And I am here – in your tent – sitting at your table – There are some wallflower petals on the table & a dead match, a blue pencil and a Magdeburgische Zeitung. I am just as much at home as they.

When dusk came – flowing up the silent garden – lapping against the blind windows – my first & last terror started up – I was making some coffee in the kitchen. It was so violent so dreadful I put down the coffee-pot – and simply ran away – *ran ran* out of the studio and up the street with my bag under one arm and a block of writing paper and a pen under the other. I felt that if I could get here & find Mrs [*illegible*] I should be 'safe' – I found her and I lighted your gas, wound up your clock – drew your curtains – & embraced your black overcoat before I sat down – frightened no longer. Do not be angry with me, Bogey – ça a été plus fort que moi . . . That is why I am here.

When you came to tea this afternoon you took a brioche broke it in half & padded the inside doughy bit with two fingers. You always do that with a bun or a roll or a piece of bread – It is your way – your head a little on one side the while . . .

– When you opened your suitcase I saw your old feltie & a french book and a comb all higgledy piggledy – 'Tig. Ive only got 3 handkerchiefs' – Why should that memory be so sweet to me? . . .

Last night, there was a moment before you got into bed. You stood, quite naked, bending forward a little – talking. It was only for an instant. I saw you – I loved you so – loved your body with such tenderness – Ah my dear – And I am not thinking now of 'passion'. No, of that other thing that makes me feel that every inch of you is so precious to me. Your soft shoulders – your creamy warm skin, your ears, cold like shells are cold – your long legs & your feet that I love to clasp with my feet – the feeling of your belly – & your thin young back – Just below that bone that sticks out at the back of your neck you have a little mole. It is partly because we are young that I feel this tenderness – I love your youth – I could not bear that it should be touched even by a cold wind if I were the Lord.

We two, you know have everything before us, and we shall do very great things – I have perfect faith in us – and so perfect is my love for you that I am, as it were, still, silent to my very soul. I want nobody but you for my lover and my friend and to nobody but you shall I be *faithful*.

I am yours for ever

Tig.

Katherine Mansfield to John Middleton Murry from The Collected Letters of Katherine Mansfield, *edited by Vincent O'Sullivan and Margaret Scott (1984). Katherine Mansfield (1888–1923), a New Zealander, moved to London in 1908. Her first stories were published in Alfred Orage's periodical* The New Age *in 1910. In 1918 she married the publisher John Middleton Murry, with whom she had lived for six years. Her younger brother was killed in the First World War. Her first volume of stories,* In A German Pension, *was published in 1911,* Prelude *in 1918 and* The Garden Party *in 1922. She died from tuberculosis, aged thirty-five.*

A WIDER VIEW OF THINGS

'Some Chinese gentlemen told me they objected to the higher education of women, because if the women were better educated they would want to rule. That must be what Englishmen think, though they do not say it. They say that our brains are lighter, and that therefore we must not be taught too much. But why not educate us to the limit of our capacity, and leave it there? Why, if we are inferior, should there be any fear of making us superior? We must stop when we cannot go any farther, and all this old-womanish cackle on the subject, the everlasting trying to prove what is already said to be proved – the looking for the square in space after laying it down as a law that only the circle exists – is a curious way of showing us how to control the "exuberance of our own verbosity." They say we shall not be content when we get what we want, and there they are right, for as soon as our own "higher education" is secure, we shall begin to clamour for the higher education of men. For the prayer of every woman worth the name is not "Make me superior to my husband," but, "Lord, make my husband superior to me!" Is there any more pitiful position in the world than that of a right-minded woman who is her husband's superior and knows it? There is in every educated and refined woman an inborn desire to submit, and she must do violence to what is best in herself when she cannot. You know what the history of such marriages is. The girl has been taught to expect to find a guide, philosopher, and friend in her husband. He is to be head of the house and lord of her life and liberty, sole arbiter on all occasions. It is right and convenient to have him so, the world requires him to fill that position, and the wife prefers that he should. But the probabilities are about equal that he, being morally her inferior, will not be fit for it, and that, therefore, she will find herself in a false position. There will then be an interval of intense misery for the wife. Her education and prejudices will make her try to submit at first to what her sense knows to be impossible; but eventually she is forced out of her unnatural position by circumstances. To save her house and family she must rebel, take the reins of government into her own hands, and face life, a disappointed and lonely woman.'

'Heaven help her!' said Claudia. 'One knows that the future of a woman in that state of mind is only a question of circumstance and temperament; she may rise, but —— '

Ideala looked up quickly. 'But she may fall, you were going to say – yes. But you know if she does it is her own fault. She *must* know better.'

'She may not be quite mistress of herself at the time – she may be fascinated; she may be led on!' I interposed, quickly. Claudia seemed to have forgotten. 'But one thing is certain, if she has any real good in her she will always stop before it is too late.'

'I think,' said Claudia, 'it would be better, after all, if women were taught to expect to find themselves their husband's equals – the disappointment would not be so great if the husband proved inferior; but when a woman has been led to look for so much, her imagination is full of dreams in which he figures as an infallible being; she expects him to be her refuge, support, and comfort at all times; and when a man has such a height to fall from in any one's estimation, there can be but little of him left if he does fall.'

Ideala sighed, and after a short pause, she said: 'I have been wondering what makes it possible for a woman to love a man? Not the flesh that she sees and can touch, though that may attract her as the colour of the flower attracts. It must be the mind that is in him – the scent of the flower, as it were. If she finds eventually that his mind is corrupt, she must shrink from it as from any other form of corruption, and finally abandon him on account of it, as she would abandon the flower if she found its odour fetid – indeed, she has already abandoned her husband when she acknowledges that he is not what she thought him.' She paused a moment, and then went on passionately: 'I cannot tell you what it was – the battling day by day with a power that was irresistible because it had to put forth no strength to accomplish its work; it simply was itself, and by being itself it lowered me. I cannot tell you what it was to feel myself going down, and not to be able to help it, try as I would; to feel the gradual change in my mind as it grew to harbour thoughts which were reflections of his thoughts, low thoughts; and to be filled with ideas, recollections of his conversations, which had caused me infinite disgust at the time, but remained with me like the taste of a nauseous drug, until I almost acquired a morbid liking for them. Oh, if I could save other women from that!'

Claudia hastily interposed to divert her. 'That is a good idea, the higher education of men,' she said. 'I don't know whether they have abandoned hope, or whether they think themselves already perfect, certain it is the idea of improving themselves does not seem to occur to them often. And we want good men in society. If the clergy and priests are good, it is only what is required of them, what everybody expects, and, therefore, their goodness is accepted as a matter of course, and is viewed as indifferently as other matters of course. One good man in society has more effect as an example than ten priests.'

'But you have not told us what you propose to do, Ideala?' I said.

'I hope it is nothing unwomanly,' Claudia interposed, anxiously.

Ideala looked at her and laughed, and Claudia laughed too, the moment after she had spoken. The fear of Ideala doing anything unwomanly was absurd, even to herself.

'An unwomanly woman is such a dreadful creature,' Claudia added, apologetically.

'Yes,' said Ideala, 'but you should pity her. In nine cases out of ten there is a great wrong or a great grief at the bottom of all her unwomanliness – perhaps both; and if she shrieks you may be sure that she is suffering; ease her pain, and she will be quiet enough. The average woman who is happy in her marriage does not care to know more of the world than she can learn in her own nursery, nor to see more of it, as a rule, than she can see from her own garden gate. She is a great power; but, unfortunately, there is so very little of her!

'What I want to do is to make women discontented – you have heard of a noble spirit of discontent? I thought for a long time that everything had been done that could be done to make the world better; but now I see that there is still one thing more to be tried. Women have never yet united to use their influence steadily and all together against that of which they disapprove. They work too much for themselves, each trying to make their own life happier. They have yet to learn to take a wider view of things, and to be shown that the only way to gain their end is by working for everybody else, with intent to make the whole world better, which means happier. And in order to accomplish this they must be taught that they have only to *will* it – each in her own family, and amongst her own friends; that, after having agreed with the rest about what they mean to put down, they have only to go home and use their influence to that end, quietly, consistently, and without wavering, and the thing will be done. Our influence is like those strong currents which run beneath the surface of the ocean without disturbing it, and yet with irresistible force, and at a rate that may be calculated. It is to help in the direction of that force that I am going to devote my life. Do not imagine,' she went on hurriedly, 'that I think myself fit for such a work. I have had conscientious scruples – been sorely troubled about my own unworthiness, which seemed to unfit me for any good work. But now I see things differently. One may be made an instrument for good without merit of one's own. So long as we do not deceive ourselves by thinking we are worthy, and so long as we are trying our best to become so, I think we may hope; I think we may even know that we shall eventually —— ' she stopped and looked at me.

'Be made worthy,' said Claudia, kissing her.

From Ideala, *1888, by 'Sarah Grand'.*

THE BATTLE GROUND HAS CHANGED

I have watched two of the human beings nearest me die slowly in the hands of a pure sweet loving woman. I have seen her put her lips to them and suck and suck all their life. You have perhaps not seen this – but were I or any man-friend about to take this step you would not be wholly indifferent. Love and friendship are sacred to individuals, not to be touched by the outer world. Sex-feeling and sex-relationship on the other hand are matters on which a man should seek the widest advice from the widest circle of friends; firstly, because sex-feeling has an aberrant effect on the intellect; secondly, because the results of sex-relationship, are matters more of social than private importance. With the brain worker who has anything to give the world marriage is a peculiarly difficult question, it may benefit the general health and so lengthen life, but what if while it makes the flame burn longer it makes it burn *duller*! I think when you take into consideration my strong feeling on the subject of sex relationships (I regard marriage as other people regard death. My feeling of profoundest gratitude is to the woman who once saved me from it) you will understand my sending you the allegory and anything which may have appeared uncalled for. In our brief acquaintance there has been an equal absence of sex feeling on your side and on mine, in other respects our relationship has been very unequal. The life of a woman like myself is a very solitary one. You have had a succession of friendships that have answered to the successive stages of your mental [growth]. When I came to England a few years ago, I had once, only, spoken to a person who knew the names of such books as I loved. Intellectual friendship was a thing I had only dreamed of. Our brief intellectual relations and our few conversations have been common-place enough to you, to me they have been absolutely unique. I have known nothing like it in my life. You will be generous and consider this when you remember how I have tortured you with half-fledged ideas, and plans of books that could never be written.

A woman has a great many lovers. When she comes near to a man it comes at last, generally, to this – 'Will you love me' – that is, 'Will you have no object or aim in the world but *me*. Let *me* be the little glass through which you see life. Let me be the wall round you beyond which you do not grow. You shall be all the world to me!' This seems a beautiful ideal, and to the woman at the present day who still wishes to be dependent on the man it may answer. But to the woman who has to fight for freedom it is exactly *this* ideal which is immoral! It is this demand upon her intellect that she has to fight against, as the savage woman had to resist the physical nature of men! It is this demand which women and men have to teach each other is *immoral*. Is it not the anarchist principle of perfect freedom cutting through life, dealing not with material property, but with affections? It is this spiritual demand that we have to fight against, not now the material. The battle ground has changed. (One feels here more clearly than one sees, one's hands are still only feeling after the truth!)

If a cat were accustomed to regard all boys as beings whose aim it was to circumscribe the liberty of cats and prevent their free locomotion; if she should discover a boy who showed no inclination in this direction, and who appeared absolutely oblivious of the possibility of capturing *any* cat, can you not imagine the infinite placid satisfaction with which that cat would trot at his side? Must men and women in their friendships always stand on the defensive, not because of any brutal instinct, but because of subtle desire to circumscribe each other's liberty? I think not: I see the hope of the world in the passing away of this.

Olive Schreiner to Karl Pearson, 30 January 1887, from Olive Schreiner Letters, Vol. I: 1871–1899, *edited by Richard Rive (1988).*

LOVE AND MISS POTTER

---

12 January [1884]. *The Argoed*
Another small episode of my life over. After six weeks of feverish indecision, the day [of Chamberlain's arrival] comes. House full of young people and the three last days passed in dancing and games: I feel all the while as if I were dancing in a dream towards some precipice. Saturday 5th remainder of the ball party chatting round the afternoon tea table, the great man's son and daughter amongst them. The door opens – 'Mr Chamberlain', general uprising. I advance from amongst them, and in my nervousness almost press six pounds just received into his hand. General feeling of discomfort; no one quite understanding the reason of Mr Chamberlain's advent. There exists evidently no cordiality between him and his host, for Father in a few minutes returns to play patience with an absent and distressed look, utterly

disgusted at the *supposed* intentions of his visitor.

At dinner, after some shyness, we plunged into essentials and he began to delicately hint his requirements. That evening and the next morning till lunch we are on 'susceptible terms'. A dispute over state education breaks the charm. 'It is a question of authority with women; if you believe in Herbert Spencer you won't believe in me.' This opens the battle. By a silent arrangement we find ourselves in the garden. 'It pains me to hear any of my views controverted', and with this preface he begins with stern exactitude to lay down the articles of his political creed. I remain modestly silent; but noticing my silence he remarks that he requires 'intelligent sympathy' from women. 'Servility, Mr Chamberlain,' think I, not sympathy, but intelligent servility: what many women give men, but the difficulty lies in changing one's master, in jumping from one *tone* of thought to the exact opposite – *with intelligence*. And then I advanced as boldly as I dare my feeble objections to his general proposition, feeling that in this case I owe it to the man to show myself and be absolutely sincere. He refutes my objections by re-asserting his convictions passionately, his expression becoming every minute more gloomy and determined. He tells me the history of his political career, how his creed grew up on a basis of experience and sympathy, how his desire to benefit 'the many' had become gradually a passion absorbing within itself his whole nature. 'Hitherto the well-to-do have governed this country for their own interests; and I will do them this credit, they have achieved their object. Now I think the time is approaching for those who work and have not. My aim in life is to make life pleasanter for this great majority. I do not care in the process if it becomes less pleasant for the well-to-do minority. Take America, for instance; cultured persons complain that the society there is vulgar, less agreeable to the delicate tastes of delicately trained minds, but it is infinitely preferable to the ordinary worker.' I suggest meekly that this characteristic of American society does not appear to have any relation to a superior equalization of conditions, brought about by American institutions. That no doubt the working class are better off, but that that surely is due to the unlimited space and power of development of the American continent; on the other hand, huge fortunes are accumulated and *seem* to be more limitless than in England and to wield more power. That in fact the plutocracy, owing to the generally corrupt nature of American institutions, *is said* to be more powerful there than in any country.

And so we wandered up and down the different paths of the Standish garden, the mist which had hid the chasm between us gradually clearing off. Not a suspicion of feeling did he show towards me. He was simply determined to assert his convictions. If I remained silent he watched my expression narrowly, I felt his curious scrutinizing eyes noting each movement as if he were anxious to ascertain whether I yielded to his absolute supremacy. If I objected to or ventured to qualify his theories or his statements, he smashed objection and qualification by an absolute denial, and continued his assertion. He remarked as we came in that he felt as if he had been making a speech. I felt utterly exhausted, we hardly spoke to each other the rest of the day. The next morning, when the Playnes had left, he suggested some more 'exercise'. I *think* both of us felt that all was over between us, so that we talked more *pleasantly*, but even then he insisted on bringing me back from trivialities to a discussion as to the intellectual subordination of women. 'I have only one domestic trouble: my sister and daughter are bitten with the women's rights mania. I don't allow any action on the subject.' 'You don't allow division of opinion in your household, Mr Chamberlain?' 'I can't help people *thinking* differently from me.' 'But you don't allow the expression of the difference?' 'No.' And that little word ended our intercourse.

From The Diary of Beatrice Webb, Vol. I: Glitter Around: Darkness Within, 1873–1892, *edited by N. and J. Mackenzie, 1982. Webb (née Potter) conceived a passionate obsession for radical politician Joseph Chamberlain in the 1880s. The ending of this ambivalent relationship was devastating to her, revealing as it did deep conflicts between emotion and intellect, desire and duty. Six years later her relationship with the Fabian socialist, Sidney Webb, faced her with the same dilemma, but in an entirely different form: with him the accomplishment of her life's work would be assured, but would her profound emotional needs be satisfied? After many misgivings, Beatrice Potter finally married Sidney Webb, the son of a Soho shopkeeper, in July 1892 and from that day forward embarked on a lifetime partnership of work, study and companionship.*

Meanwhile, I must tell you really what I feel. I cried very bitterly over your letter – and tossed about the night through feeling how wrong it had been of me to have been led away from my better judgment last spring and to have granted your request for friendship. But that is now done – and cannot be undone – the question is what is the present position?

First – all you write about your career does not in any way affect the one question. It would suit my work – and therefore me – far better to marry a clerk in the Colonial Office than a leading politician to whose career I should have in the end to sacrifice my own. It was exactly your position which made me hesitate – it was this with your views and your moral refinement which made me try to love you.

But I do not love you. All the misery of this relationship arises from this. It is now six months that we have known each other intimately – and yet there is no change in my feeling except a growing certainty that I cannot love you.

To be perfectly frank I did at one time *fancy* I was beginning to care for you – but I was awakened to the truth by your claiming me as your future wife – then I felt – that what I cared for was not *you* but simply the fact of being loved: and this self knowledge has become clearer every day. That was a fortunate misunderstanding. I might have drifted on feeling the whole thing too remote to decide on and enjoying the meaning of love – yet refusing to give in return – and then when the time came there would have been a terrible crash – I should have refused to carry out what would have seemed to you a tacit promise.

Frankly, I do not believe my nature is capable of love. I came out of that six years agony uninjured as a worker – I came out of it less egotistical, more sympathetic, with no cynicism nor bitterness against men and the world – my whole nature rebounded into an energetic, hopeful, impersonal life – doubtless there was a great big dash of contempt which has taken a personal form. But I came out right as I told you at Glasgow – like a bit of steel – I was not broken but I was hardened – the fire must do one or the other. And this being the case –

the fact that I do not love you – I cannot, and will never, make the stupendous sacrifice of marriage. If I loved a man – if *ever* I love a man – the sacrifice of an insignificant work will seem a good riddance. But this is in itself a test of my feeling.

Beatrice Potter to Sidney Webb, 7 December 1890, from The Letters of Sidney and Beatrice Webb, Vol. I: Apprenticeships 1873–1892, *edited by Norman Mackenzie (1978).*

20 June [1891] [Norway]

Beautiful Norwegian scenery ... Definitely engaged on a new life ... At times I am afraid, and disconsolately ask myself whether from my own point of view I have been wise. But the need for a warmer and more responsible relationship with another human being has made it seem the best even for me. The world will wonder. On the face of it, it seems an extraordinary end to the once brilliant Beatrice Potter (but it is just because it is not an end that she has gone into it) to marry an ugly little man with no social position and less means, whose only recommendation, so some may say, is a certain pushing ability. And I am not 'in love', not as I was. But I see something else in him (the world would say that was proof of my love) – a fine intellect and a warm-heartedness, a power of self-subordination and self-devotion for the 'common good'. And our marriage will be based on fellowship, a common faith and a common work. His feeling is the passionate love of an emotional man, mine the growing tenderness of the mother touched with the dependence of the woman on the help of a strong lover, and in the background there is the affectionate *camaraderie*, the 'fun', the strenuous helpfulness of two young workers in the same cause. Workers have the great advantage that there is a great fund of playfulness and high spirits in the times of rest after the year's labour. Our holydays will be real holydays – nothing is too small or too trivial to yield amusement and interest to two hard-worked individuals who have given themselves a rest from work. He is in a state of happy exaltation, I am beginning to feel at rest and assured. It will not wrench me from my old life, simply raise it to a higher level of usefulness.

The long dreamy days with the beautiful scenery passing by; the mountain fiords, rivers, waterfalls all in rapid succession lend a stillness to one's mind, a lengthened brooding over the past and the future. It is well to have this time of almost religious rest, this Sabbath of emotion, for with both of us there is a long dusty road, with steep inclines, before us. Our life will be strenuous, may it not also be peaceful? We have honestly only *one* desire – the commonweal. Why may not the current of our lives be deep and unruffled by all the surface agitations of personal success and failure?

From The Diary of Beatrice Webb, Vol. I: Glitter Around: Darkness Within, 1873–1892, *edited by N. and J. Mackenzie (1982).*

HOW A STRONG-SOULED WOMAN FEELS ABOUT THE MARRIAGE TIE AS IT IS

———————————

   'Oh, to be alone!
To escape from the work, the play,
The talking every day;
   To escape from all I have done,
And all that remains to do.
To escape – yes, even from you,
   My only love, and be
   Alone and free.

   'Could I only stand
Between gray moor and gray sky,
Where the winds and the plovers cry,
   And no man is at hand;
And feel the free wind blow
On my rain-wet face, and know

I am free – not yours, but my own –
Free, and alone!

    'For the soft firelight,
And the home of your heart, my dear,
Thy heart being always here.
    I want to stand upright,
And to cool my eyes in the air,
And to see how my back can bear
      Burdens – to try, to know,
      To learn, to grow!

    'I am only you!
I am yours, part of you, your wife!
And I have no other life.
    I cannot think, cannot do;
I cannot breathe, cannot see;
There is "us," but there is not "me" –
      And worst, at your kiss I grow
      Contented so.'

From 'Woman Free' in Shafts, *March 1893.*

A WORLDLY WOMAN

You, though you love me, would want to keep a rein over me. You have ideas of a man being master, of a woman being submissive; you would want to show me clearly at times – though there had arisen no necessity – that you were master, you would think it manly to do so. But I should hate a man who kept a rein over me; it is what the men do who are not sure of themselves, the men who feel that they must always be making signs that they are strong, lest they be suspected of weakness. It would seem to me like a gaoler rattling the keys as he walked by the cells, lest the prisoners should forget that they had lost their freedom. I remember your asking me once when we were engaged if I kept an account of what I spent,

of the few odd pounds a year that were allowed me, and when
I said no, you said in a firm voice that sent a thrill through
me, a thrill of opposition, 'You will have to do it when you
are my wife, darling.' It was like the flick of a whip before
my eyes; it was the tone of the man who meant to have his
way, to make it clearly felt that he was master, and to let no
other will but his be felt within his doors. I think those words
alone did much to strengthen the impossibilities. They opened
a sudden vista of the future, and every bit of me rose in revolt. I
should have hated the life you would have expected me to lead:
its rules and obligations, its monotony. I dreaded it even when I
was only seventeen and knew nothing of the world, but now it
would kill me. You think, too, that woman should keep in the
background, that home life and duties should be sufficient for
her, that her views of the outer world should be gained from her
husband, and those views as a matter of course agree with his.
You would not approve of much going out, of social success
even, of individuality of any sort. This would fret and worry me.
I am no strong-minded woman; I do not want to go to meetings,
still less to speak at them. But I must have freedom – freedom to
think and read and speak and form my own ideas, as all thinking
men let their wives do now. Since John prospered so well, and
gave me as his sister a place in the world, I have had what I
wanted. I could not give it up to go to live in Gower Street as
your wife, to look after your house, to plan your quiet evening
dinner, to arrange your children's lessons, to let all my joys and
sorrows be your shaping, submitting always my will to yours. My
life, for all its dreams and ambitions, is not a happy one, has not
been, but ——

(*Unfinished, and not sent.*)

From Love Letters of a Worldly Woman, *1891, by Mrs W.K.*
Clifford. Lucy Clifford (c. 1853–1929) was a novelist and dramatist,
whose best-known novel is Mrs Keith's Crime *(1885), which*
deals with infanticide.

DEAR GIRL

Ruth's Diary   Saturday, 9 March 1907
On Saturday I met Eva in Ilford. She brought me two pictures for my birthday – they are so beautiful. We left about six and I saw her onto a tram, then walked on to the station to meet Wal. Would he miss his train, I wondered? Yes, and the next one as well. I felt free to give expression to vexed remarks when he *did* appear, after I had waited for nearly an hour. He did not appreciate them, and punished me by refusing to explain the cause of his lateness, and so we started out on our walk in no very amiable mood. I was then soundly berated on my obstinacy and independence – the latter quality I intend ever to cultivate and Wal must learn my intention. I am sure it would be better for many, many people if conventional ideas concerning women's dependence upon men could be altered – they are a hindrance to the true progress of women, and are not altogether good for men. I believe so strongly in the possibilities and powers of my own sex, that I deprecate all customs, though rooted in ideas of chivalry once admirable, that would retard their emancipation. Wal would shield and shelter, where I do not desire that he should.

From Dear Girl. The diaries and letters of two working women, 1897–1917, *edited by Tierl Thompson (1987). Ruth Slate was a clerk in a grocery firm in the City; Eva Slawson a legal secretary from Walthamstow. They met in 1902 and began a friendship and correspondence that spanned twenty years and ranged over such subjects as women's suffrage, disenchantment with orthodox religion, doubts about marriage and a commitment to pacifism.*

THE WOMAN WHO DID

'O Herminia,' he cried, calling her for the first time by her Christian name alone, 'how glad I am I happened to go that afternoon to Mrs. Dewsbury's. For otherwise perhaps I might never have known you.'

Herminia's heart gave a delicious bound. She was a woman, and therefore she was glad he should speak so. She was a woman, and therefore she shrank from acknowledging it. But she looked him back in the face tranquilly none the less on that account, and answered with sweet candour, 'Thank you so much, Mr. Merrick.'

'*I* said Herminia,' the young man corrected, smiling, yet aghast at his own audacity.

'And I thanked you for it,' Herminia answered, casting down those dark lashes, and feeling the heart throb violently under her neat bodice.

Alan drew a deep breath. 'And it was *that* you thanked me for,' he ejaculated, tingling.

'Yes, it was that I thanked you for,' Herminia answered, with a still deeper rose spreading down to her bare throat. 'I like you very much, and it pleases me to hear you call me Herminia. Why should I shrink from admitting it? 'Tis the Truth, you know; and the Truth shall make us Free. I'm not afraid of my freedom.'

Alan paused for a second, irresolute. 'Herminia,' he said at last, leaning forward till his face was very close to hers, and he could feel the warm breath that came and went so quickly: 'that's very, very kind of you. I needn't tell you I've been thinking a great deal about you these last three weeks or so. You have filled my mind; filled it to the brim: and I think you know it.'

Philosopher as she was, Herminia plucked a blade of grass and drew it, quivering, through her tremulous fingers. It caught and hesitated. 'I guessed as much, I think,' she answered low, but frankly.

The young man's heart gave a bound. 'And *you*, Herminia?' he asked in an eager ecstasy.

Herminia was true to the Truth. 'I've thought a great deal about you too, Mr. Merrick,' she answered, looking down, but with a great gladness thrilling her.

'I said "Herminia," ' the young man repeated, with a marked stress on the Christian name.

Herminia hesitated a second. Then two crimson spots flared

forth on her speaking face as she answered with an effort, 'About you too, Alan.'

The young man drew back and gazed at her. She was very, very beautiful. 'Dare I ask you, Herminia?' he cried. 'Have I a right to ask you? Am I worthy of you, I mean? Ought I to retire as not your peer, and leave you to some man who could rise more easily to the height of your dignity?'

'I've thought about that too,' Herminia answered, still firm to her principles. 'I've thought it all over. I've said to myself, Shall I do right in monopolizing him, when he is so great and sweet and true and generous? Not monopolizing, of course, for that would be wrong and selfish; but making you my own more than any other woman's. And I answered my own heart, Yes, yes, I shall do right to accept him if he asks me; for I love him; that is enough. The thrill within me tells me so. Nature put that thrill in our souls to cry out to us with a clear voice when we had met the soul she then and there intended for us.'

Alan's face flushed like her own. 'Then you love me?' he cried, all on fire. 'And you deign to tell me so! O Herminia, how sweet you are! What have I done to deserve it?'

He folded her in his arms. Her bosom throbbed on his. Their lips met for a second. Herminia took his kiss with sweet submission, and made no faint pretence of fighting against it. Her heart was full. She quickened to the finger-tips.

There was silence for a minute or two – the silence when soul speaks direct to soul through the vehicle of touch, the mother-tongue of the affections. Then Alan leaned back once more, and hanging over her in a rapture murmured in soft, low tones, 'So, Herminia, you will be mine! You say beforehand you will take me.'

'Not *will* be yours,' Herminia corrected in that silvery voice of hers. '*Am* yours already, Alan. I somehow feel as if I had always been yours. I am yours this moment. You may do what you would with me.'

She said it so simply, so purely, so naturally, with all the supreme faith of the good woman enamoured, who can yield herself up without blame to the man who loves her, that it hardly even occurred to Alan's mind to wonder at her self-surrender. Yet he drew back all the same in a sudden little crisis of doubt and uncertainty. He scarcely realized what she meant. 'Then, dearest,' he cried tentatively, 'how soon may we be married?'

At sound of those unexpected words from such lips as his, a flush of shame and horror overspread Herminia's cheek. 'Never!' she cried firmly, drawing away. 'O Alan, what can you mean by it? Don't tell me, after all I've tried to make you feel and understand, you thought I could possibly consent to *marry* you!'

The man gazed at her in surprise. Though he was prepared for much, he was scarcely prepared for such devotion to principle. 'O Herminia,' he cried, 'you can't mean it. You can't have thought of what it entails. Surely, surely, you won't carry your ideas of freedom to such an extreme, such a dangerous conclusion?'

Herminia looked up at him, half-hurt. 'Can't have thought of what it entails!' she repeated. Her dimples deepened. 'Why, Alan, haven't I had my whole lifetime to think of it? What else have I thought about in any serious way save this one great question of a woman's duty to herself and her sex and her unborn children? It's been my sole study. How could you fancy I spoke hastily or without due consideration on such a subject? Would you have me like the blind girls who go unknowing to the altar, as sheep go to the shambles? Could you suspect me of such carelessness? – such culpable thoughtlessness? – you, to whom I have spoken of all this so freely?'

Alan stared at her, disconcerted, hardly knowing how to answer. 'But what alternative do you propose then?' he asked in his amazement.

'Propose?' Herminia repeated, taken aback in her turn. It all seemed to her so plain and transparent and natural. 'Why, simply that we should be friends like any others – very dear, dear friends, with the only kind of friendship that nature makes possible between men and women.'

She said it so softly, with some womanly gentleness, yet with such lofty candour, that Alan couldn't help admiring her more than ever before for her translucent simplicity and directness of purpose. Yet her suggestion frightened him. It was so much more novel to him than to her. Herminia had reasoned it all out with herself, as she truly said, for years, and knew exactly how she felt and thought about it. To Alan, on the contrary, it came with the

166

shock of a sudden surprise, and he could hardly tell on the spur of the moment how to deal with it. He paused and reflected. 'But do you mean to say, Herminia,' he asked, still holding that soft brown hand unresisted in his, 'you've made up your mind never to marry any one? made up your mind to brave the whole mad world, that can't possibly understand the motives of your conduct, and live with some friend, as you put it, unmarried?'

'Yes, I've made up my mind,' Herminia answered with a faint tremor in her maidenly voice, but with hardly a trace now of a traitorous blush where no blush was needed. 'I've made up my mind, Alan; and from all we had said and talked over together, I thought you, at least, would sympathize with my resolve.'

She spoke with a gentle tinge of regret, nay, almost of disillusion. The bare suggestion of that regret stung Alan to the quick. He felt it was shame to him that he could not rise at once to the height of her splendid self-renunciation. 'You mistake me, dearest,' he answered, petting her hand in his own (and she allowed him to pet it). 'It wasn't for myself or for the world I hesitated. My thought was for you. You are very young yet. You say you have counted the cost. I wonder if you have. I wonder if you realize it.'

'Only too well,' Herminia replied, in a very earnest mood. 'I have wrought it all out in my mind beforehand, covenanted with my soul that for women's sake I would be a free woman. Alan, whoever would be free must himself strike the blow. I know what you will say – what every man would say to the woman he loved under similar circumstances – "Why should *you* be the victim? Why should *you* be the martyr? Bask in the sun yourself. Leave this doom to some other." But, Alan, I can't. I feel *I* must face it. Unless one woman begins, there will be no beginning.' She lifted his hand in her own, and fondled it in her turn with caressing tenderness. 'Think how easy it would be for me, dear friend,' she cried, with a catch in her voice, 'to do as other women do; to accept the *honourable marriage* you offer me, as other women would call it; to be false to my sex, a traitor to my convictions; to sell my kind for a mess of pottage – a name and a home; or even for thirty pieces of silver – to be some rich man's wife – as other women have sold it. But, Alan, I can't. My conscience won't let me. I know what marriage is – from what

167

vile slavery it has sprung; on what unseen horrors for my sister women it is reared and buttressed; by what unholy sacrifices it is sustained and made possible. I know it has a history. I know its past: I know its present: and I can't embrace it. I can't be untrue to my most sacred beliefs. I can't pander to the malignant thing, just because a man who loves me would be pleased by my giving way, and would kiss me and fondle me for it. And I love you to fondle me. But I must keep my proper place, the freedom which I have gained for myself by such arduous efforts. I have said to you already, "So far as my will goes, I am yours; take me and do as you choose with me." That much I can yield, as every good woman should yield it, to the man she loves, to the man who loves her. But more than that – no. It would be treason to my sex. Not my life, not my future, not my individuality, not my freedom.'

'I wouldn't ask you for those,' Alan answered, carried away by the torrent flood of her passionate speech. 'I would wish you to guard them. But, Herminia, just as a matter of form – to prevent the world from saying the cruel things the world is sure to say – and as an act of justice to you and your children! A mere ceremony of marriage; what more does it mean nowadays than that we two agree to live together on the ordinary terms of civilized society?'

Still Herminia shook her head. 'No, no,' she cried vehemently. 'I deny and decline those terms. They are part and parcel of a system of slavery. I have learnt that the righteous soul should avoid all appearance of evil. I will not palter and parley with the unholy thing. Even though you go to a registry office and get rid as far as you can of every relic of the sacerdotal and sacramental idea, yet the marriage itself is still an assertion of man's supremacy over woman. It ties her to him for life; it ignores her individuality; it compels her to promise what no human heart can be sure of performing; for you can contract to do or not to do, easily enough: but contract to feel or not to feel – what transparent absurdity! It is full of all evils, and I decline to consider it. If I love a man at all, I must love him on terms of perfect freedom. I can't bind myself down to live with him to my shame one day longer than I love him; or to love him at all if I find him unworthy of my purest love, or unable to retain it; or if I discover some other more fit to be loved by me. You admitted the other day that all this was

168

abstractly true; why should you wish this morning to draw back from following it out to its end in practice.'

Alan was only an Englishman, and shared, of course, the inability of his countrymen to carry any principle to its logical conclusion. He was all for admitting that though things must really be so, yet it were prudent in life to pretend they were otherwise. This is the well-known English virtue of moderation and compromise; it has made England what she is, the shabbiest, sordidest, worst organized of nations. So he paused for a second and temporized. 'It's for your sake, Herminia,' he said again. 'I can't bear to think of your making yourself a martyr. And I don't see how, if you act as you propose, you could escape martyrdom?'

Herminia looked up at him with pleading eyes. Tears just trembled on the edge of those glistening lashes. 'It never occurred to me to think,' she said gently but bravely, 'my life could ever end in anything else but martyrdom. It must needs be so with all true lives and all good ones. For whoever sees the truth, whoever strives earnestly with all his soul to be good, must be raised many planes above the common mass of men around him; he must be a moral pioneer, and the moral pioneer is always a martyr. People won't allow others to be wiser and better than themselves unpunished. They can forgive anything, except moral superiority. We have each to choose between acquiescence in the wrong, with a life of ease, and struggle for the right, crowned at last by inevitable failure. To succeed is to fail, and failure is the only success worth aiming at. Every great and good life can but end in a Calvary.'

'And I want to save you from that,' Alan cried, leaning over her with real tenderness, for she was already very dear to him. 'I want to save you from yourself. I want to make you think twice before you rush headlong into such a danger.'

'Not to save me from myself, but to save me from my own higher and better nature,' Herminia answered with passionate seriousness. 'Alan, I don't want any man to save me from that. I want you rather to help me, to strengthen me, to sympathize with me. I want you to love me – not for my face and form alone, not for what I share with every other woman – but for all that is holiest and deepest within me. If you can't love me for that, I don't ask you to love me. I want to be loved for what I am

169

THE NEW WOMAN

in myself, for the yearnings I possess that are most of all peculiar
to me. I know you are attracted to me by those yearnings above
everything; why wish me untrue to them? It was because I saw
you could sympathize with me in these impulses that I said to
myself, "Here, at last, is the man who can go through life as an
aid and a spur to me." Don't tell me I was mistaken; don't belie
my belief. Be what I thought you were – what I know you are!
Work with me and help me. Lift me! – raise me! exalt me! Take
me on the sole terms on which I can give myself up to you.'

She stretched her arms out pleading. She turned those subtle
eyes to him appealingly. She was a beautiful woman. Alan Merrick
was human. The man in him gave way. He seized her in his clasp,
and pressed her close to his bosom. It heaved tumultuously.

'I could do anything for you, Herminia,' he cried; 'and, indeed,
I do sympathize with you. But give me at least till to-morrow to
think this thing over. It is a momentous question. Don't let us be
precipitate.'

Herminia drew a long breath. His embrace thrilled through her.

'As you will,' she answered, with a woman's meekness. 'But
remember, Alan, what I say I mean. On these terms it shall be, and
upon none others. Brave women before me have tried for a while to
act on their own responsibility, for the good of their sex; but never
of their own free will from the very beginning. They have avoided
marriage, not because they thought it a shame and a surrender,
a treason to their sex, a base yielding to the unjust pretensions of
men, but because there existed at the time some obstacle in their
way in the shape of the vested interest of some other woman.
When Mary Godwin chose to mate herself with Shelley, she took
her good name in her hands; – but still, there was Harriet. As soon
as Harriet was dead, Mary showed she had no deep principle of
action involved, by marrying Shelley. When George Eliot chose
to pass her life with Lewes on terms of equal freedom, she defied
the man-made law – but still, there was his wife to prevent the
possibility of a legalized union. As soon as Lewes was dead,
George Eliot showed she had no principle involved, by marrying
another man. Now, *I* have the rare chance of acting otherwise. I
can show the world from the very first that I act from principle,
and from principle only. I can say to it in effect, "See, here is the
man of my choice; the man I love, truly and purely; the man any

170

one of you would willingly have seen offering himself in lawful marriage to your own daughters. If I would, I might go the beaten way you prescribe, and marry him legally. But of my own free will I disdain that degradation. I choose rather to be free. No fear of your scorn, no dread of your bigotry, no shrinking at your cruelty, shall prevent me from following the thorny path I know to be the right one. I seek no temporal end. I will not prove false to the future of my kind in order to protect myself from your hateful indignities. I know on what vile foundations your temple of wedlock is based and built, what pitiable victims languish and die in its sickening vaults; and I will not consent to enter it. Here, of my own free will, I take my stand for the right, and refuse your sanctions! No woman that I know of has ever yet done that. Other women have fallen, as men choose to put it in their odious dialect; no other has voluntarily risen as I propose to do." ' She paused a moment for breath.

'Now, you know how I feel,' she continued, looking straight into his eyes. 'Say no more at present: it is wisest so. But go home and think it out, and talk it over with me to-morrow.'

From The Woman Who Did, *1895, by Grant Allen (1848–1899). The most notorious, and successful, of the 'New Woman' novels – albeit written by a man – the book, which chronicled the ultimate tragedy of the free-thinking Herminia, ran to nineteen editions in its first year of publication and drew several responses, including* The Woman Who Didn't *(1895) by 'Victoria Cross(e)' (Vivian Cory).*

THIS WAS THE GOAL

Serious admirers were not lacking, and with one of these, a young man some eight years older than herself, she had had for the past three months a sort of understanding. For her, as for so many others, the time she had still to spend at school was as purgatory before paradise. To top all, one of the day-scholars in Laura's class was actually engaged to be married; and in no

171

boy-and-girl fashion, but to a doctor who lived and practised in Emerald Hill: he might sometimes be seen, from a peephole under the stairs, waiting to escort her home from school. This fiancée was looked up to by the class with tremendous reverence, as one set apart, oiled and anointed. You really could not treat her as a comrade – her, who had reached the goal. For this *was* the goal; and the thoughts of all were fixed, with an intentness that varied only in degree, on the great consummation which, as planned in these young minds, should come to pass without fail directly the college-doors closed behind them. – And here again Laura was a heretic. For she could not contemplate the future that was to be hers when she had finished her education, but with a feeling of awe: it was still so distant as to be one dense blue haze; it was so vast, that thinking of it took your breath away: there was room in it for the most wonderful miracles that had ever happened; it might contain anything – from golden slippers to a Jacob's ladder, by means of which you would scale the skies; and with these marvellous perhapses awaiting you, it was impossible to limit your hopes to one single event, which, though it saved you from derision, would put an end, for ever, to all possible, exciting contingencies.

From The Getting of Wisdom, *1910, by Henry Handel Richardson.*

THE MARRIAGE?

1894: 26. To Edward Carpenter. The Homestead, Kimberley,
8 October 1894.

Dear old E.C.

The marriage pamphlet has come. I think it splendid! You don't perhaps dwell QUITE enough on the monetary independence of woman as the first condition necessary to the putting of things on the right footing: but you do mention it.

You see the monetary question between man and woman is not the same as the monetary question between two close friends of the same sex. Were a man to live with a closely loved friend on whom he was dependent, there would be no antecedents and traditions implying inferiority on one side and superiority on the other to be fought against as well as the monetary inequality, before the true equality of true friendship can be reached.

A man and a woman stand in the same relation to each other as a white man and a black man, supposing the two to have struck up a deathless friendship and to have determined to live together. It would not do for the black man to be dependent on the white because, at least in this country, there are such centuries of traditions of the inferiority of the black and the superiority of the white; of submission on one side and masterhood on the other; and these traditions and the force of education would so deeply, if unconsciously, have affected both, that if the monetary power were on one side, I believe a friendship [of] true equality would be impossible between the two. Even if this was a perfect monetary equality, even if the black man were supporting the white, and even if in his heart the white man believed the black man to be much his superior and deeply honoured him, yet even *then* there would [be] difficulty in the small things of life; there would be an unconscious tendency on the part of the white man to expect, and of the black man a subservience which culture would expect or give to those born their equals. It would be rather desirable than otherwise that the black man should have money and the white not; it would tend to put things in a truer and more beautiful relation to each other. Just so with a man and a woman; with two thousand years of slavish submission on one side and animal dominance on the other as the tradition of their race, they can *neither* of them afford anything which tends to keep up those traditions. I can believe the most ideally happy fellowship might exist between a man and woman where the woman had material wealth and the man none. I think it would tend to make them both happier in the deepest sense but I can't picture the opposite. The newly freed slave has to stand a little on his dignity!!

From Olive Schreiner Letters, Vol. I: 1871–1899, *edited by Richard Rive (1988).*

SINGLE WOMEN, WORLD LOVERS

Eva's Diary   Wednesday, 21 May 1913

I ran round to see Mrs Taverner in my lunch hour – we sat in the summer house and chatted. Mrs Taverner said she thought so many young married women shut themselves away from outside interests because at first the love of husband and children seemed all sufficient. She believed this was a mistake – but a mistake of ignorance. Ah! homes would not be closed at least to a single woman, if the married once realized how the hearts of their sisters yearn after companionship. Mrs Taverner also gave me a verse upon the lonely woman. It is a comfort to me to believe that we single women have a very definite part to play in the battle of life. If all women could marry would they have sufficient leisure and opportunity to study the position of woman and to represent her cause to the world? This is work which single women can make their own. So enriched we can become world lovers – the companions of the lonely!

From Dear Girl. The diaries and letters of two working women, 1897–1917, *edited by Tierl Thompson (1987).*

FAMILY AND HOME

My brothers were all older than I; the eldest eleven, the youngest five years older; and my mother, when I was born, was in her forty-seventh year; a circumstance which perhaps makes it remarkable that the physical energy and high animal spirits of which I have just made mention came to me in so large a share. My old friend Harriet St. Leger, Fanny Kemble's 'dear H.S.,' who knew us all well, said to me one day laughing: 'You know *you* are your Father's *Son!*"' Had I been a man, and had possessed my brother's facilities for entering Parliament or any profession,

174

I have sometimes dreamed I could have made my mark and done some masculine service to my fellow-creatures. But the woman's destiny which God allotted to me has been, I do not question, the best and happiest for me; nor have I ever seriously wished it had been otherwise, albeit I have gone through life without that interest which has been styled 'woman's whole existence.' Perhaps if this book be found to have any value it will partly consist in the evidence it must afford of how pleasant and interesting, and withal, I hope, not altogether useless a life is open to a woman, though no man has ever desired to share it, nor has she seen the man she would have wished to ask her to do so. The days which many maidens my contemporaries and acquaintances,–

> 'Lost in wooing
> In watching and pursuing,'–

(or in being pursued, which comes to the same thing); were spent by me, free from all such distractions, in study and in the performance of happy and healthful filial and housewifely duties.

From Life of Frances Power Cobbe: As Told by Herself, *1894.*
A philanthropist, philosopher and feminist, Frances Power Cobbe (1822–1904) established societies to help workhouse girls and wrote pamphlets on various aspects of the 'woman question'. She was active in the suffrage movement from the 1870s.

MARRIAGE AS A TRADE

If it be granted that marriage is, as I have called it, essentially a trade on the part of woman – the exchange of her person for the means of subsistence – it is legitimate to inquire into the manner in which that trade is carried on, and to compare the position of the worker in the matrimonial with the position of the worker in any other market. Which brings us at once to the fact – arising from the compulsory nature of the profession – that it is carried on under disadvantages unknown and unfelt by those who earn their living by other methods. For the regulations governing compulsory service – the institution of slavery and the like – are always framed, not in the interests of the worker, but in the interests of those who impose his work upon him. The regulations governing exchange and barter in the marriage market, therefore, are necessarily framed in the interests of the employer – the male.

The position is this. Marriage, with its accompaniments and consequences – the ordering of a man's house, the bearing and rearing of his children – has, by the long consent of ages, been established as practically the only means whereby woman, with honesty and honour, shall earn her daily bread. Her every attempt to enter any other profession has been greeted at first with scorn and opposition; her sole outlook was to be dependence upon man. Yet the one trade to which she is destined, the one means of earning her bread to which she is confined, she may not openly profess. No other worker stands on the same footing. The man who has his bread to earn, with hands, or brains, or tools, goes out to seek for the work to which he is trained; his livelihood depending on it, he offers his skill and services without shame or thought of reproach. But with woman it is not so; she is expected to express unwillingness for the very work for which she has been taught and trained. She has been brought up in the belief that her profession is marriage and motherhood; yet though poverty may be pressing upon her – though she may be faced with actual lack of the necessities of life – she must not openly express her desire to enter that profession, and earn her bread in the only way for which she is fitted. She must stand aside and wait – indefinitely; and attain to her destined livelihood by appearing to despise it.

That, of course, is the outcome of something more than a convention imposed on her by man; nature, from the beginning, has made her more fastidious and reluctant than the male. But with this natural fastidiousness and reluctance the commercialism imposed upon her by her economic needs is constantly at clash and at conflict, urging her to get her bread as best she can in the only market open to her. Theoretically – since by her wares she lives – she has a perfect right to cry those wares and seek to push them to the best advantage. That is to say, she has a perfect right to seek, with frankness and with openness, the man who, in her judgment, can most fittingly provide her with the means of support.

This freedom of bargaining to the best advantage, permitted as a matter of course to every other worker, is denied to her. It is, of course, claimed and exercised by the prostitute class – a class which has pushed to its logical conclusion the principle that woman exists by virtue of a wage paid her in return for the possession of her person; but it is interesting to note that the 'unfortunate' enters the open market with the hand of the law extended threateningly above her head. The fact is curious if inquired into: since the theory that woman should live by physical attraction of the opposite sex has never been seriously denied, but rather insisted upon, by men, upon what principle is solicitation, or open offer of such attraction, made a legal offence? (Not because the woman is a danger to the community, since the male sensualist is an equal source of danger.) Only, apparently, because the advance comes from the wrong side. I speak under correction, but cannot, unaided, light upon any other explanation; and mine seems to be borne out by the fact that, in other ranks of life, custom, like the above-mentioned law, strenuously represses any open advance on the part of the wo-man. So emphatic, indeed, is this unwritten law, that one cannot help suspecting that it was needful it should be emphatic, lest woman, adapting herself to her economic position, should take the initiative in a matter on which her livelihood depended, and deprive her employer not only of the pleasure of the chase, but of the illusion that their common bargain was as much a matter of romance and volition on her part as on his.

As a matter of fact, that law that the first advances must come from the side of the man is, as was only to be expected, broken, and broken every day; sometimes directly, but far more often in-directly. The woman bent on matrimony is constantly on the alert to evade its workings, conscious that in her attempt to do so she can nearly always count on the ready, if unspoken, co-operation of her sisters. This statement is, I know, in flat contravention of the firmly-rooted masculine belief that one woman regards another as an enemy to be depreciated consistently in masculine eyes, and that women spend their lives in one long struggle to gratify an uncontrollable desire for admiration at each other's expense. (I

have myself been told by a man that he would never be so foolishly discourteous as to praise one woman in another's hearing.
I, on my part, desirous also of being wisely courteous, did not
attempt to shake the magnificent belief in his own importance
to me which the statement betrayed.) Admiration is a very real
passion in some women, as it is a very real passion in some men;
but what, in women, is often mistaken for it is ambition, a desire
to get on and achieve success in life in the only way in which
it is open to a woman to achieve it – through the favour of man.
Which is only another way of saying what I have insisted on before
– that a good many feminine actions which are commonly and
superficially attributed to sexual impulse have their root in the
commercial instinct.

It is because women, consciously or unconsciously, recognize the commercial nature of the undertaking that they interest
themselves so strongly in the business of matchmaking, other than
their own. Men have admitted that interest, of course – the thing is
too self-evident to be denied – and, as their manner is, attributed
it to an exuberant sexuality which overflows on to its surroundings; steadfastly declining to take into account the 'professional'
element in its composition, since that would necessarily imply
the existence of an *esprit de corps* amongst women.

I myself cannot doubt that there does exist a spirit of practical, if largely unconscious, trade unionism in a class engaged
in extracting, under many difficulties and by devious ways, its
livelihood from the employer, man. (I need scarcely point out
that man, like every other wage-payer, has done his level best
and utmost to suppress the spirit of combination, and encourage
distrust and division, amongst the wage-earners in the matrimonial
market; and that the trade of marriage, owing to the isolation of the
workers, has offered unexampled opportunities for such suppres-
sion of unity and encouragement of distrust and division.) But, in
spite of this, women in general recognize the economic necessity
of marriage for each other, and in a spirit of instinctive comradeship seek to forward it by every means in their power. There must
be something extraordinarily and unnaturally contemptible about
a woman who, her own bargain made and means of livelihood
secured, will not help another to secure hers; and it is that
motive, and not a rapturous content in their own unclouded

destiny, not an unhesitating conviction that their lot has fallen in a fair ground, which makes of so many married women industrious and confirmed matchmakers. What has been termed the 'huge conspiracy of married women' is, in fact, nothing but a huge trade union whose members recognize the right of others to their bread. To my mind, one of the best proofs of the reality of this spirit of unconscious trade unionism among women is the existence of that other feminine conspiracy of silence which surrounds the man at whom a woman, for purely mercenary reasons, is making a 'dead set'. In such a case, the only women who will interfere and warn the intended victim will be his own relatives – a mother or a sister; others, while under no delusions as to the interested nature of the motives by which the pursuer is actuated, will hold their tongues, and even go so far as to offer facilities for the chase. They realize that their fellow has a right to her chance – that she must follow her trade as best she can, and would no more dream of giving her away than the average decent workman would dream of going to an employer and informing him that one of his mates was not up to his job and should, therefore, be discharged. In these emergencies a man must look to a man for help; the sympathies of the practical and unromantic sex will be on the other side.

I shall not deny, of course, that there is active and bitter competition amongst women for the favour not only of particular men, but of men in general; but, from what I have said already, it will be gathered that I consider that competition to be largely economic and artificial. Where it is economic, it is produced by the same cause which produces active and bitter competition in other branches of industry – the overcrowding of the labour market. Where it is artificial, as distinct from purely economic, it is produced by the compulsory concentration of energy on one particular object, and the lack of facilities for dispersing that energy in other directions. It is not the woman with an interest in life who spends her whole time in competing with her otherwise unoccupied sisters for the smiles of a man.

From Marriage as a Trade, *1909, by Cicely Hamilton.*

THE VARIATIONS OF LOVE

The marriage tie is a way of keeping people together while they undergo the various disillusions and jealousies that are inevitable, unless one of them is prepared to give way in everything. Is there any better way? In most cases, no.

The marriage tie will always exist, because it is the natural impulse of the majority of young people to wish to love each other alone, and to remain with each other for ever. The honeymoon having elapsed, they very likely find they are about to become parents, and they spend the intervening months in making happy preparations. Then the baby is born, and has to be brought up until it is old enough to go to school. If there are three children, they have to be looked after for about fourteen years. The wife is now thirty-four, and the husband thirty-eight. The children are placed in various schools away from home. Is there any alternative to the rather boring life that has to be lived out until death parts the parents? None. They are not rich enough to travel and amuse themselves, so the wife goes on housekeeping and calling on neighbours, and changing her servants, and the husband goes to the City, plays golf, and reads trashy novels. The marriage tie must always persist while these people exist.

But what are the six million bachelors and the seven million spinsters to do? Some of them are very young; thousands of them do not wish to marry, their sexual nature is hardly developed more than a child's; others are invalids, openly or secretly; and a good number are leading illegally arranged lives because the present marriage laws do not suit their constitutions. Among the grown-up population about half the number are married, and the other half unmarried. Many of these marriages are unhappy, and it is to be presumed that at least six million of each sex do not wish to marry enough to overcome the terrors of saying what they want for ever, and getting it.

Now, having regard to the natural variations of love, I must suggest that the stigma might be removed from those who are not capable of lifelong fidelity. There seems good proof that a

180

few millions of men and women are bringing misery upon the
rest because they are treated as unworthy of social consideration.
Medical men are saying that the disease which is undermining the
health of the nation is dangerous only because it is shameful. It
could be easily cured in its early stages if it could be treated openly
and without ruining the reputation of those whom it attacks. Even
when health is retained, reputations are lost and careers are ruined
in order to prop up the tottering institution of marriage by making
it the only refuge for the respectable.

But until it is acknowledged that it is not respectable to live
together when the temperaments are incompatible, there will
be no real virtue in the married state. Never to want the same
thing at the same time is a more far-reaching cause of emotional
degradation than one violent outbreak of temper under extreme
provocation. It is more degrading to the finer feelings than a
temporary alienation of marital love. One would imagine that the
men who refuse to alter the divorce laws really do believe in the
sacrament of the marriage ceremony, instead of in the sacrament
of the true love, which abides when there is a real compatibility
of temperament.

From Modern Woman. Her Intentions, *1910, by Florence Farr
(1860–1917). Farr was a theatre manager, scribe to the occultist
Golden Dawn and author of several novels and plays. G.B. Shaw
and W.B. Yeats were among her lovers.*

THE FARMER'S BRIDE

Three Summers since I chose a maid,
Too young maybe – but more's to do
At harvest-time than bide and woo.
   When us was wed she turned afraid
Of love and me and all things human;
Like the shut of a winter's day.
Her smile went out, and 'twasn't a woman –

More like a little frightened fay.
    One night, in the Fall, she runned away.

'Out 'mong the sheep, her be,' they said,
'Should properly have been abed;
But sure enough she wasn't there
Lying awake with her wide brown stare.
So over seven-acre field and up-along across the down
We chased her, flying like a hare
Before our lanterns. To Church-Town
    All in a shiver and a scare
We caught her, fetched her home at last
    And turned the key upon her, fast.

She does the work about the house
As well as most, but like a mouse:
    Happy enough to chat and play
    With birds and rabbits and such as they,
    So long as men-folk keep away.
'Not near, not near!' her eyes beseech
When one of us comes within reach.
    The women say that beasts in stall
    Look round like children at her call.
    I've hardly heard her speak at all.

Shy as a leveret, swift as he,
Straight and slight as a young larch tree,
Sweet as the first wild violets, she,
To her wild self. But what to me?

The short days shorten and the oaks are brown,
    The blue smoke rises to the low grey sky,
One leaf in the still air falls slowly down,
    A magpie's spotted feathers lie
On the black earth spread white with rime,
The berries redden up to Christmas-time.
    What's Christmas-time without there be
    Some other in the house than we!

    She sleeps up in the attic there
    Alone, poor maid. 'Tis but a stair

Betwixt us. Oh! my God! the down,
 The soft young down of her, the brown,
The brown of her – her eyes, her hair, her hair!

'The Farmer's Bride', 1914, by Charlotte Mew (1869–1928). A poet, Mew contributed short stories to The Yellow Book *('Passed' in 1894) and* The Egoist, *published two volumes of poetry,* The Farmer's Bride *(1915) and* The Rambling Sailor *(1929), essays, criticism and memoirs. She killed herself in 1928, aged fifty-nine.*

MARRIAGE À LA MODE

Dramatis Personae: EDWIN AND ANGELINA.
Scene: ANYWHERE IN ENGLAND.
Time: A MONTH BEFORE THE WEDDING DAY.

EDWIN: And you have really, really, never loved another? Oh, I know, I know! But tell it me once more!

ANGELINA: Oh, Edwin! Can you doubt it? Do you think that in return for the virgin heart you tell me you are giving me, I would palm off on you a jaded love unworthy of yours? I know that men always say that women have no sense of honour comparable to a man's; but, believe me – even if you will believe it of no other of my sex – I would no more act dishonestly in such a matter than you would yourself! There, my Edwin! Can I say more?

EDWIN: No, darling; and of course I trust you ——

ANGELINA: As completely as I do you! Our records are exactly equal.

EDWIN: Impossible! I will never believe ——

ANGELINA: Impossible? You do not believe me, then? Why, what do you think of me?

EDWIN: Pardon, my darling, you don't understand. I was going to say that a man's and a woman's honour are quite different. 'Truth is the masculine, purity the feminine, of honour,' as – is it Hare? – says so well.

ANGELINA (*thoughtfully*): That means – if it means anything –

183

that an honourable man may be impure, but must not deceive; and an honourable woman may lie, but must not be impure.

EDWIN: Exactly, darling.

ANGELINA (*as before*): So that if your life had been impure you would not be to blame; but if you deceived anyone about that life, you would be dishonourable.

EDWIN: My darling, you put things too severely. No one is perfect. I doubt if any man or woman – if everything could be known about him or her – would be found quite honourable.

ANGELINA: And, on your morality, if I had failed in purity I should be dishonourable; but as I have a perfect right to tell as many fibs as I choose, no one could blame me for any deception I practised about it. You can't blame me if I am deceiving you about my past.

EDWIN: My darling, that is absurd. Of course it would be wrong of you to deceive.

ANGELINA (*surprised*): Edwin, dearest, I do not understand you. You think the rule you yourself gave me too stringent for your sex, and too lax for mine. Yet it only asks one virtue from each of us, and as a man wrote it, it is to be presumed man had the first choice. Are you quite fair?

EDWIN (*hurriedly*): Angelina, darling, you can't understand these things ——

ANGELINA (*as before*): Not understand? But if one is to obey a moral law one *must* understand it.

EDWIN: No, darling – moral laws are for men, of course – women must obey the individual instructions of the men. There – that's it! You mustn't bother your little head with abstract laws – women can't understand them – even such a clever woman as you, my darling! Leave those hard nuts for our tough brains to crack. My Angelina will do what her Edwin wishes – that is her law, is it not, dearest?

ANGELINA: And will her Edwin never do what his Angelina wishes?

EDWIN: Yes, always; always, darling. (*Reflectively*): Angelina, my dearest, when we marry we will mean every word we say in that beautiful service of our Church, won't we?

ANGELINA: Of course, darling. How can anyone dare to stand before the altar and commit perjury – take oaths they have no intention of keeping? I can hardly conceive a deadlier sin.

EDWIN: Nobly spoken, my own. So many wicked women nowadays grumble at having to promise to obey – a woman's noblest privilege. You, my pet, are not such a modern unsexed creature.

ANGELINA: No, indeed, I have thought it carefully over. I gladly promise to obey. It is but a just return; for I note that in that beautiful service you will solemnly undertake to endow me with all your earthly goods. Oh, Edwin! It is too noble of you! Everything of yours will be my very own, to spend and use as I please. No conditions are mentioned; you will have no more right to anything that is yours.

EDWIN (*alarmed*): My dear girl, you totally misunderstand the word 'endow.' It doesn't mean that at all.

ANGELINA: No? Then what does it mean?

EDWIN: Oh, it means – it means – of course it means that you will pay the weekly bills and the servants' wages, and your dress – no, not your dress – at least you would if you hadn't your own money – and house expenses and all that out of my income. It can't mean more than that. (*Excitedly*): It would be absurd.

ANGELINA (*reproachfully*): Edwin, you know we are to take no vows we do not absolutely mean to keep.

EDWIN: Yes – but there must be some mistake! Is it *likely* you are right? Remember the service was composed by men!

ANGELINA: True, darling; but is it reverent to suppose that influenced them?

EDWIN: The word is antiquated – it is a sort of legal fiction, which it would be ridiculous to follow literally.

ANGELINA: Does that apply to the word 'obey'?

EDWIN: No, of course not! That's plain enough. But the other is ridiculous – stay! Ha, ha! Of course! I *thought* the old fellows who made up that service couldn't have been such duffers! Don't you see, darling? I can safely vow to endow you with all my earthly goods, because the moment you have vowed to obey me I can simply order you to give them all back again! It's a trump card over all the pack! See?

ANGELINA (*gravely*): Yes, I see, Edwin, dear. Do you think that is taking a vow one really means, if one intends immediately to get out of it?

EDWIN: Be reasonable! Would any man marry if he had to take such a vow seriously? It is too much to ask of anyone!

ANGELINA: Well, shall we reverse the vows? You take mine and I will take yours, and I promise to keep it faithfully. You are no loser, for my three hundred a year is more than you will earn for a long time to come, and I will endow you absolutely with it, if you will with equal sincerity vow to obey me.

EDWIN (*much excited*): Preposterous! A really preposterous idea, Angelina! O come! This is reversing things with a vengeance! Oh, Angelina! I never thought you were a New Woman!

ANGELINA: But I'm not, darling. I am your own loving Angelina. I only suggest that, as you said your vow was too hard for you, you should take mine, which you seem to consider quite an easy little one.

EDWIN: Quite easy for *you*, I said – but that is so different.

ANGELINA: I see; any sacrifice is a trifle to ask of a woman; her money or her liberty or both she should readily render up. But a man cannot give up anything.

EDWIN: Well, if marriage is to be a choice of beggary or slavery, why should a man marry?

ANGELINA: Then why should a woman?

EDWIN (*after a pause*): I really don't know! I suppose because she has such a beastly time of it if she doesn't!

ANGELINA: Well, Edwin, obedience and endowment are not the whole of marriage! There is love and honour.

EDWIN: Yes, we must not look only on the dark side. If it is difficult to vow obedience and endowment, at all events love and honour and cherishing are easy vows!

ANGELINA: Yes, dear! What a comfort to think that whatever one does or becomes, there is one person bound always to love, honour and cherish one! (*dreamily*): You will always love me, Edwin. Though I take to drink, became a slattern, nag by day and by night – nay, do all that I shouldn't do – yet you will love me always, till death us do part.

EDWIN: Don't speak like that! You could never do anything like that! I love you with all my heart! But I don't think I could love you if you were to become as you describe. How could I? I should be kind to you – I hope – but could I love you? Could you love me as you do if I were to turn into a dissolute drunken brute?

186

ANGELINA: No, Edwin; if I could love a dissolute drunken brute I should be unworthy of you. I should have to be depraved and coarse. How can we vow to love one another? How can one love and honour anyone because one has vowed it? Love and honour must be inspired by the object! How can one love what one thinks unloveable? or honour what one thinks dishonourable? One can pretend – that is all.

EDWIN (*gloomily*): Yes, as you say, one can't love at will. One can only pretend. – But why torture ourselves? My Angelina will always be loveable.

ANGELINA: Edwin! What is a vow? Surely it is a dead letter so long as it jumps with one's desire. Where is the good of vowing you will be angry for such time as you are angry? You needn't vow that. Your vow to remain angry is only of use to bind you to be angry when you are no longer angry.

EDWIN: That sounds absurd, dear.

ANGELINA: Yes, doesn't it? That proves that we should only vow to do those things over which we believe ourselves to have control; to perform actions or to make mental efforts; but not to have certain ideas or sentiments, for that can only lead to forswearing ourselves.

EDWIN (*helplessly*): Then what can we vow?

ANGELINA: We can vow to cherish – that means to act kindly.

EDWIN: But we can't vow to love?

ANGELINA: We can vow that if love flies we will faithfully try to love, and conscientiously pretend that we have succeeded.

EDWIN: I'm not quite sure that I should want you to pretend to love me if you really didn't do so, Angelina.

ANGELINA: Then we must reduce the vow to trying. Do you think the clergyman would help us if we explained to him that we meant to be sincere?

EDWIN: I fear not! He is bound by rules, you know.

ANGELINA: How dreadful! Oh, Edwin! And how can it be a dignified or sincere thing for poor papa to come in his Sunday coat and pretend to give me away when never a day passes but he and mamma both declare I am throwing myself away! And if they could stop our marriage they would.

EDWIN (*with dignity*): Your parents are strangely unappreciative of true worth. If they should finally refuse, some of my people would give you away. Anyone can do it, you know.

ANGELINA: That makes it more dignified and sincere, doesn't it? And why should I pretend I am being given like a bale of goods, when I am not? I am of full age, and I give myself because I love you, Edwin. No one gives me. Why should I pretend I am a slave? I'm not!

EDWIN (*desperately*): We must go to a Registrar's Office.

ANGELINA: Oh, Edwin! Nobody who is anybody does that. It sounds so vulgar! And then, my beautiful white satin and my bridesmaids! The splash I hope to make! The organ voluntary and the surpliced choir! The flowers, the vaulted arches, and oh! – the Church's blessing!

EDWIN: True, Angelina; I dare not ask you to give that up! I will vow endowment, not meaning to endow; you will vow obedience, not meaning to obey; we will both vow to love, knowing we vow what we could not, if called upon, perform; and your father will pretend he is giving you away, well knowing he is doing nothing of the sort. So we will obtain society's approval and the Church's blessing, and enter holily the holy estate.

Marriage à la Mode *by Olga Sann in* The Humanitarian, *Vol. VIII, January–June 1896.*

GLORIANA

'Hulloa, Trevor! you there? Didn't see you, old man. What! you haven't read an Eton boy's "Essay on Woman's Position"? Every one is talking about it. It's deuced clever and original, whatever one may think of the opinions, and is clearly written by a lad who will make his mark in the world.'

'Let's have a look at it, Vereton, if you don't want it, there's a good chap. I want something to read,' exclaims Mr. Trevor eagerly, reaching out his hand for the periodical, which the baronet passes to him good-naturedly. It is open at the page of honour, the first page in the book, and as Mr. Trevor scans the heading he reads it as follows: 'Woman's Position in this World. By Hector D'Estrange, an Eton boy.' He starts reading it, languidly at first, as if the remarks of a boy on such a subject cannot possibly be worth reading, but he is soon absorbed in the article, and never budges in his chair until he has read it through and through.

And there are some parts to which he turns again and again, as though he would burn their truths into his brain, and keep them there never to be forgotten. One in especial rivets his attention, so much so that he commits it to memory.

'When a girl is born,' it ran, 'no especial difference is made in the care of her by doctor or nurse. Up to a certain age the treatment which she and her brother receive is exactly the same. Why, I ask, should there be ever any change in this treatment? Why should such a marked contrast be drawn later on between the sexes? Is it for the good of either that the girl should be both physically and mentally stunted, both in her intellect and body, – that she should be held back while the boy is pressed forward? Can it be argued with any show of reason that her capacity for study is less, and her power of observation naturally dwarfed in comparison with that of the boy? Certainly not. I confidently assert that where a girl has fair play, and is given equal opportunities with the boy, she not only equals him in mental capacity, but far outruns him in such; and I also confidently assert, that given the physical opportunities afforded to the boy, to develop and expand, and strengthen the body by what are called "manly exercises," the girl would prove herself every inch his equal in physical strength. There are those, I know, who will sneer at these opinions, but in the words of Lord Beaconsfield, I can only asseverate that "the time will come," when those who sneer will be forced to acknowledge the truth of this assertion.

'Well then, granting, for the sake of argument, that what I have stated is correct, why, I ask, should all that men look forward to and hold most dear, be denied to women? Why should the professions which men have arrogated to themselves be entirely monopolized by their sex, to the exclusion of women? I see no manner of reason why, if women received the same moral, mental, and physical training that men do, they should not be as fit – nay, infinitely more fit – to undertake the same

189

duties and responsibilities as men. I do not see that we should be a wit less badly governed if we had a woman Prime Minister or a mixed Cabinet, or if women occupied seats in the Houses of Parliament or on the bench in the Courts of Justice.

'Of course woman's fitness to undertake these duties depends entirely on the manner in which she is educated. If you stunt the intellect, tell her nothing, and refuse to exercise the physical powers which Nature has given her, you must expect little from such an unfortunate creature. Put man in the same position in which you put woman, and he would be in a very short time just as mentally and physically stunted as she is.

'All very well to declare that it is a woman's business to bear children, to bring them up, to attend to household matters, and to leave the rest to men. A high-spirited girl or woman will not, in every instance, accept this definition of her duties by man as correct. That such a definition is clearly man's, it is not difficult to see, for woman would never have voluntarily condemned herself to a life of such inert and ambitionless duties as these. But so long as this definition of woman's duty and position be observed and accepted by Society, so long will this latter be a prey to all the evils and horrors that afflict it, and which are a result of woman's subjection and degradation.

'Think you, you who read these words, that hundreds of women now unhappily married would ever have contracted that terrible tie had they been aware of what they were doing, or had they had the smallest hope of advancement and prospects of success in life without? Certainly not. Marriage is contracted in ninety-nine cases out of a hundred by women desirous of making for themselves a home, and because in no other quarter can they adopt agreeable and pleasant professions and occupations like men. Were it possible, they would either not have married, or at least have waited until, with the knowledge of man which they *should* possess – but which, unfortunately, nowadays comes to them only with marriage – they could select for themselves, with their eyes open, a partner suited to them in every respect. As it is, what does one see? Women, especially in the higher grades of society, marry only to escape in many instances the prim restraints of home. Others marry for money and position, because they know that the portals, through which men may pass to try for these, are closed to them. The cruel laws by which men have shut women out from every hope of winning name and fame, are responsible for hundreds of wretched marriages, which have seared the world with their griefs. If, in the narrow sphere within which she moves, a woman errs, let not the man blame her, but rather look to the abolition of unnatural laws which have brought about her degradation.'

Mr. Trevor sits very still in his chair. A flood of thoughts have come to fill his brain. They keep him very busy and occupied. The revelations thrown upon woman's position by the straight-forward, truth-breathing article of Hector D'Estrange, have taken him by storm, and have completely revolutionized his ideas. He has hitherto been so accustomed to look upon and treat women with the self-satisfied, conscious feeling of superiority assumed by men, that such ideas as these before him are startlingly strange and extraordinary. His position with Vivi, and hers in regard to him, presents itself now to his mind in a totally different light to that in which he has hitherto been accustomed to regard it. He remembers how he first met her hardly a year ago, a beautiful, lively, healthy girl, whose scheming mother, knowing no better, had thrust her into the busy mart, willing to sell her to the highest bidder. He remembers how passionately he fell in love with this girl, how he never paused to ask himself if his love were returned. He recalls full well the bitter look that had crossed her face when he had asked her to be his wife, and the cold, matter-of-fact way in which she had accepted him. Then his thoughts fly back to his wedding day, and a shudder runs through Launcelot Trevor as he recalls the utter absence of love on her part towards him. And, remembering all this, he cannot but feel that Hector D'Estrange is right. If, in the narrow sphere within which poor Vivi had moved, she had, according to the notions of propriety laid down by Mrs. Grundy, erred, Launcelot Trevor feels that the blame must rest not so much with her, as with the cruel laws that had left that beautiful girl no other option but to sell herself for gold; for be it remembered, she had been educated up to no higher level, been imbued with no better aim. She had been taught that the only opening for a girl is to get herself well married, that while men could go forth into the world with a score of professions to

191

choose from, she must for ever regard herself as shut out from that world of enterprise, daring, and fame, created, so says man, solely for himself.

He sits on in his chair, his thoughts still busy with the new problem that has presented itself so startlingly to his mind. The luncheon hour is far past, much of the afternoon has slipped away, still Launcelot Trevor remains where he had seated himself many hours before. Men keep coming in and out; friends and acquaintances nod to him as they pass. He scarcely heeds them, or pays attention to what they say. His mind is absorbed by the truths which he has faced for the first time.

From Gloriana; or the Revolution of 1900, *1890, by Lady Florence Dixie. A novelist, travel writer, journalist and feminist, Dixie pioneered the cross saddle for British women and explored Patagonia and Brazil (where she acquired a pet tiger) in 1878–9. She wrote a bestseller,* Across Patagonia, *in 1880 and was appointed war correspondent for the* Morning Post *in South Africa. Several of her novels are autobiographical; all are concerned with women's issues. The 'hero' of the utopian novel* Gloriana, *Hector D'Estrange, is in fact a woman, Gloria.*

A RATIONAL MARRIAGE

'Besides, Larry, marriage itself is responsible for half these scandals. There is too much familiarity, too much uxoriousness, too much of the fettering business about it, not to make its victims long to jump over the traces. They are so soon sick of one another. Now, if it could be conducted on a rational plane —— '

'What do you mean by a rational plane?' interrupted her companion.

'Just what I say! If people want to be married, to have a license for being the closest of friends, well, let them – but why in the name of goodness should they alter all their lives on that account – give up their ambitions, their fancies, their friends, and settle down in the same house to bore each other from morning till night!'

'How could they marry without living together?'

'Very well indeed! Now, for instance, if I were married – which I am not such a fool as to contemplate – why should I not continue to occupy my own little flat, and to be secretary to Lord Mauleverer, and generally to look after myself, whilst my husband – ugh! what a horrible idea! – would do the same.'

'A nice sort of a marriage!' said Larry, shrugging his shoulders.

'You're quite right, my dear boy, a very nice sort of a marriage! Think how pleasant it would be, after knocking about the Strand all day, to have a comfortable little room to come to and have your afternoon tea, and a cheerful wife full of news to pour it out for you, instead of a woman who had been bored to extinction with housekeeping during your absence and had nothing but complaints of her servants to amuse you with. Then what a little excitement would hover round the chances whether you would come or not; how pleasant the secret outings in the evenings, with a little supper perhaps to follow; and how nice to be able to reckon up your liabilities without including the item of your wife's bills for millinery. Following my plan, men and women would remain friends to the very end. They wouldn't tire so soon of one another. A trip to Paris would be a honeymoon for them each time it occurred. And then, if you were sick or sorry, you would always feel that you had a home to creep to – a shelter from the outside world – a ——— '

'Then I might come to your flat as often as I liked,' interposed Larrikins.

'You!' exclaimed Joan; 'good gracious! who was talking of you? I was only depicting a rational marriage for your edification. I bet it would last twice as long as the ordinary ones. You male creatures get so soon tired of your possessions. A little doubt and uncertainty – to have to take a little trouble to find out if your wife would be at home, or willing to receive you, or had got hold of some nicer fellow than yourself, would prove a panacea against infidelity. Don't you agree with me?'

'Not a bit,' said Mr. O'Donnell; 'your plan would do away with all the good or the meaning of marriage. What a man wants is a woman always ready to welcome him, and a home which is his very own from cellar to garret, and over the threshold of which no one can cross without his permission.'

'Exactly! – a very pleasant idea for the man when he wants rest and quiet and attention; but what about the woman who has to remain at home to await his coming, and to give up half her own friends at his bidding? However, have it your own way, Larry; but I shall not follow your example for one. And now, about the manuscript. Whilst we have been wasting our time over this rubbish, I have been longing to tell you how glad I am to think that you are going to do something big at last!'

From A Rational Marriage, *1899, by Florence Marryat (1838–1899), novelist, dramatist, actress and singer. Daughter of Captain Marryat* (Children of the New Forest), *she was the prolific author of seventy-five novels, mainly sensational romances, although several dealt with female emancipation and questions of spiritualism.*

A QUIET MIDDLE-CLASS MARRIAGE

Wednesday evening [*May, 1915*]   *Hurstbourne Tarrant*
I am writing again, as I promised I would. It has been a lovely day, a beautiful hot sun, and cobalt blue sky with passing clouds. I have been hard at work on my picture of saint John the Baptist it was good having a model this morning, as I got on much better with it. Mancini's figure is quite good to draw. But his face fills me with depression. Curious how no models have good heads to draw. He comes again tomorrow and Friday. I am so glad all this wedding is over, you have no idea how terrible a real English wedding is. Two people, with very ordinary minds want each other physically, at least the man does, the woman only wants to be married and have his possessions and position. To obtain all this they go through a service, which is comprised of worthy sentiments uttered by the old apostles and Christ! Many relatives come and friends all out of curiosity to see this presumably religious rite; afterwards they all adjourn to the house, and eat like animals and talk, and view each other's clothes and secretly criticize everyone and then

return home. All this costs a great deal of money: a bouquet of flowers which the bride carries into the church for 15 mins, and afterwards leaves in the house behind her, which dies the next day as none of the flowers have stalks, costs £2. It seems curious. The dress she wears for about 1 hr. costs about £10. And yet this is a so called 'quiet' middle class wedding. But it astounds one, the ridiculous farce, the sham festivity. If only they all got merry and drunk, and danced: or if only they were all moved and religious it wouldn't matter. But to be nothing real. Thank god it cannot happen again now. I was almost glad it rained. I felt my sky and country here anyrate were not 'pretending' to shine and be happy.

It makes it much worse for me now, coming up to London. I long, and long for you to talk to. Everything they say jars so terribly. They are so commonplace and material. This morning I just longed to run away from them all, and escape to London. You can never know what it is to have a Mother and family, and surroundings like those people in 'the Way of all Flesh'. Like 'Anne Veronica's' parents. The only thing to do is to make up your mind not to be irritated by it all, but to love the country, the trees and the good hot sun. Soon I will pick you some flowers but there aren't many out just now. I had a long letter from both my brothers which made me happy. I have a beautiful little bantam cock and hen now of my own; a farmer gave them to me. They look like a lovely Chinese silk painting.

Dora Carrington to Mark Gertler from Carrington: Letters and Extracts from her Diaries, *edited by David Garnett (1979). Dora Carrington (1893–1932) was a painter, trained at the Slade School of Fine Art. She was part of the Bloomsbury Group through her friendship with Virginia and Leonard Woolf and Lady Ottoline Morrell. She had an intense friendship with the artist Mark Gertler, but refused to marry him. In 1917 she moved into Lytton Strachey's house in Berkshire as his housekeeper. Carrington was in love with Strachey, but his homosexuality limited their relationship and in 1921 she married Ralph Partridge. She killed herself soon after Strachey died of cancer in 1932.*

WOMEN WHO SHOULD NEVER MARRY

The woman who proudly declares that she cannot hem a pocket-handkerchief, never made up a bed in her life, and adds with a simper that she has 'been in society ever since she was fifteen.'

The woman who would rather nurse a pug dog than a baby.

The woman who thinks that men are angels.

The woman who would rather die than wear a hat two seasons old.

The woman who thinks that the cook and nurse can keep house.

The woman who expects a declaration of love three times a day.

The woman who buys ornaments for the drawing-room and borrows kitchen utensils from her neighbours; and who thinks table decorations are of more importance than good food.

The woman who wants things just because 'other women' have them.

From The Young Woman, *Vol. VIII, October 1899–September 1900.*

THE FUNDAMENTAL PULSE

The judgments of men concerning women are very rarely matters of cold scientific observation, but are coloured both by their own sexual emotions and by their own moral attitude toward the sexual impulse. . . . [Men's] Statements about the sexual impulses of woman often tell us less about women than about the persons who make them.

H. Ellis

By the majority of 'nice' people woman is supposed to have no spontaneous sex-impulses. By this I do not mean a sentimental 'falling in love', but a physical, a physiological state of stimulation which arises spontaneously and quite apart from any particular man. It is in truth the *creative* impulse, and is an expression of a

196

high power of vitality. So widespread in our country is the view that it is only depraved women who have such feelings (especially before marriage) that most women would rather die than own that they *do* at times feel a physical yearning indescribable, but as profound as hunger for food. Yet many, many women have shown me the truth of their natures when I have simply and naturally assumed that of course they feel it – being normal women – and have asked them only: *When?* From their replies I have collected facts which are sufficient to overturn many ready-made theories about women.

Some of the ridiculous absurdities which go by the name of science may be illustrated by the statement made by Windscheid in *Centralblatt für Gynäkologie*:

> In the normal woman, especially of the higher social classes, the sexual instinct is acquired, not inborn; when it is inborn, or awakens by itself, there is *abnormality*. Since women do not know this instinct before marriage, they do not miss it when they have no occasion in life to learn it. (Ellis trans.)

The negation of this view is expressed in the fable of Hera quoted by Ellen Key. Hera sent Iris to earth to seek out three virtuous and perfectly chaste maidens who were unsoiled by any dreams of love. Iris found them, but could not take them back to Olympus, for they had already been sent for to replace the superannuated Furies in the infernal regions.

Nevertheless it is true that the whole education of girls, which so largely consists in the concealment of the essential facts of life from them; and the positive teaching so prevalent that the racial instincts are low and shameful; and also the social condition which places so many women in the position of depending on their husband's will not only for the luxuries but for the necessaries of life, have all tended to inhibit natural sex-impulses in women, and to conceal and distort what remains.

It is also true that in our northern climate women are on the whole naturally less persistently stirred than southerners, and it is further true that with the delaying of maturity, due to our everlengthening youth, it often happens that a woman is approaching or even past thirty years before she is awake to the existence of the profoundest calls of her nature. For many years before that, however, the unrealized influence, diffused throughout her very system, had profoundly affected her. It is also true that (partly due to the inhibiting influences of our customs, traditions and social code) women may marry before it wakes, and may remain long after marriage entirely unconscious that it surges subdued within them. For innumerable women, too, the husband's regular habits of intercourse, claiming her both when she would naturally enjoy union and when it is to some degree repugnant to her, have tended to flatten out the billowing curves of the line of her natural desire. One result, apparently little suspected, of using the woman as a passive instrument for man's need has been, in effect, to make her that and nothing more. Those men – and there are many – who complain of the lack of ardour in good wives, are often themselves entirely the cause of it. When a woman is claimed at times when she takes no *natural* pleasure in union, and claimed in such a way that there is no *induced* romantic pleasure, the act reduces her vitality, and tends to kill her power of enjoying it when the love-season returns.

It is certainly true of women as they have been made by the inhibitions of modern conditions, that most of them are only fully awake to the existence of sex after marriage. As we are human beings, the social, intellectual, spiritual side of love-choice have tended to mask the basic physiological aspect of women's sex-life. To find a woman in whom the currents are not all so entangled that the whole is inseparable into factors, is not easy, but I have found that wives (particularly happy wives whose feelings are not complicated by the stimulus of another love) who have been separated from their husbands for some months through professional or business duties – whose husbands, for instance, are abroad – are the women from whom the best and most definitive evidence of a fundamental rhythm of feeling can be obtained. Such women, yearning daily for the tender comradeship and nearness of their husbands, find, in addition, at particular times, an accession of longing for the close physical union of the final sex-act. Many such separated wives feel this; and those I have asked to keep notes of the dates, have, with remarkable unanimity, told me that these times came specially just before and some week or so after the close of menstruation, coming, that is, about every fortnight.

198

It is from such women that I got the first clue to the knowledge of what I call the law of Periodicity of Recurrence of desire in women. For some years I have been making as scientific and detailed a study as possible of this extremely complex problem. Owing to the frank and scientific attitude of a number of women, and the ready and intimate confidence of many more, I have obtained a number of most interesting facts from which I think it is already possible to deduce a generalization which is illuminating, and may be of great medical and sociological value... A more detailed and scientific consideration of my data will be published elsewhere.

My law of Periodicity and Recurrence of desire in women it is possible to represent graphically as a curved line; a succession of crests and hollows as in all wave-lines. Its simplest and most fundamental expression, however, is generally immensely complicated by other stimulations which may bring into it diverse series of waves, or irregular wave-crests. We have all, at some time, watched the regular ripples of the sea breaking against a sand-bank, and noticed that the influx of another current of water may send a second system of waves at right angles to the first, cutting athwart them, so that the two series of waves pass through each other.

Woman is so sensitive and responsive an instrument, and so liable in our modern civilized world to be influenced by innumerable sets of stimuli, that it is perhaps scarcely surprising that the deep, underlying waves of her primitive sex-tides have been obscured, and entangled so that their regular sequence has been masked in the choppy turmoil of her sea, and their existence has been largely unsuspected, and apparently quite unstudied.

From Married Love, *1918, by Marie Charlotte Stopes (1880–1958). Born in Edinburgh, she graduated with honours in botany and geology after only two years at University College, London, and became Britain's youngest* DSC *in 1905. She travelled in Japan doing scientific research and married a Canadian botanist. The marriage was annulled on the grounds of non-consummation in 1916. In 1918 she married Humphrey Verdon Roe, an early aeroplane manufacturer, and went on to write several books on marriage and motherhood, plays, novels and fairy stories. Following the success of* Married Love *and* Wise Parenthood *(1918) – both of which caused an uproar and sold millions of copies – Stopes and her husband opened a birth-control clinic in Islington, in the face of strong opposition. She continued her writings with* Radiant Motherhood *(1920),* Contraception: its History, Theory and Practice *(1923) and* Enduring Passions *(1928).*

THE SPINSTER [1911]

BY ONE

I write of the High Priestess of Society. Not of the mother of sons, but of her barren sister, the withered tree, the acidulous vestal under whose pale shadow we chill and whiten, of the Spinster I write. Because of her power and dominion. She, unobtrusive, meek, soft-footed, silent, shamefaced, bloodless and boneless, thinned to spirit, enters the secret recesses of the mind, sits at the secret springs of action, and moulds and fashions our emasculate Society. She is our social Nemesis. For the insult of her creation, without knowing it she takes her revenge. What she has become, she makes all. To every form of social life she gives its complexion. Every book, every play, every sermon, every song, each bears her inscription. The Churches she has made her own. Their message and their conventions are for her type, and of their Ideal she has made a Spinster transfigured. In the auditorium of every theatre she sits, the pale guardian. What the players say and do, they say and do never forgetting her presence. She haunts every library. Her eye will pierce the cover of every book, and her glance may not be offended. In our schools she takes the little children, and day by day they breathe in the atmosphere of her violated spirit. She tinges every conversation, she weights each moral judgment. She rules the earth. All our outward morality is made to accommodate her, and any alien, wild life-impulse which clamours for release is released in secret, in shame, and under the sense of sin. A restive but impotent world writhes under her subtle priestly domination. She triumphs, and we turn half expecting to see in her the joy of triumph. But no, not that even. She has no knowledge of it. All is pure fatality. She remains at once the injured and the injuring. Society has cursed her and the curse is now roosting at home.

The indictment which the Spinster lays up against Society is that of ingenious cruelty. The type of intelligence which, in its immaturity, conceived the tortures of a Tantalus might have essayed the creation of a spinster as its ripe production. See how she is made, and from what. She is mothered into the world by a being, who, whatever else she may be, is not a spinster, and from this being she draws her instincts. While yet a child these instincts are intensified and made self-conscious by the development, in her own person, of a phenomenon which is unmistakable, repellent, and recurrent with a rapid and painful certainty. This development engenders its own lassitude, and in this lassitude new instincts are set free. Little by little, the development of her entire form sets towards a single consummation, and all the while, by every kind of device, the mind is set towards the same consummation. In babyhood, she begins, with her dolls. Why do not the parents of a prospective spinster give her a gun or an engine. If Society is going to have spinsters, it should train spinsters. In girlhood, she is ushered into an atmosphere charged with sex-distinctions and sex-insinuations. She is educated on a literature saturated with these. In every book she takes up, in every play she sees, in every conversation, in every social amusement, in every interest in life she finds that the pivot upon which all interest turns is the sex interest. So body, mind, training, and environment unite to produce in her an expectation which awaits definite fulfilment. She is ready to marry, ripe to marry, needing marriage, and up to this point Society has been blameless. It is in the next step that she sins. Did Society inculcate nothing more, Nature would step in to solve her own difficulties, as she does where Society and its judgments have little weight. Among the very poor there is no spinster difficulty, because the very poor do not remain spinsters. It is from higher up in the social scale, where social judgments count, where the individual is a little more highly wrought, better fashioned for suffering, that we draw the army of actual spinsters. It is in the classes where it is not good form to have too much feeling, and actual bad form to show any; where there is a smattering of education, and little interests to fill in the time, that their numbers rally and increase. It is here that Society, after having fostered just expectations, turns round arbitrarily on one perhaps in every four and says, 'Thou shalt not.' No reason given, only outlawry prescribed if the prohibition is disregarded. And because Society has a dim consciousness of its own treachery – for its protection and like a coward – it lays down the law of silence, and in subtle fashion makes the poor wretch the culprit. (It is probably this sense of self-defection which keeps these cheated women from committing rape. Imagine an equal proportion of any male population under similar circumstances!) Probably, one will ask, What is all the fuss about? Is it all because a man did not turn up at the right time? Well, partly yes and partly no. Not *any* man; *any* man was not what she had been led to expect. She had, in fact, been specially warned against *any* man. It was the right man she was expecting, HER man. Rightly or wrongly, the theory of the right man has been dinned into the consciousness of the ordinary middle-class woman. It may be merely a subtle ruse on the part of a consciously inadequate society to prepare its victims for the altar. However that may be, the result is the same. The Spinster stands the racket. She pays the penalty. She is the failure, and she closes her teeth down and says nothing. What can she say? Is she not the failure? And so the conspiracy of silence becomes complete. Then, mind and body begin. *They* get their pound of flesh, and the innermost Ego of the Soul, the solitary Dweller behind the Mind, stands at bay to meet their baiting. Day by day, year by year, the baiting goes on. To what end – for what temporal or final good is all this? This is the question to which Society, in sheer amends, has to find an answer. This unfair war waged by instinct and training against poor ordinary consciousness can only be rendered decent by some overwhelming good accruing to someone or something. To whom and for what? These are questions to which we demand an answer as a right. Then, being answered, if any woman considers the benefit conferred upon Society great enough to outweigh the suffering entailed upon herself she may possibly undertake it in the spirit of some magnanimous benefactor. Because this inward warfare cannot truthfully be considered for one moment as benefiting the Spinster herself. Her character for instance, is not in need of that kind of tonic. For, be it noted, the Spinster does not overcome Sex as a Saint overcomes Sin. She does not, save rarely, crush out of existence that part of her which is threatening her life's reasonable calm. Driven inward, denied its rightful ordained fulfilment, the instinct becomes diffused. The field of consciousness is charged with an all-pervasive unrest and sickness, which changes all meanings, and queers all judgments, and which, appearing outwardly, we recognize as sentimentality. It is to this sentimentality that all reason and intelligence has to bow. It is by this means that we are all made to pass under the yoke. It is not, however, to be believed that every spinster will thus suffer mind and body to enter into bondage. Some are finding a way of escape. Some women have taken this way, and more will take it. It is the final retort. It is the way of the Saint. It would be the right way in overcoming sin. But in overcoming the life instinct itself, who shall say it is right? The way is to destroy the faculty. With a strong will and a stern régime it can be done. Women are doing it with a fierce joy that would have gladdened the heart of some old Puritan. You take the body and tire it out with work, work, work. In any crevice of time left over you rush here and there, up and down, constantly active. And for the mind, you close down the shutters on that field. No image, no phrase, no brooding, nothing there which speaks of emotions which produce life. And this sort of Spinster, more and more, is bringing up the younger generation. Another unconscious revenge! But this is the way of the few. As for the many, they go the sentimental way. For there is no shuffling possible in this matter. The Spinster must either keep her womanhood at the cost of suffering inordinate for the thing it is, and be compelled to turn what should be an incidental interest into the basis of all interest; or she must destroy the faculty itself, and know herself atrophied. There is no alternative. To offer work, pleasure, 'doing good', in lieu of this is as much to the point and as sensible as to offer a loaf to a person who is tortured with thirst.

Let the social guardians remember that in the fulness of time physical developments show themselves, and that as they appear, so must they be provided for. This social slaughter can no longer pass without challenge, and they may remember for their comfort that if prurience has slain its thousands, chastity has slain its tens of thousands. In this matter, it remains for Society to justify itself.

From The Freewoman, *23 November 1911.*

I WANT LIFE

I walked on today and came to a garden behind Notre Dame. The pink and white flowering trees were so lovely that I sat down on a bench. In the middle of the garden there was a grass plot and a marble basin. Sparrows taking their baths turned the basin into a fountain and pigeons walked through the velvety grass pluming their feathers. Every bench and every chair was occupied by a mother or a nurse or a grandfather and little staggering babies with spades and buckets made mud pies or filled their buckets with fallen chestnut flowers or threw their grandfathers caps on to the forbidden grass plot. And then there came a chinese nurse trailing 2 babies. Oh, she was a funny little thing in her green trousers and black tunic, a small turban clamped to her head. She sat down with her darning and she kept up a long bird like chatter all the time, blinking at the children and running the darning needle through her turban. But after I had watched a long time I realised I was in the middle of a dream. Why haven't I got a real 'home', a real life – Why haven't I got a chinese nurse with green trousers and two babies who rush at me and clasp my knees – Im not a girl – Im a woman. I *want* things. Shall I ever have them? To write all the morning and then to get lunch over quickly and to write again in the afternoon & have supper and *one* cigarette together and then to be alone again until bed-time – and all this love and joy that fights for outlet – and all this life drying up, like milk, in an old breast. Oh, I want life – I want friends and people and a house. I want to give and to spend (the P.O. savings bank apart, darling.)

Tig.

Katherine Mansfield to J.M. Murry, ? May 1915, from The Collected Letters of. Katherine Mansfield, *edited by Vincent O'Sullivan and Margaret Scott (1984).*

CHAPTER FIVE

A VOICE
IN THE LAND

The New Woman might declaim against the laws that men made, but she had no representation to get these laws changed. On issues like divorce reform, equal pay, sweated labour and prostitution, women had no voice in a male Parliament. By the end of the nineteenth century, this absence seemed a pertinent barrier to further reform regarding the 'woman question', and women of different political persuasions, and with a variety of reform agendas, banded together to demand votes for women.

The first women's suffrage committee had been set up in 1866. The following year, John Stuart Mill pressed for the terms of the 1867 Reform Act to be amended to include women's suffrage. He was unsuccessful, though supported by eighty MPs.

In 1897, under the chairmanship of Millicent Garrett Fawcett, the various suffrage societies that had mushroomed in the intervening years, to petition and lobby for the extension of the franchise to women, came together to form the National Union of Women's Suffrage Societies (NUWSS): a nationwide movement committed to obtaining the vote for women by constitutional means.

But this was not enough for some reformers. In 1903 a new dimension to the struggle emerged when Emmeline Pankhurst, a Manchester suffragist and social reformer, decided that the constitutional route would never succeed – 'so willing to sit, so incorrigibly leisurely,' she castigated the NUWSS. In her view the campaign needed to force itself on to the male agenda. It needed more urgency, dynamism, a higher profile. Together with her daughters, Sylvia and Christabel, Mrs Pankhurst founded the Women's Social and Political Union (WSPU) with the slogan 'Deeds, Not Words'.

The debate over the next ten years focused both on objectives and methods. The militant tactics of the WSPU members – hurling bricks through the windows of shops and government buildings, heckling at political meetings and in Parliament, burning letter-boxes, holding carefully orchestrated mass rallies and demonstrations – brought the suffragettes (as they were called in the press) publicity, prison sentences and resulted in a campaign of hunger and thirst strikes. The Liberal government tried to bring these to an end by passing the notorious 'Cat and Mouse Act' in 1912, under the terms of which a hunger-striker would be released from prison to regain her strength and would then be re-arrested.

Militant tactics also brought division and dissent, together with criticism of the Pankhursts' alleged despotism. At the same time, the NUWSS began to grow into a mass movement, composed by 1909 of some 50,000 members – women who wanted the vote but felt unable to support the militancy of the WSPU.

There was also debate over exactly who should get the vote: should it be granted to women on the same terms as it was granted to men? Or, since only about 58 per cent of the male population was entitled to vote, should the goal be universal adult suffrage – the enfranchisement of working men and women, as well as householders? If so, how should the working classes and organized labour be involved in the campaign? And should the demand for the vote be above party politics? An appeal to natural justice? Or should a strategic electoral pact ensure the political clout of the suffrage movement?

It was these issues that continued to exercise the votes for women campaign on the outbreak of the First World War.

A GIRL'S LIFE

To MRS. FRANCIS SMITH.

TAMBOER'S KLOOF, CAPE TOWN, *27th June [1908]*

. . . I seem to have so strangely little connection with South
African life or people now. But my only friends in Cape Town,
the Purcells, will be back in about two weeks, I hope, and she
will bring the sweet little baby to see me. Oh, I do long for it
so. I know how I shall love it. My heart feels so tender over a
baby girl because of all the anguish which may be before it. I
always think of it when I touch and hold in my arms the dear
little female bodies; which no love can shield from the anguish
which may be waiting for them. I have done all I can to help to
free women, but oh it is so little. Long ages must pass before we
really stand free and look out on a world that is ours as well as
man's. The poor little political franchise is just a tiny, little, wee
step towards it. I don't think you can understand a little how I love
those suffragettes in London, those that I do know, and those that
I don't. They are women who have freed themselves spiritually
fighting for freedom: we, here, have in our little movement only
slaves clanking their little chains along as they go, asking for
their little franchise. You know when I was a young girl and
a child I felt this awful bitterness in my soul because I was a
woman, because there were women in the world. I felt [like] the
wonderful Kaffir woman, who once was talking to me and said,
'There may be a God, I do not say there is not; but if there is he is
not good – why did he make woman?' During those ten or twelve
happy middle years of my life the bitterness went; I realized the
evils of woman's position but I was so full of infinite hope. Every
thing seemed coming right quite soon – just on the other side of
the hill. I loved all my beautiful men friends in England and the
Kingdom of Heaven on Earth seemed just here. Now, especially
during the last eight years, I seem struggling with more than the
old bitterness; it seems choking me, suffocating me sometimes.
I try to fix my eye on the future but the future seems so far. It
wouldn't matter a bit that one will never reach it if one knew

207

it were coming *soon* to others. These dear suffragettes are just making life possible to me. It's not what they are trying to *get*, it's what they are becoming – they *are* breaking free!!

From The Letters of Olive Schreiner, 1876–1920, *edited by S.C. Cronwright-Schreiner (1926).*

VOTES FOR WOMEN

Ruth's Diary   Saturday, 13 June 1908
Met Eva and May Liverpool St. Station 2.30. Took bus to Charing Cross – saw 'Votes for Women' procession – a *really marvellous sight*. Thousands upon thousands of women, carrying small banners and large – some exceedingly beautiful. Most of the notable women were represented – George Eliot, Charlotte Brontë, Josephine Butler, Madame Curie, Black Agnes of Dunbar, Joan of Arc, Boadicea, Vashti – I could not name *half*. The smaller banners showed us the class to which each group belonged – clerks, typists, scriveners, lace-makers, doctors, nurses, painters etc. There were some splendid bands too. The entire procession took exactly an hour to pass, and there was no halting. The crowd stood through it all, cheering and applauding often, but I did not hear one sound of mockery or contempt. It was a most impressive sight. We came home, had tea, and then went a little walk, taking Daisy with us. Some music – and bed.

Ruth's Diary   Sunday, 21 June 1908
Up to City 12 o'clock. Met by Wal at Charing Cross. Hyde Park Demonstration by Women's Social and Political Union. *Most* marvellous sight, outreaching the procession of the previous week in numbers – I should think by thousands – but my sympathies are more with the others. We joined the throng around Miss Pankhurst's stand for a time, but the crush was becoming very dangerous, so we fought our way out. Miss Pankhurst was wearing her robes and college cap, and made an inspiring figure

in an inspiring spectacle. I should very much have liked a picture of her as she stood, a smile on her almost beautiful face, a slender arm outstretched, appealing for an audience, which a gang of roughs, stationed right in the front, refused for some time to give her. It was all very wonderful, but I could not help thinking their object would not be half-attained – the crowd seemed more intent on amusement than anything else.

I went on with Wal to Ealing. His friend Mr Reynolds and the young lady he is marrying in September came to tea, and we spent the evening in talking and music. I had been curious to see this pair, but strive as I would to keep them away, some bitter and jealous thoughts tormented me and toned my impressions. They knew so much more about Wal than I did. I felt all out in the cold, and felt too that Wal is often needlessly and thoughtlessly cruel. It hurts me almost more than I can bear, that he should treat me so affectionately one time and so coolly another – I cannot understand it.

Ruth's Diary   Tuesday, 23 June 1908
Have nearly cried myself silly this morning – very foolishly. Later – learned that some orange coloured pamphlets displayed in the window of Wal's lodgings, offering to explain the case *against* Women's Suffrage, had been placed there by him.

From Dear Girl. The diaries and letters of two working women, 1897–1917, *edited by Tierl Thompson (1987).*

THE CASE OF THE HELOTS

The last class to be enfranchised in this country – last, so long as representation is based upon taxation – is that of the helots. For a quarter of a century helots have been asking for the Parliamentary vote, and they are asking for it still. They have seen class after class enfranchised, sometimes with very little trouble and after slight demand, but the time for the helots is not yet.

Why do they want the vote? The simplest answer to this question is another question; why does anyone want the vote? This sets the first questioner thinking; and thought is good.

A great statesman, speaking of another class, once used words like these: 'They had no votes, and therefore they could be safely neglected.' And it is a fact that grievances are not easily redressed, and usually remain unredressed, while those who suffer are unrepresented in our Parliament.

An exasperated helot sometimes says to an adversary, 'Am I not a householder? do I not pay rates and taxes? have I not property of this, that, and the other kind? have I not to keep the laws as well as you? and is it not true that laws are made on purpose to arrange my affairs for me? Why should I not have a voice in the making of them?'

'Yes, oh, yes!' hurriedly and impatiently, 'I grant all that, but – oh, it would never do.'

'Why not?'

'Well, you see – er – you are only a helot!'

On which the helot has much ado not to lose her temper – on some occasions, alas, she loses it – and begs to know what the fact of her helothood has to do with the question of the franchise.

'Here I am,' she cries, 'living next door to a man who pays exactly the same rates and taxes as myself. He has a vote; I have not. How is that?'

'Well, don't you see? It is as plain as possible. Of course he is not a helot!'

There is no other argument. Yet the men who use it are accounted sane.

Helots are scolded for wanting class-legislation. 'You are making divisions in the body politic,' they are told; 'you are setting class against class. No one would dream of wrongs, rights, jealousies, grievances, if only you would keep quiet.' Then helots humbly submit that as long as they are left out in the cold there is division, but not of their making. Some people have votes, others have none; some have rights, to others these rights are denied. And they throw the accusation of class-opposition back upon the law-makers, which, if one thinks of it, seems only reasonable.

210

There are at present signs that the old method of representation, based upon taxation, is coming to an end, and that manhood suffrage is to take its place, but here comes in another inequality. An outsider might naturally consider that manhood signified humanity; but no, the helot part of humanity is still to be excluded.

Helots are in a minority, then, in this country? On the contrary, they number nearly a million more than the privileged persons. If the figures happened to be reversed we should hear them quoted continually as proof positive of the survival of the fittest.

For twenty-five years the majority has been asking for the franchise. Twenty-five years: is that all? Helots knew these grievances years, centuries ago, but they were taught to believe that they were heaven-sent, and therefore good, and good-producing. Submission was enjoined upon them, and beauteous self-abnegation. They were apt scholars, all the more apt because they could not help themselves; and they carefully impressed their beliefs upon their children. Little by little, however, one here, and another there, they began to ask, 'Is it right? is it just? Why should we bear tamely all our lives what our brethren, our masters, would not bear for a day?'

The first important book written in vindication of the rights of helots appeared about a hundred years ago; a second was produced in this century by a man who was not a helot, and to whose memory, therefore, helots owe undying gratitude.

And what were the wrongs which exasperated helots at last to claim their rights?

They were many, and of various kinds. Helots who had to earn their own living knew that their work was often harder than other people's, and never commanded the same remuneration. Some helots were teachers, others were household servants, others again, were in business; but every one of them who was employed by anyone else had to take small pay, on the one ground – so simple, so easy to comprehend – that she was a helot.

The Universities were shut against them, and so were many trades, and all professions.

Preach! oh, dear no. There is something dreadful, even blasphemous, in the thought! But act, sing, recite in public, by all

211

means; you do it so well, and it amuses Us. The ornamental and amusing is distinctly your mission in life, 'O Helot, in Our hours of ease!'

As for being lawyers, helots had not brains enough; and, as for being doctors, it was so indelicate, don't you know, even if a helot desired to practise only upon other helots. It was not indelicate or out of place to be a hospital nurse. There was, and is, a great demand for helot-nurses, the more highly educated, the more perfectly refined, the better. Not forty years ago, however, the pioneer of helot-nurses was treated with contempt, and had to fight her way against great opposition. To volunteer to nurse wounded soldiers was thought to be so 'unhelotic' as to argue something like depravity of nature. But the pioneer had courage and the consciousness of right, and accomplished so grand a work, that she was put upon a pedestal for all time, and praised as being 'most helotic,' and an example to the whole body of helots . . .

No wonder that at last a few helots . . . banded together and said, 'These things must come to an end. Those who make the laws may possibly mean well, but they clearly do not understand us, and they legislate for us from their own point of view. We must have the franchise.'

A cry of horror arose from one end of the country to the other. The poor helots were argued with, shouted at, hustled and badgered. Worse than all, they were laughed at.

'What wrongs have you, my dears?' asked one.

'Ho, ho!' laughed another; 'only a helot, and wanting a vote! Why, you will be wanting to sit in Parliament next!'

'I don't believe in "Helot Rights," ' was a growl from another quarter; 'all moonshine! fudge!'

They were called 'strong-minded,' under the impression that this was a term of reproach, and in utter obliviousness of the fact that the antithesis of 'strong' is 'weak.'

They were told that home was their sphere, their only sphere; and they had quoted to them such sweet sayings as 'The hand that rocks the cradle rules the world,' the quoters forgetting that the world is not always in its cradle, and that many and many a helot never has a chance of rocking. There was also thrown at them that nice little poem which begins –

212

The rights of helots, what are they?
The rights to labour and to pray.

'That is all very well,' said one helot after another, 'we are quite willing to labour, and we are thankful that we can pray; but don't you do the same? And, if you don't, why don't you? The poem has nothing to do with what we are talking about.'

Their opponents drew pictures of the helots who wanted to vote, and they made them as ugly as they could, with blue spectacles and big umbrellas, so that people should laugh; and they had their reward, for the laughter was loud and long. It was so long, indeed, that some of it can be heard to this day.

And they drew beautiful pictures of the dear, sweet helots who did not want the vote; for, unfortunately, there were some so very comfortable that they did not realize that their fellows were suffering, and so selfish that they did not care even when these sufferings were described over and over again. Some of them would say – parrot-like, for they could only repeat what they had been taught – 'It is so unhelotic, don't you know, so unfashionable, too! Nobody likes a helot who goes in for helot's rights.'

And people who knew them were fond of making, on platforms, such speeches as these:

'I have asked several helots whether they desired the suffrage, and they have invariably said, "No, not on any account;" and I am quite convinced, for I know them very well, that they have no wrongs, and that, therefore, no helot has any. All the best helots are with us.'

The helots whose eyes were open to see the way in which unjust and unequal legislation pressed upon them, grieved greatly over the attitude of their rich, comfortable sisters. For they were drags upon the wheels. They lived sheltered lives, and never thought of anything but themselves, their relations and friends. They talked a great deal about 'their sphere,' and all the men who petted and admired them talked about it too, but no-one knew exactly what it meant.

So the 'best' helots sat still, and came not to the help of the 'shrieking sisterhood.' But these worked on, worked harder and

213

harder, and yet did not gain what they wanted – the Parliamentary franchise.

In consequence, however, of their continuous demand, statesmen were at last driven to ask, 'Why do you want the suffrage?'

The answer was the recital of a whole chapter of grievances.

'Stop!' cried the great men, putting their hands to their ears. 'What shrieking this is! you deafen us.'

And they retired to consult. They then agreed to redress one small grievance rather than have this clamour go on any longer: and an Act of Parliament, hedged about with many restrictions, was thrown to them as a sop. In the course of years one or two other things were bestowed upon them with a 'take-this-and-be-satisfied' kind of air. Behind the scenes, grave politicians said to each other,

'If those stupid helots want the franchise because of all the things they call grievances, let us redress the "grievances" one by one, as far, of course, as is compatible with the preservation of our own interests, and then they will have nothing to complain about. Anything, anything, rather than give them the vote!'

'*The* vote' was not granted, but several lesser ones were granted as the years went on. Helots began to vote councillors into Town Councils, and soon found that people treated them with a little respect when they complained of the state of the streets, for instance, or the way in which the rates had gone up. The franchise for the Board of Guardians was also given, and helots were allowed, besides, actually to sit upon these Boards and watch over the interests of those poorer than themselves. And when the School Boards were formed, a friend of helots managed to put a word or two into the Parliamentary Act, which allowed helots from the first not only to vote for members of the board but to be members themselves. Then came the County Council, with a vote for householders all round, helot-householders included. But may helots sit in these Councils? Oh, no, that would be too shocking; it would be almost like going into Parliament.

It is only fair, however, to say, that the members of the greatest County Council in the kingdom would welcome helots as fellow-members if the law would but allow them to come.

But, to-day, though so much has been gained, helots are still unsatisfied, are still asking for the Parliamentary franchise. Why?

214

For the simple reason that they are taxed exactly as their fellow subjects are taxed, and ought to have the same right as they to say how the money shall be spent. They see their money taken to build an unnecessary ironclad, or to promote an unrighteous war against barbarians; and many a helot grudges her money for such purposes, and wishes to say so with effect.

In these latter days, another and more insidious danger has arisen. Helots have come more and more to the front, and their fellow-men, speaking generally, have discovered that they really have the brains that were so long denied, and that they can, in consequence, be made of very great use. It was often said at first, when helots began to creep out into public life, 'How well they get on, considering that they are only helots! It is really quite surprising!' But after a time people began to acknowledge that helots could speak on platforms, and conduct business-meetings as admirably as themselves; and they often complimented them on their most astonishing success.

Then, when the helots turned upon them with the old demand, 'Give us the suffrage,' there was a look of shocked solemnity on many faces, and a sudden slipping away at side doors, and the helots were left alone to wonder why, *why*, WHY their brethren were so much afraid of them.

Both political parties are every day making more and more use of helot-labour. It is not 'unhelotic' now to speak from platforms, or to canvass for votes; and helots who will do either, especially the latter, are courted and caressed. Nothing is too good for them – except the franchise.

The root-mistake which has caused helots to be treated differently from other people has been the regarding of Helothood as a special, and greatly inferior, variety of Humanity, not Humanity itself, but created to wait upon Humanity.

Condescending editors often reserve one little column in their newspapers which they call 'The Helots' Column'. It is supposed to suit exactly the humble range of the helotic mind. It deals almost invariably with cookery and clothes, and with the doings of the Royal Family. Many of its appointed readers peruse this column and the lists of births, marriages, and deaths, and nothing else in the paper. Why meddle with matters that are known to be too high for them: politics, the state of trade, the prospects of the crops, and the election of Mr Brown as vestryman? I cannot blame these people. The power of thinking for themselves has been drilled out of them. Their food has been not only selected but cut up for them on their plates, and they have never yet seen the absurdity of the thing. Let us admire those helots who have dared to think for themselves (how they ever began to do it I cannot imagine), whose sense of humour and strength of originality have broken through the tradition of the elders. And let us be patient with the readers of 'The Helots' Column', and do our best to enlarge their vision. Let us also remember that a very great many people who are not helots, and have never been shut up in a sphere, but have always had full liberty of thought and action, prefer *Titbits* and *Scraps* to politics and metaphysics, and a glass of beer and a pipe to anything else in the wide world. Yet no kind editor provides a column for these lowly minds.

Then there are sayings which are accepted without question, and passed on from mouth to mouth, in parrot-fashion, generation after generation. More evil is done by unreflective, unquestioning people than can be calculated. 'Helots are such talkers', 'so fond of dress', 'always looking at themselves in the glass', 'always gossiping', 'never able to keep a secret', etc. It is very seldom that anyone stops to ask. Are these sweeping assertions true? and, if they are, are they not true of humanity in general and not of one species only? There are helots who are uninterested in dress, others who rarely open their mouths, others again who will keep a secret to the death. And there are people who are not helots who look long at themselves in the glass, and are fastidious about the breadth of a hat-brim and the set of a coat. There are also people, not helots, who sit for hours in public-houses, or stand at street-corners with their hands in their pockets, gossiping, gossiping, chattering, chattering, yet no-one calls attention to their behaviour as being peculiar to one section of humanity; and no one sneers.

The very word 'helotic' is a question-begging word. What does it mean? Used by you, dear sir, it simply means your idea of what a helot ought to be. We do not speak of 'a sheeply sheep', or 'a pigly pig'; and I do not know that our conception of either sheep or pig would be enlarged if we did. Why go on talking, then, of 'helotic helots'?

216

It may be worth while to imagine a country where only helots
live, a circumscribed area – oh, most circumscribed! – which
may be called, for want of a better name, Helot's Sphere. Outside
the boundary line people are doing, thinking, saying anything
they please. Inside, there is restriction in the air, repression,
artificiality. It is not proper, for instance – though everything
is being rapidly modified by self-assertion – for a helot to be
out late at night alone, to go unattended to concert or theatre,
to ride outside an omnibus, or to be carried about in a hansom.
A young helot cannot live alone in rooms without losing caste,
even though she has to earn her own living, and has no home.
A well-to-do young helot is thought to be more than peculiar
if she attempts to inhabit her own house alone. She is always
expected to hire a 'companion', or find some elderly relation,
who will 'play propriety'. As for travelling alone, especially in
'foreign parts', such a thing is shocking to the Grundy mind.
Did you ever hear a youthful helot say anything like this: 'I think
of running over to Paris for a few days?' did you ever see her
pack her portmanteau and depart, just to look at Paris and 'enjoy
herself', with no protecting, chaperoning friend at her heels?

Again, a helot must dress, not so much for considerations
of suitability, or convenience, but to 'look nice' in the eyes
of those outside the sphere. If they are pleased, all is well.
Many a helot would like to be clothed so as to be able to
go about easily and in all weathers. She is often taunted with
not walking much, and laughed at for being easily fatigued,
but the regulation garb is rigidly enforced, and any modifica-
tions thereof are denounced as 'fast', 'eccentric', 'advanced';
worse than all, 'unhelotic'; and the small boy laughs in the
street.

It used to be the fashion in the sphere to be physically delicate.
Pale faces and languid movements were cultivated, and appetites
that could scarcely be seen. Outdoor exercise of any kind, riding
and a little walking excepted, was not to be thought of. Perhaps
the idea was that weakness of body would help to promote that
gentle dependence of mind so sweet to the feelings of the governing class.

There are all sorts of curious little unwritten regulations for
the decorous conduct of the helot-world. A helot must keep her

hat on in church and at a public meeting. Everybody would sit and gaze at her if she took it off. She may, however, go without it to concert, theatre, or opera, if in what is called 'full dress', which, being interpreted, means less dress than usual. If in ordinary dress the hat must be carefully kept on, as in church. At balls a helot must uncover shoulders and arms. No one can give a reason for this regulation. Other people never have to do it, and it would be thought 'not quite the thing' if they did. The Lord Chamberlain would most certainly turn anyone back who came to Court in such guise – anyone, except a helot; and the rules for helots who attend Court are very severe, and are written and printed so that even she who runs may read. No helot can appear before her sovereign except with bare, exceeding bare, shoulders, neck and arms. Within the last few years, however, a slight concession has been made. If a helot will bring a medical certificate stating that her lungs or throat are likely to suffer from exposure, or if she choose to proclaim herself advanced in years, court-etiquette will grant her absolution. But the latter part of the concession accomplishes little because it is accounted somewhat disgraceful in a helot to be elderly. Curiously enough it does not greatly matter if she be married; but, if unmarried, the helot who is approaching middle age is made to feel in many ways that she is a failure and ridiculous. And so helots in general are driven to pretend that they are younger than they are, to avoid reference to birthdays, and to dread the coming of the census.

Of late the sphere has widened.

Much, very much, has been changed. But nothing would have been changed if helots themselves had not had some little originality, some perception that whatever is is not necessarily right, some love of freedom, some determination that right shall be had, and justice shall be done, had by all, done for all, though the skies come down upon our heads.

By Elizabeth Martyn, 1894.

WHAT WOMEN DEMAND

The Women's Social and Political Union are asking for votes for women on the *same terms* as they are possessed by men.

They are not asking for the vote for every woman, but that a woman shall not be refused a vote simply because she is a woman.

At present men who pay rates and taxes, who are owners, occupiers, lodgers, or have the service or university franchise possess the Parliamentary vote. The Women's Social and Political Union claim that women who fulfil the same conditions shall also enjoy the franchise. This means that those women who pay taxes, and bear the responsibilities imposed upon men voters, will have the same political rights. Married women will obtain the vote, provided they possess the necessary qualifications; thus, where a married woman, and not her husband, is the householder, or where a woman is in business on her own account, she will become a voter.

It is estimated that when this claim has been conceded about a million and a-quarter women will possess the vote, in addition to the seven and a-half million men who are at present enfranchised.

The Women's Social and Political Union claim that the following simple measure, giving the vote to women on these terms, shall be passed this Session:

WOMEN'S ENFRANCHISEMENT BILL

That in all Acts relating to the qualification and registration of voters or persons entitled or claiming to be registered and to vote in the election of Members of Parliament, wherever words occur which import the masculine gender the same shall be held to include women for all purposes connected with and having reference to the right to be registered as voters, and to vote in such election, any law or usage to the contrary notwithstanding.

WSPU leaflet, c. 1908–9.

THE FIGHTING SUFFRAGIST TO THE FRIGHTENED POLITICIAN

'Why can they not be satisfied with constitutional methods?' – Mrs. Asquith

Through sixty years of days and nights,
  Our mothers fought a quiet campaign;
Petitioned humbly for their rights –
      In vain.

They worked and waited long and late,
  For justice to a Suffrage Bill:
Their hair grows white, and they are wait-
      ing still!

No 'patient' methods now for us,
  No empty pledge shall take *us* in;
It is the folks who make a fuss
      That win.

Oh, gentlemen, who make our laws,
  While we sit mum behind the grill –
You say we should behave – like men.
      We will!

We've proved we'll never get from you
  The vote because it's just and right:
There is but one thing left to do –
      To fight.

You think by 'pledges' you may buy
  A respite from our tactics rough?
No, thank you, gentlemen, we've had
      Enough!

The future's much too vaguely planned,
  Too 'speculative and remote' –
We've paid our taxes, and demand
      Our vote.

Winifred Auld in Votes for Women.

WOMAN, OR – SUFFRAGETTE?

A great question is before the country. It is this: Shall we sacrifice our Womanhood to Politics? Shall we make a holocaust of maidens, wives and mothers on the brazen altars of Party? Shall we throw open the once sweet and sacred homes of England to the manoeuvres of the electioneering agent? Surely the best and bravest of us will answer No! – ten thousand times no! Rather let us use every means in our power to prevent the consummation of what would be nothing less than a national disaster. For Great Britain is already too rapidly losing many of the noble ideals and institutions which once made her the unrivalled mistress of the world; the sanctity of the private household is being exchanged for the scrambling life of public restaurants and hotels – preachers of all creeds are reproaching women (and rightly too) for their open and gross neglect of their highest duties, – for their frivolity, waste of time, waste of money and waste of love, – the grace of hospitality, the beauty of sincerity, the art of good manners are all being forgotten under an avalanche of loose conduct and coarse speech, – and if the mothers of the British race decide to part altogether with the birthright of their simple *womanliness* for a political mess of pottage, then darker days are in store for the nation than can yet be foreseen or imagined. For with women alone rests the Home, which is the foundation of Empire. When they desert this, their God-appointed centre, the core of the national being, then things are tottering to a fall.

'Votes for women!' is the shrill cry of a number of apparently discontented ladies who somehow seem to have missed the best of life. And it is well-nigh useless to re-iterate the plain, trite truth that Woman was and is destined to *make* voters rather than to be one of them. Such is Nature's evident intention; and to contradict Nature is not an easy matter. With singular short-sightedness and obstinacy the Suffragette seeks to be what Woman *naturally* is not. She is unable to see that Woman, as pure womanly, has the whole game of life in her own hands, without 'suffrage.' She loses sight of the fact that if it be true that Man is her master, Woman has trained him into that position. And that therefore, it is perfectly puerile to try and undo now what she has been doing ever since she came into the world. There are bad men, of course, who take unfair and even criminal advantage of the position given them by the wholesale adulation and tenderness of women, – but there are millions of good men and true, who still keep the 'ideal' woman enshrined in their hearts as something exquisite, God-given and sacred – who only seek to honour her, never to degrade her, and who, from this very excess of honour, try to keep her if they can, out of political storm and contention, with which they, in their rough strength are better fitted to deal.

From Woman or Suffragette? A Question of National Choice, *1907, by 'Marie Corelli' (Mary Mackay, 1855–1924). Corelli was a bestselling novelist with an invented past and a profound interest in spiritualism and scientific phenomena. Her novel* The Sorrows of Satan *(1895) was the first English 'bestseller' and* The Treasures of Heaven *sold 100,000 copies on the day of publication.* The Soul of Lilith *(1892) remained Corelli's most famous work.*

MEMORIES OF A MILITANT [1906]

If it was necessary for us to ask a question at the Free Trade Hall meeting, it was vital that a question should be asked at the first great Liberal rally in London. The Manchester Labour Party organized a social gathering and Mrs. Pankhurst gave one of her daughter's pictures to be raffled to raise money for our fares to London. All the money that was necessary for the work in the very early days came out of Mrs. Pankhurst's pocket.

Tickets were bought, and I was chosen to be one of the women to make a protest. This was my first visit to London, and I have no impression of it except of buying hot chestnuts and eating them as I walked up the Strand and Fleet Street!

Through a friendly Labour-man two tickets were secured

for Mr. John Burns' private box, and they were given to me. Before the meeting I was disguised in a fur coat and a thick veil. My companion was an East End woman who was to come as my maid. We were almost the first arrivals in the hall, which action in itself would have given the game away later in the fight.

We waited patiently for the meeting to start. An express letter had been sent to Sir Henry Campbell-Bannerman, which was timed to arrive as the meeting commenced, and it asked that a pronouncement be made on Woman Suffrage. Unless a favourable reply were given it said, I (which meant we) should feel called upon to make a protest.

No reply was given, much less a favourable one, so in the middle of his speech I got up and asked whether the Liberals, if elected, would give Votes to women.

As soon as the audience heard that sentence it rose in anger. I had pinned a banner round my waist, bearing the simple motto, 'Give Votes to Women.' I brought this out and hung it over the box. As I did so everybody roared with laughter, for it was upside-down! The only person in the assembly who could read it was myself!

From Memories of a Militant, 1924, *by Annie Kenney (1879–1953). A trade unionist and suffragette, Kenney was born near Oldham and went to work in a mill when she was ten years old. She organized textile workers and became a correspondence student at Ruskin College, Oxford. In 1905 Kenney moved to London, where she lived with the Pankhursts and became an active speaker for the WSPU. She was imprisoned several times and was a victim of the 'Cat and Mouse Act' used against hunger-strikers.*

QUEEN VICTORIA AND WOMEN'S RIGHTS

The advocates of Women's Suffrage have made great play with the names of eminent women of the nineteenth century. Let Anti-Suffragists answer with the greatest name of all, the name of Queen Victoria! 'We women are not *made* for governing,' said the Queen, who governed the more effectively because she governed in a woman's way, by effacing herself, by putting her husband forward – 'Albert grows daily fonder and fonder of politics and business, and is so wonderfully fit for both' – by keeping herself aloof from all parties and fixing her gaze steadfastly on the highest good of her people. In a word, Victoria was great as a Queen because she was great as a wife and mother, and in place of Women's Rights she thought only of Women's Duties.

Writing to Sir Theodore Martin in 1870 the Queen spoke anxiously of 'this mad, wicked folly' on which my 'poor feeble sex is bent, forgetting every sense of womanly feeling and propriety.' If she spoke thus of advocates of Women's Rights thirty years ago, what would she have said of the scenes in Parliament Square in 1908?

Queen Victoria governed greatly, because she governed with common sense. Wild talk might rage round her, of equality between the sexes, of the grievances of women, of the iniquity of man-made law; the Queen knew better. 'God created men and women different; let them remain each in their own position.' 'We women are not *made* for governing, and if we are good women, we must *dislike* these masculine occupations; but there are times which force one to take *interest* in them.'

There are, indeed, and this is one of them. **Every woman is bound to take an interest in the question of whether a vote shall be forced upon her, and whether laws shall in future be made for her by women, who mistake their true place in the State.** It will happen, if we do not exert ourselves to stop it. Let us be wise in time, and do not let us be afraid of being called stupid and reactionary. We are stupid in good company; we stand side by side with Queen Victoria!

Leaflet published by the National League for Opposing Woman Suffrage.

VOTES FOR WOMEN

About this time I realized that if women did not bestir themselves the Socialists would be quite content to accept Manhood Suffrage in spite of all their talk about equality. I began to help the Pankhursts, who were trying to fan into flame the smouldering fire of discontent lit by the older suffrage societies. These had worked quietly and constitutionally in Manchester for over fifty years, by means of petitions, pleading with M.P.'s and candidates to demand the immediate extension of the franchise to women on the same terms 'as it is (or *may* be) granted to men'. Strangely enough, Mrs. P. and her followers found some of their bitterest opponents amongst the Socialists.

When we began to approach Labour candidates for support we were often snubbed. When I went myself with a deputation to interview a candidate, who later held high office in a Labour Government, he listened with ill-concealed impatience while we stated our case; then he said very grandly 'I am an adult suffragist,' and so dismissed us from his presence. We heard a lot about adult suffrage at this time from men who never seemed to have thought about it before. George Bernard Shaw with his usual incisive touch, summed them up in these terms:

'If a man owes you a sovereign,' he said, 'and being able to pay you fifteen shillings, refuses to do so, depend upon it, ladies, he never intends to pay the lot.' As I knew my Adult Suffragist pretty well I knew the candidate was one of the intending defaulters.

We began a vigorous campaign with the slogan 'Votes for Women'. In Manchester, The Women's Social and Political Union – W.S.P.U. – with Mrs. Pankhurst as its founder and chief, recruited at first mainly from the women members of the I.L.P., became very active. I joined them, and shared in the intensive

225

propaganda which preceded the outbreak of militancy in October 1905. How well I remember being invited to the Pankhurst home in Nelson Street, Manchester, to meet two girls from Oldham who were already helping in the work there, Annie Kenney and her sister Jenny. They were good-looking, well-mannered young women, wearing dark costumes of excellent quality, with white silk blouses. Both were fine examples of the self-respecting Lancashire mill girl, intellectual and independent. All the Kenney girls became active in the W.S.P.U. but Annie flung herself into the struggle with all the fervour of a religious crusader. In the winter of 1904–1905, we visited Trades Councils, Debating Societies, Women's Guilds. During the summer we went round all the Lancashire towns; we held outdoor meetings, stood on the steps of shows or roundabouts, on the market grounds, or at a street corner, on a chair, or a soap box from the nearest shop, often lent only in the hope of seeing some fun. Mrs. Pankhurst and her three daughters led the campaign; Christabel was studying for the Bar, Sylvia was an art student with a scholarship to the Kensington Art School and Adela was training to become a teacher. There was also their brother, Harry, a Manchester Grammar School boy, who, still in his early teens, had taken the affirmative in a school debate on 'Votes for Women' when the arrogant young bloods of Manchester solemnly decided that their mothers were not capable of casting a vote. I think it possible, however, that some of them may have thought differently after they reached home. Women were waking up, and in those days many mothers still believed that Solomon knew a thing or two.

With one or other of the small band of speakers I must have worked the Colne Valley from end to end, often under the auspices of the Colne Valley Labour Party. Sometimes we just went on our own and held little meetings in the streets, going first from door to door to ask the women to come out and listen, which the Colne Valley women were usually willing to do. We sold suffrage literature, and if the crowd was large enough, we took a collection; if this was sufficient we got our train fares out of it; if not we all paid our own. If we got a few shillings extra we bought more literature.

It was a strenuous time for us all, but for me it was particularly hard. Between my home duties and the Poor Law work I had little time for rest, and for study or reading, none at all. Indeed, I was so hard-pressed for time, that when another vacancy occurred on the Board of Guardians the candidate, Will Chapman, a keen feminist and a good comrade, came to ask for some help in compiling his election address. I said:

'I can't. I'm baking, and I've just put the bread in the oven.'

Whereupon he offered to look after it, while I wrote his election address. Both the bread and the address turned out all right, and Will thought the latter so good that it went out to the electors pretty much as I wrote it. When he was complimented on his knowledge of the Poor Law, he said gravely that he had given a good deal of thought to the subject before preparing his election address. He said to me afterwards that this was quite true, as he had thought about it all the time I was writing the address, and wondered what I was putting in it. He did not win the election though, and I did not regret this, much as I would have welcomed his presence on the Board, because he was a great help in our suffrage campaign. His wife, also a keen feminist, was helped and encouraged by him to take part in the work, and we badly needed the help of our male relatives, many of whom became 'anti' if their wives were out too often. No cause can be won between dinner and tea, and most of us who were married had to work with one hand tied behind us, so to speak. Public disapproval could be faced and borne, but domestic unhappiness, the price many of us paid for our opinions and activities, was a very bitter thing. But neither deterred us, and we carried on this intensive, but perfectly constitutional propaganda until the autumn of 1905.

Many attempts had been made by our friends in the House to get a hearing for a Suffrage Bill, and in May we had got second place in the Ballot for a private members' Bill. The first place was won for a measure to compel carts on the road to carry rear lights. Typical of the contempt for women shown by M.P.'s at that time was the gleeful manner in which they used this paltry bill as the means to 'talk out' the Women's Bill, with silly speeches and foolish jokes. This so angered the anxious women in the lobby that, led by Mrs. Pankhurst, they gathered outside for a meeting of protest, but they were twice moved on by the police before being allowed to hold their meeting.

Apropos of this Bill, Will Chapman remarked bitterly to me:

'Your only hope lies in the death rate.' Some time later, when one of our bitterest opponents died, Will obtained a photo of him, and sent it to me, with this message written on the back: 'Cheer up, your hopes are beginning to flower.'

From The Hard Way Up, The Autobiography of Hannah Mitchell, *edited by Geoffrey Mitchell (1968). Hannah Mitchell (1871–1956), the daughter of a farmer in the Derbyshire Peak District and one of six children, had an unhappy childhood with almost no formal schooling. She left home in 1885 and supported herself with a variety of jobs. In 1895 she married Gibbon Mitchell, a socialist, and in 1897 started to become involved in the Independent Labour Party and women's suffrage. She helped the Pankhursts in their work, speaking and demonstrating for women's rights, and was appointed an organizer for the Women's Social and Political Union. After 1907, disagreeing with some of the Pankhursts' tactics, she joined the Women's Freedom League led by Charlotte Despart. As a pacifist, Mitchell opposed the war in 1914, and afterwards became active in politics and civic life in Manchester and fought for the cause of feminism there.*

WOMEN'S RIGHTS

Down by Glencar Waterfall
There's no winter left at all.

Every little flower that blows
Cold and darkness overthrows.

Every little thrush that sings
Quells the wild air with brave wings.

Every little stream that runs
Holds the light of brighter suns.

But where men in office sit
Winter holds the human wit.

In the dark and dreary town
Summer's green is trampled down.

Frozen, frozen everywhere
Are the springs of thought and prayer.

Rise with us and let us go
To where the living waters flow.

Oh, whatever men may say
Ours is the wide and open way.

Oh, whatever men may dream
We have the blue air and the stream.

Men have got their towers and walls,
We have cliffs and waterfalls.

Oh, whatever men may do
Ours is the gold air and the blue.

Men have got their pomp and pride –
All the green world is on our side.

From Poems of Eva Gore-Booth, *with a biographical introduction by Esther Roper (1929). Eva Gore-Booth (1870–1926) was the daughter of Anglo-Irish landowners. Her sister Constance (later Countess Markievicz) was a famous Irish patriot and the first woman elected to the House of Commons. Eva was a poet, mystic and feminist, a close friend of Christabel Pankhurst, sympathetic to the suffragist cause, though never a militant. She was also an ardent worker for the Women's Peace Crusade and, after the Easter Rising in 1916, for Home Rule for Ireland.*

THE FREEDOM OF WOMEN

To MRS. FRANCIS SMITH.　　　　　DE AAR, *27th Aug.* [1912]
... I'll write about the suffragettes another day. I can under-

stand your position if you condemn *all* force – all fighting for freedom and justice and right – Washington and the Americans who fought *because they would not be taxed but by their own representatives* – Oliver Cromwell and Pym and Hampden – the Greeks who died at Thermopylae. If you say no wrong; no wickedness, no injustice must be opposed by force, in that case the Boers were wicked in fighting for freedom to save their little Republics, William the Silent and the Dutch of Holland were wicked to fight against Philip of Spain, Garibaldi, Cavour and the Italians when they fought against the Austrians, &c. &c. &c.! If you really hold this principle, if you feel that if a Russian army was landed in England to-morrow it would be the duty of English people to sit quite still and let them burn down houses, kill people, and take possession of and rule England – and that to use force to expel them was wrong – then you are *quite* justified in thinking the militants wrong. But those people who think of Washington and Pym and Hampden and William the Silent and the Dutch who fought with him as heroes, who glory in Italy's war against Austria, and the Greek wars against the Persians, and the war of modern Greece against Turkey – those people, who, if the working classes in England gained power and passed a law that all men with more than £300 a year should not vote, would advise their rising and fighting for their right – such have no justification for morally condemning the militant suffragettes. The freedom of women is yet more important than any question which humanity has yet fought out. If it was right for Garibaldi and the Italians to cause the death of thousands fighting for their freedom, or the Americans in resisting 'taxation without representation,' how infinitely more right it would be for the women of England to cause twenty thousand deaths in their fight for justice – a fight which would help not only to put them in a new position, but all the women of the world! I, myself, am opposed to all using of force personally. I, personally, would use *passive resistance* and argument. But I recognize this is an eccentricity on my part. It is the religion of the future, not of the present and the past. *I* would take no human life in revenge – not the life of a man who had committed ten murders. But, while we execute criminals or sentence them to solitary confinement for life; while we admire

230

soldiers, hired to fight against any nation or class of persons the Prime Minister of England and his Cabinet may at any moment desire to fight against and kill; while our whole system is based on the use of force – police, prisons, repressive laws – it is to me simply hypocrisy for anyone upholding this system and approving of it, to talk of the wickedness of women in fighting for freedom in using a little force. If the use of force is ever justified it is justified in fighting against social oppression. Of course there is quite another question – the question of tactics – which is not a moral question at all. Granted that it is right for men and women to fight for freedom and against injustice and oppression, what under the conditions is the *wisest* way of doing it? I cannot judge from this distance, but I think, under the conditions, their later tactics are not wise. If they could kidnap Asquith and Winston Churchill and *force-feed* them for six weeks, I think that would be a mode of warfare which the world must approve as perfectly just; I, personally, am a non-force-using *passive resister*. The only life I would ever punish anyone by taking is my own; I have always since I was a little child, long before I had heard of the Japanese custom, thought the punishment one would have a right to inflict on those who had injured one too much was to go and stand before them and stab or shoot oneself and say – 'my blood be upon you.' But that is a wholly un-English idea. An Englishman would probably laugh and have a whiskey and soda if a woman killed herself on his door-step – but a Japanese is forever disgraced.

I feel, personally, as you do about the use of physical force against others; but I cannot possibly be so unjust as to make one rule for one set of persons and another for another. I have a horrible idea that many people condemn the militants because they are women. The glory to me of the militant movement is that women are showing they *can* fight; there are higher things than fighting physically, the quiet *resistance* of wrong even to the death; but it is a great step forward when the slave shows any kind of fight. I am not going to condemn those who are fighting in a method that is not my method. Personally I prefer the martyr to the warrior – but I admire the warrior too. I think, I may be mistaken, but I think their later tactics are unwise – but their brave fight will never be forgotten while the world lasts. In forced-feeding and treating the women fighting for justice as they have done, Asquith and his followers have committed a crime which brands them forever. I would rather be Con. [Lady Constance Lytton] lying broken and shattered there than any one of those men who have been false to every principle of the Liberalism they have professed. If they had been Conservatives it would have been quite another matter. I do not believe that any civilized government has ever committed a greater crime, given the enlightenment of their age and surroundings. I do not think I could bear the thought of their treatment of those women, if it were not for my deep Jewish faith – 'Be not deceived, God is not mocked. Whatsoever a man soweth, that shall he reap.' How glorious to be one of those women, now to-day, rather than Asquith. Talk of 'force'; who has used the force of their whole social organization to crush a small body of human creatures fighting for justice? I don't think, darling, you hate the use of force at all more than I do, especially when it's organized force used to crush individuals. But I think, my own darling, perhaps you haven't felt so deeply and bitterly as I have, ever since I was a little tiny child, the evil and injustice of woman's position. I would always have been so glad, so glad, to give my life, if I could have done a little to free woman. The vote may seem to you a little thing, but nothing is small that is a step towards the large freedom. I believe the whole future development of the race depends on woman's freeing *herself* – no one can do it for her. If Con had died it seems to me she would have died so gloriously. Good-bye, dear one. I hope you can make out this scribble.

From The Letters of Olive Schreiner, *1876–1920, edited by S.C. Cronwright-Schreiner (1926).*

THE MILITANT SUFFRAGE MOVEMENT

PERSONAL FOREWORD

I write this book in criticism of the militant suffrage movement because I am impelled to do so by forces as strong as those which kept me five years within its ranks. I write because I am convinced that speech is necessary, because I know that no one else so well acquainted with the facts is prepared to speak, because I cannot keep silent longer without self-contempt.

I would be clearly understood from the first, and so I set down here at the beginning my confession of faith and the articles of my unbelief. I am a feminist, a rebel, and a suffragist – a believer, therefore, in sex-equality and militant action. I desire to see woman free and human; I seek her complete emancipation from all shackles of law and custom, from all chains of sentiment and superstition, from all outer imposed disabilities and cherished inner bondages which unite to shut off liberty from the human soul borne in her body. I believe that woman is in freedom the equal of man, and that any disabilities imposed by man upon woman or by woman upon man are evil. Against all such evils I believe in the sacred duty of insurrection. Women, along with every other unjustly restricted class, are not only entitled to revolt but have revolt imposed upon them; it is their gateway to liberty. This, and all that it implies, I believe.

I do not believe in the modern militant suffrage movement. I have believed in it, worked in it, suffered in it, and rejoiced in it, and I have been disillusioned. I do not believe in votes for women as a panacea of all evils. I do not believe that any and every interest and consideration and principle should be sacrificed to the immediate getting of any measure of suffrage legislation. Votes for women we must have, and many other things for women; but votes for women over-hurried and at any price may cost us too dear. I do not believe that woman is the superior of man any more than I believe that she is his inferior. Pretensions of sex-superiority are like bad coins; they are just as bad whichever face is turned up. I do not believe that the best

233

avenue for the emancipation of women is through emotionalism, personal tyranny, and fanaticism. To none of these things do I subscribe.

I am setting out to condemn the militant suffrage movement, but not to condemn militancy, for I shall be a militant rebel to the end of my days. I am setting out to expose the tone and tactics of the Women's Social and Political Union and the suicidal weakness of the Women's Freedom League. I have served in both these societies, have shared the burdens of the early days in both, have had my part in their successes and in their failures, and now I find both inadequate, fallen from a high estate full of promise to narrowness and incapacity. I do not condemn the present day militancy because it has gone too far. I fear that it has not gone far enough, and that it will never rise to the heights to which it originally showed potential claim. What I condemn in militant tactics is the small pettiness, the crooked course, the double shuffle between revolution and injured innocence, the playing for effects and not for results – in short, the exploitation of revolutionary forces and enthusiastic women for the purposes of advertisement. These are the things by which militancy has been degraded from revolution into political chicanery, these are the means by which it has been led to perjure its soul: it is against these evils that I mean to use the whole strength of my power of protest. I am not at all concerned that the militant movement has outraged convention, that it has shocked self-satisfied and blind benevolence, that it has made the exquisite and dainty suffer pangs of revulsion against sordid realities; it is not for convention that I plead. The crime of the militant suffrage movement in my eyes is that it is not real, that it is itself dangerously and determinedly conventional, that its militancy claims to be but is not revolution, that it has given itself over to the demon of hurry and has abused the great cleansing forces by means of which the world is carried into purgatorial fires and brought out purified. Other movements have failed in rebellion, but it has been left to this woman's movement to ape rebellion while belittling and abusing it. Other rebellions have failed; this movement has failed rebellion.

From The Militant Suffrage Movement, *1911, by Teresa Billington-Greig, one of the first suffragists to be imprisoned in Holloway.*

OVER ONE THOUSAND WOMEN
HAVE GONE TO PRISON [April 1913]

'Over one thousand women have gone to prison in the course of this agitation, have suffered their imprisonment, have come out of prison injured in health, weakened in body, but not in spirit. I come to stand my trial from the bedside of one of my daughters, who has come out of Holloway Prison, sent there for two months' hard labour for participating with four other people in breaking a small pane of glass. She has hunger-struck in prison. She submitted herself for more than five weeks to the horrible ordeal of feeding by force, and she has come out of prison having lost nearly two stone in weight. She is so weak that she cannot get out of her bed. And I say to you, gentlemen, that is the kind of punishment you are inflicting upon me or any other woman who may be brought before you. I ask you if you are prepared to send an incalculable number of women to prison – I speak to you as representing others in the same position – if you are prepared to go on doing that kind of thing indefinitely, because that is what is going to happen. There is absolutely no doubt about it. I think you have seen enough even in this present case to convince you that we are not women who are notoriety hunters. We could get that, heaven knows, much more cheaply if we sought it. We are women, rightly or wrongly convinced that this is the only way in which we can win power to alter what for us are intolerable conditions, absolutely intolerable conditions.

'From the moment I leave this court I shall quite deliberately refuse to eat food – I shall join the women who are already in Holloway on the hunger-strike. I shall come out of prison, dead or alive, at the earliest possible moment; and once out again, as soon as I am physically fit I shall enter into this fight again. Life is very dear to all of us. I am not seeking, as was said by the Home Secretary, to commit suicide. I do not want to commit suicide. I want to see the women of this country enfranchised, and I want

235

to live until that is done.' [*Mr. Justice Lush passed sentence on Mrs. Pankhurst of three years' penal servitude.*]

As soon as the sentence was pronounced the intense silence which had reigned throughout the trial was broken, and an absolute pandemonium broke out amongst the spectators. At first it was merely a confused and angry murmur of 'Shame. Shame.' The murmurs quickly swelled into loud and indignant cries and then from gallery and court there arose a great chorus uttered with the utmost intensity and passion. 'Keep the flag flying,' shouted a woman's voice, and the response came in a chorus: 'We will,' 'Bravo,' 'Three cheers for Mrs. Pankhurst.' Then the women filed out, singing the 'Women's *Marseillaise*':

March on, march on
Face to the dawn
The dawn of liberty.

'At three o'clock, when I left the court by a side entrance in Newgate Street, I found a crowd of women waiting to cheer me. With the two wardresses I entered a four-wheeler and was driven to Holloway to begin my hunger-strike. Scores of women followed in taxi-cabs, and when I arrived at the prison gates there was another protest of cheers for the cause and boos for the law. In the midst of all this intense excitement I passed through the grim gates into the twilight of prison, now become a battleground.'

My Own Story: The Autobiography of Emmeline Pankhurst, 1914. *Born in Manchester, Emmeline Pankhurst (née Goulden, 1858–1928) married Dr Richard Pankhurst, a legal scholar and radical reformer, came to London in the mid-1860s, supported Annie Besant's 'Match Girls' Strike' and convened the inaugural meeting of the Women's Franchise League. On her return to Manchester and her husband's death in 1898, Mrs Pankhurst worked for the Registrar of Births, Marriages and Deaths and, with her daughters Christabel and Sylvia, found the Women's Social and Political Union (WSPU) in 1903, committed to gaining suffrage for women on the same terms as men – using militant tactics to do so. On the outbreak of the First World War, Mrs Pankhurst suspended the activities of the WSPU and directed its energies towards conscription propaganda and her campaign for 'social purity'.*

WINDOW BREAKING: TO ONE WHO HAS SUFFERED

Dear Sir,

You, a prosperous shopkeeper, have had your windows broken and your business interfered with, you are very angry about it, and no wonder. But you are angry with the wrong people. You are angry with the women who broke your windows, whereas you ought really to be angry with the people who drove them to it. These people are the members of the present Government.

You know as well as I do that the Suffragettes bear no grudge against you personally, though perhaps they have some reason to do so. On the contrary, the women are good friends to you, and without them and their support what would become of that flourishing business of yours?

The people the Suffragettes are angry with, and the people you must blame for your broken windows, are, as I have said, the present Liberal Government. They are robbing women of their just right to vote for the Members of Parliament who levy taxes upon them and make laws for them. What is worse, the Government are constantly cheating and deluding the women who demand the Vote.

How would you like it yourself if you were treated in that fashion, and what would you do to get your rights? We know what men did a few years ago in South Africa for the sake of votes. It was not a question of a few broken windows then; it was a question of thousands of lives and millions of money.

'Well,' you may say, 'I sympathize with the women, but what have I got to do with it? Why should my windows be broken because Cabinet Ministers are a pack of rogues and tricksters?'

My dear Sir, you have got everything to do with it. You are a voter, and, therefore, the Members of the Government are your servants, and if they do wrong, you are really responsible for it. That is why your windows have been broken – to make you realize your responsibility in the matter.

Let me remind you again that women are your best supporters. You can get on very well without Mr Asquith and Mr Lloyd George, but you can't get on without the women who are your good friends in business. Surely one good turn deserves another? The women have been having a very hard time in this Votes for Women fight. **What have you done, what are you doing, and what are you going to do to help them?**

You as voters and as business men have got enormous influence. Last time there was window breaking, some people clamoured for severe punishment for the women. What good did that do? Long sentences of imprisonment, hunger strikes, forcible feeding, which, as the Recorder in a recent trial admitted, is torture! What man likes to think of women going through all that, even if his window *has* been broken?

Don't let it happen again. Put a stop to window breaking, and put a stop to the sufferings and sacrifices of the women, by telling the Liberal Government that you will **stand no more of it and that women must have the Vote**.

Believe me, the women will never give in, and you would think the less of them if they did. It is the politicians who must give in, and you and your fellow electors can make them do it.

The day will come when you will be as proud as can be of your broken windows, and of the orders you delivered to the Government to give women the vote.

I am, Sir,

Yours faithfully,

A SYMPATHIZER

WSPU leaflet, c. 1912–13.

THE LIFE OF EMILY DAVISON

I never dreamed how terrible the life of Emily Davison must have been. Yet she was to me quite a familiar personality ever since I first met her just after her first imprisonment four years ago. She was a wonderful talker. Her talk was an expression of that generosity which was her master-passion, which she has followed till today she is beggared even of her body; it was as though, delighted by the world, which her fine wits and her moral passion had revealed to her, she could not rest till you had seen it too. So I knew her, though I never spoke to her again. I saw her once more; last summer I saw her standing in some London street collecting for the wives and children of the dockers, her cheerfulness and her pyrotechnic intelligence blazing the brighter through a body worn thin by pain and the exactions of good deeds.

But for her last triumph, when in one moment she, by leaving us, became the governor of our thoughts, she led a very ordinary life for a woman of her type and times. She was imprisoned eight times; she hunger-struck seven times; she was forcibly fed forty-nine times. That is the kind of life to which we dedicate our best and kindest and wittiest women; we take it for granted that they shall spend their kindness and their wits in ugly scuffles in dark cells. And now in the constant contemplation of their pain we have become insensible. When enlightened by her violent death, we try to reckon up the price that Emily Davison paid for wearing a fine character in a mean world, we realize that her whole life since she joined the Women's Social and Political Union in 1906 was a tragedy which we ought not to have permitted. For if, when we walked behind her bier on Saturday, we thought of ourselves as doing a dead comrade honour, we were wrong. We were making a march of penitence behind a victim we allowed the Government to do to death.

Emily Davison was a woman of learning: she had taken honours in both the English schools of Oxford and classics and mathematics in London University. When she became a militant suffragist she turned her back on opportunities of distinction as a journalist and teacher. More than that, she entered into a time of financial insecurity; no comfortable background offered her ease between her battles. And eight times she went to prison. So many women have been brave enough to pass through prison unconsumed that, doubting if our race could furnish so much courage at one time, we have come to wonder whether prison is such a place of horror after all. But it was a hell through which she passed eight times. Once, indeed, the law of the land pursued those who maltreated her in gaol. A more than common ruffianly gang of visiting magistrates, who turned a hose of icy water on to her as she barricaded herself in her cell against forcible feeding, had to answer for their offence in the law courts. But we have our own description of an ordeal when her tormentors kept well within the law:

> On Wednesday 19 June, from 10 a.m. onwards, we were kept in solitary confinement.
> On Saturday we decided that most of us would barricade our cells after they had been cleaned out. At ten o'clock on the Saturday a regular siege took place in Holloway. On all sides one heard crowbars, blocks and wedges being used; men battering on doors with all their might. The barricading was always followed by cries of the victims, groans and other horrible sounds. These sounds came nearer and nearer in my direction. My turn came. I fought like a demon at my door, which was forced open with crowbars till at last enough room was made for one of the besiegers to get in. He pulled open the door, and in came wardresses and a doctor. I protested loudly that I would not be fed by a junior doctor, and tried to dart out into the passage; then I was seized by about five wardresses, bound into the chair still protesting; and they accomplished their purpose. They threw me on my bed, and at once locked the door and went off to the next victim.

If we subjected the most infamous woman, expert in murder, to such mental and physical torture, we should make ourselves criminals. And this woman was guiltless of any crime. Such torture, so unprovoked, would have turned most of us to the devising of more bitter violence against the Government; but there was a generous twist even to her rebellion. She longed not for a satisfying revenge, but for the quickest end to the tormenting of her friends. And then it was she conceived the idea of the need for a human sacrifice to buy the salvation of women:

I lay like a log for some time. When I did recover a little, I got up and smashed out the remaining panes of my window, then lay down again until I was able to get out into the corridor. In my mind was the thought that some desperate protest must be made to put a stop to the hideous torture which was now being our lot. Therefore, as soon as I got out I climbed on to the railing, and threw myself out on to the wire-netting, a distance of between 20 and 30 feet. The idea in my mind was 'one big tragedy may save many others'; but the netting prevented any severe injury. The wardress in charge ran forward in horror. She tried to get me off the netting, and whistled for help. Three others came and tried their best to induce me to go into my cell. I refused.

After a time their suspicions were allayed, and the matron came through into the ward to visit some of the prisoners; while she was there the wardresses relaxed their watch, and I began to look again. I realized that my best means of carrying out my purpose was the iron staircase. When a good moment came, quite deliberately I walked upstairs and threw myself from the top, as I meant, on to the iron staircase. If I had been successful I should undoubtedly have been killed, as it was a clear drop of 30 to 40 feet. But I caught once more on the edge of the netting. A wardress ran to me, expostulating, and called on two of my comrades to try and stop me. As she spoke I realized that there was only one chance left, and that was to hurl myself with the greatest force I could summon from the netting on to the staircase, a drop of about ten feet. I heard someone saying 'No surrender!' and threw myself forward on my head with all my might. I knew nothing more except a fearful thud on my head. When I recovered consciousness, it was to

241

a sense of acute agony. Voices were buzzing around me; in the distance someone said, 'Fetch the doctor.' Someone tried to move me, and I called out, 'Oh, don't!' Then the doctor came and asked for me to be moved to a cell close by. They lifted me as gently as possible. He asked me to go to hospital, but I begged him to leave me there – which he did. I also managed to say, 'For heaven's sake, don't feed me, because I shall fight.'

That was a year ago. For twelve months she was brooding over this plan to close a bloody war by giving her body to death. We belittle her if we think that her great decision can have made that decision to die an easy one; her last months before death must have been a time of great agony. To a woman of such quick senses life must have been very dear, and the abandonment of it a horror which we, who are still alive and mean to remain so, who have not even had the pluck to unseat the Government and shake it into sense, cannot conceive. And this decision was made by a soul harried by a body whose state was such as would have killed the courage in most of us. For the harsh treatment to which she subjected herself was nothing to the treatment she received from the prison officials, and between the two her body was shattered:

To my amazement the doctors came to forcibly feed me that afternoon. The operation, throughout which I struggled, caused me such agony that I begged the three comrades who were being released that afternoon to let friends know outside what was being done.

From that time on they fed me twice a day, in spite of the torture it caused me, until Thursday when, to our intense relief, they fed me only once. We all said that any food that could have been poured into us in a second operation could not possibly have done us the good that the relief from a second torture did.

Meantime nothing was being done to make my condition better. My head was dressed on Sunday. Nothing further was done to it. By the examination I knew that besides the two injuries to my head the seventh cervical vertebra was injured, and another at the base of my spine. They seemed very much worried about my right shoulder-blade. The sacrum bone was also injured, not to mention the many bruises all over my arms and back. All the vertebrae at the back of the head are very painful, and it is torture to turn.

From these injuries she never quite recovered. Till the day she died her spine still hurt her. Twelve months of misery of body and soul we inflicted on her by tolerance of this vile Government.

Many of the women in that funeral march were weeping; the sight of the broad arrows on her purple pall kept me from tears. Surely it was the most merciful thing that ever befell Emily Davison that her death, unlike her life, was unshadowed by prison walls. To the end the sunlight was on her face. Mr McKenna had no part in her sick-room; he paid no delicate deathbed attentions with the stomach-pump and nostril-tube. I was glad that for her executioner she had an unmalicious brute. But except for these kind circumstances of her death it was all grief.

When I came out of the memorial service where, in our desire to testify that the way of high passion which she had trodden was the only way, we had said and sung rather inadequate things over her coffin, I heard that Mrs Pankhurst had been re-arrested. And for a moment I was choked with rage at the ill-manners of it. Imagine a government arresting an opponent simply and solely to prevent her doing honour to the body of another opponent! But then I realized what it meant. Mrs Pankhurst was very ill, so ill that her nurse had tried to dissuade her from rising for the funeral, lest she should die on the way. And now she was taken back to Holloway and the hunger-strike. I felt a feeling that is worse than grief. It was the feeling that one has when one is very ill and has not slept all night. There comes an hour in the early morning when one realizes that one will not sleep again for a long, long time; perhaps never. So now it was not only that England had passed through a hot restless night of delirious deeds. But England has murdered sleep. Before us stretch the long, intolerable weeks during which they are going to murder Mrs Pankhurst. During that time we shall know no innocent rest, and surely some plague should fall upon us afterwards.

They have released her since. It must be for the last time. We dare not bear the double guilt of the death of Emily Davison and of Mrs Pankhurst. We must avoid it at the risk of turning the British Constitution upside down, at the risk of driving from the Cabinet 'the best-dressed man in Parliament', at the risk of breaking Mr Asquith's evil, obstinate heart. We must drop this masochist attitude of long-suffering, which is the mistake of the revolutionary movements, and show ourselves an angry England. We must have a demonstration in Trafalgar Square that will tell an astonished government that positively in the beginning of the twentieth century, in the centre of civilization, after seven years of Liberal government, there are still people who object to the murder of women. And when the Government absurdly asks: 'But what are we to do?' we must tell them that we prefer law-breakers to be at liberty; that if the women must burn grandstands they must; but that at any cost these wonderful law-breakers must go free, for they are the stuff of which England is built. And if the Government dislikes the resulting state of chaos it can give Votes for Women.

What a foe we have to fight! Can we hand Mrs Pankhurst over to that foe? This mishandling of women has its roots in horror. Doctors know that there is an obscene kind of madness that makes men torture women. Twenty-five years ago London was sick with fear because one such maniac crept through the dark alleys of Whitechapel mutilating and murdering unfortunate women. In those days people cursed him. They tried to hunt him out of his black hiding-place and make him pay for his crime. But today Jack the Ripper works free-handed from the honourable places of government: he sits on the Front Bench at St Stephen's or in those vast public sepulchres of conscience in Whitehall, and works not in secret but through Home Office orders and scarlet-robed judges. Scotland Yard is at his service; the medical profession, up to the President of the Royal College of Surgeons, places its skill at his disposal, that his mutilations may be the more ingenious. And for his victims he no longer seeks the shameful women of mean streets. To him, before the dull eyes of the unprotesting world, fall the finest women of the land, the women of the most militant honour and the wisest courage. How times can change in a quarter of a century!

And the backing behind this Government! The *Manchester Guardian* whimpered evil of the dead last week; so party passion can turn fools to knaves. The unspeakable *Pall Mall Gazette*, whose pages in their technical excellence and spiritual nauseousness remind one of an efficiently managed sewage farm, had a vulgar leader with a comic title on the death of Emily Davison. The dreary mob of Pecksniffs and heavy-jowled stockbrokers that stand behind these papers! And poverty has made many allies for the perverted Government. Near King's Cross there was a horrible crowd that jeered at the hearse. Old men, that looked like wicked little boys, little boys that looked like wicked old men, lively young prostitutes with bare arms scrawled with tattooing, old women putrescent with sin. They cried out lovingly upon the name of one Jones, the King's jockey, for these were betting people. Again I was glad that Emily Davison was killed by a horse and not by the kind of person she was fighting with.

Now that she is laid to earth, will we break up the procession and melt into the wicked crowd? Or will we continue to follow in the hard path of tolerance and defence of a cause that is fighting under extraordinarily difficult and perplexing conditions, till her spirit, eased by our achievements, may rest in peace, all being won?

'The Life of Emily Davison' by Rebecca West in The Clarion, *20 June 1913. Rebecca West (Cecily Isabel Fairfield, 1892–1983), feminist, journalist and novelist, took her* nom de plume *from the heroine of Ibsen's* Rosmersholm. *West was a staff writer for the suffragist periodical* The Freewoman, *and it was after reviewing his book* Marriage *that she met the writer H.G. Wells, with whom she had a ten-year relationship. Her books included* The Return of the Soldier *(1918),* The Fountain Overflows *(1957) and* Black Lamb and Grey Falcon: A Journey through Yugoslavia *(1941).*

THE EAST END CAMPAIGN

I regarded the rousing of the East End as of utmost importance. My aim was not merely to make some members and establish some branches, but the larger task of bringing the district as a whole into a mass movement, from which only a minority would stand aside. The need of our cause I believed to be such a movement. This was the meaning of Herbert Gladstone's challenge to the suffragists in 1908, and the still more pointed challenge of Hobhouse in February 1912, which had caused so much excitement. Not by the secret militancy of a few enthusiasts, but by the rousing of the masses, could the gage be taken up which not merely some Cabinet Ministers, but history itself had flung to us. The East End was the greatest homogeneous working-class area accessible to the House of Commons by popular demonstrations. The creation of a woman's movement in that great abyss of poverty would be a call and a rallying cry to the rise of similar movements in all parts of the country.

I induced the local W.S.P.U.'s to assist in organizing it: Kensington, Chelsea, and Paddington made themselves responsible for shops in Bethnal Green, Limehouse, and Poplar respectively, and Unions, even so far afield as Wimbledon, sent speakers and canvassers. W.S.P.U. headquarters agreed to be responsible for the rent of a shop in Bow. An intensive campaign like that of an election, to include deputations to local M.P.'s, was to culminate in a demonstration in Victoria Park.

Strange women of the underworld came to us eagerly: 'I have seen the Suffragettes in Holloway. They have made things better there! I remember you. I saw you when you was there.' One of these poor ones came asking for me in my absence and left her address. I went to seek for her, and knocked at the door with the given number in a neighbouring alley. From the window, close beside me, an old man leant out, wrapped in a filthy blanket, displaying his naked breast and shoulders. He shouted and swore at me, and looked so evil and menacing that I fled precipitately; but chiding myself for cowardice, returned to

246

knock again. Thereto came no response, but fearing the woman might be in trouble, I went again later in the day. Again the old fellow appeared at the window, extending a bare arm from his blanket to shake his fist in my face with horrible epithets. From others I learnt he was the landlord of a common lodging-house, expressing his objection to being disturbed during the day. The woman, who usually slept there, had merely left the address in case I should want to see her. For some time she was an eager attender at the meetings, then ceased to come. I learnt she was again in prison.

Women in sweated and unknown trades came to us, telling their hardships: rope-makers, waste-rubber cleaners, biscuit-packers, women who plucked chickens, too often 'high,' for canning, and those who made wooden seeds to put in raspberry jam. Occupants of hideously unsavoury tenements asked us to visit and expose them. Hidden dwellings were revealed to us, so much built round that many of their rooms were as dark as night all day. Exorbitant rents were charged in wretched barracks for so-called furnished rooms, containing nothing but a dilapidated bedstead with the poorest of covering, and a couple of chairs. In one such, I met a fragile orphan girl earning seven shillings a week and her food, minus threepence insurance, for washing up in a city restaurant until nine each night, and paying six shillings a week in rent. It was 'hard to keep straight,' she said. I procured for her an offer of better work, but when I returned she was gone. I could find no trace. Her words haunted me. In a one-roomed dwelling were a crowd of little children, and a man lying ill on a heap of rags. He had been a blackleg in the dock strike, and the strikers had thrown him from the Embankment. His leg had been broken and had not recovered. His wife had just been released from prison, where she had served a sentence for begging. She had been standing in the gutter offering bottlaces for sale, but several people had given her pennies without troubling to take the laces. The policeman declared her trading merely a blind to cover appeals for alms.

Women flocked to our meetings; members joined in large numbers. I at once began urging them to speak, taking classes for them indoors, and inducing them to make a start outdoors by taking the chair for me at a succession of short meetings in

247

the side streets where the workers lived, or by the market stalls in the shopping hours.

'The East End Campaign' by Sylvia Pankhurst, October 1912. Sylvia Pankhurst (1882–1960), suffragette and social reformer, was the daughter of Emmeline and Richard Pankhurst of Manchester, and an artist, speaker and organizer for the WSPU. After 1912 she was active in building a democratic mass movement in the East End of London, and edited its journal The Worker's Dreadnought. *Frequently imprisoned under the notorious 'Cat and Mouse Act', Sylvia was a pacifist during the First World War, fought for workers' rights and organized welfare provisions in the East End.*

THE ANTI-SUFFRAGIST

The princess in her world-old tower pined
A prisoner, brazen-caged, without a gleam
Of sunlight, or a windowful of wind;
She lived but in a long lamp-lighted dream.

They brought her forth at last when she was old;
The sunlight on her blanchèd hair was shed
Too late to turn its silver into gold.
'Ah, shield me from this brazen glare!' she said.

From Poems of Eva Gore-Booth, *with a biographical introduction by Esther Roper (1929).*

A CHAT WITH MRS CHICKY

Characters
MRS CHICKY, *a charwoman*
MRS HOLBROOK, *an Anti-Suffrage canvasser*

Scene: *A Room in the house of* MRS HOLBROOK's *brother. Window on left with desk and writing chair in front of it. Door left centre. Fireplace right with armchair (on castors) drawn towards it, facing audience. Bookshelf right centre. Table up centre. One small chair on top of another left of desk. Fender drawn away from hearth. Broom leaning against the wall. Pail of water, flannel, dustpan and brush, hearthbox with hearthcloth, scouring-stone, blacking brushes, old gloves, etc., up near door. Desk, table, bookshelf and armchair covered with dust sheets.*

N.B. – Although the effect of this duologue is much enhanced by the setting, it can quite well be played without it on small platforms, etc. Where this is desired, MRS HOLBROOK *should be discovered on rising of curtain, seated at a table with paper and pencil. She says,* 'Come in!' *in answer to a knock at the door, and* MRS CHICKY *appears, saying,* 'Sarah said you wanted to speak to me, 'M.' MRS HOLBROOK *answers:* 'So I do, Mrs Hicky. Sit down,' *and the duologue proceeds as written, except that instead of asking* MRS CHICKY *to go on with her work,* MRS HOLBROOK *says* 'I won't keep you from your work more than a few moments.' *Subsequent chance references to the 'turning-out' would, of course, be omitted.*

On rising of the curtain MRS CHICKY, *with sleeves rolled up, skirts pinned high, etc., is discovered scattering tea-leaves from a jar over the carpet. She stops short as* MRS HOLBROOK, *in outdoor things, bustles into the room.*

MRS HOLBROOK: Oh, you're here, Mrs Hicky! I just want to –

MRS CHICKY (*briefly*): Chicky.

MRS HOLBROOK: What do you say? Oh, Chicky – yes, of course. You're not the same charwoman my brother employed last time I came to see him, are you?

MRS CHICKY: I couldn't say.

MRS HOLBROOK: Ah, but I remember. I've such a memory for faces. She was short and stout, and –

MRS CHICKY (*interrupting*): If you're alludin' to Martha Buggins, 'M., she 'ad a cock-eye.

MRS HOLBROOK: Oh, poor woman, yes. She *had* a slight squint.

MRS CHICKY: 'Ope I may never see a severe one, then!

MRS HOLBROOK (*ignoring remark*): My brother said I might have a little chat with you, Mrs Chicky.

MRS CHICKY (*setting jar on table, pulling down sleeves, and looking round at general disorder*): Shall I come into the 'all, 'M.?

MRS HOLBROOK: No, no! I haven't come to keep you from your work. Please go on with it just as if I wasn't here – I shan't interfere with you. (*Laughs pleasantly.*) You and I are the sort of women who like to stick to our work and not interfere with other people's, aren't we?

MRS CHICKY: I'll answer for meself.

MRS HOLBROOK: It's a pity everybody can't say as much. (*Looks round for somewhere to sit down. MRS CHICKY takes up small chair, puts it centre and dusts it with apron.*) Ah, thank you! (*Sits down.*) Now please go on with whatever you're doing. We can talk just as well while you're working.

MRS CHICKY (*takes up broom leaning against wall*): Thank you, 'M.

MRS HOLBROOK (*as MRS CHICKY begins to sweep round the room*): That's right. Well, I'm trying to collect opinions wherever I go on a subject that a handful of women are making a great fuss about just now. I wonder if you know what I mean by Women's Suffrage?

MRS CHICKY (*looks thoughtfully at MRS HOLBROOK, then shakes her head and goes on sweeping*): No, 'M.

MRS HOLBROOK: All the better! *You* haven't got time to trouble your head about politics, have you?

MRS CHICKY (*sweeping tea-leaves and dust almost into MRS HOLBROOK*): I don't interfere with what don't interfere with me!

MRS HOLBROOK (*gathering skirts round her and putting feet on chair-rail.*): Splendid! Well, the fact is, Mrs Hicky –

MRS CHICKY: Chicky!

MRS HOLBROOK: Chicky – I beg your pardon. The fact is that a few women who haven't got anything else to do have some ridiculous idea that they ought to have votes, and do men's work instead of their own and interfere with the government of the country, and if you and I and millions of other women who know better don't stop them at once we shall simply have England going to rack and ruin!

MRS CHICKY (*pauses, leans on broom, and asks as if seeking light*): Then I 'ave got to trouble me 'ead about pollytics after all?

MRS HOLBROOK: Oh no! Let me put it a little differently! If you don't want a thing you certainly oughtn't to be made to have it, ought you?

MRS CHICKY (*giggling as she goes on sweeping*): That's what John Joseph says when 'e sees me with 'is lickrice powder. 'E's my third, is John Joseph.

250

MRS HOLBROOK (*coughing as dust rises, but evidently determined not to show irritation*): And a credit to you, I'm sure. Well, what *we* want to do is to show everybody that by far the greater number of women *don't* want votes, and I'm doing my part by asking a hundred women, taken as far as possible from every station in life, and putting down their replies so that I can send the result to a newspaper.

MRS CHICKY: An' 'ow might you be gettin' on, 'M.?

MRS HOLBROOK: Oh – er – of course one can't quite tell till one's got to the end. But when once we show in figures that most women are *against* having the vote, of course nobody can go on saying anything in favour of it.

MRS CHICKY: Well I 'ope you won't be disappointed 'M., I'm shore. But some people are that obstinate you can't make 'em see nothin'.

MRS HOLBROOK: Oh those kind of people needn't be considered at all.

MRS CHICKY: No 'M. (*Stops sweeping again.*) Why if you took one o' them lists of yours, down our Court to find out 'ow many wanted to wash theirselves every day I could tell you before 'and which side you'd 'ave a big balance on, an' yet I dessay you'd find some folks pig-'eaded enough to go on sayin' as they all orter use soap and water.

MRS HOLBROOK (*looks sharply at* MRS CHICKY *whose face remains impassive*): Please don't let me stop your work, Mrs Chicky. I don't think we need go into the question of your neighbours' cleanliness this afternoon. I merely want to know if I may put you down on my list as being against votes for women?

MRS CHICKY (*still pausing*): Well o' course 'M., if I was to set out to explain to you –

MRS HOLBROOK (*patiently*): I don't want *you* to explain anything to *me*, Mrs Chicky. I'm here to explain things to *you* this morning. (MRS CHICKY *still hesitates.*) You'd like to hear something more from me about it before you say yes, perhaps?

MRS CHICKY: I should, 'M.

MRS HOLBROOK: I thought so. Well, I can make the whole thing clear to you in a few minutes. Yes, please go on. (MRS CHICKY *begins to sweep again.*) You see *we* think that women have their own special work to do in their homes, and of course some of them have a Council vote already about things they can understand, like lighting streets and making roads.

251

MRS CHICKY (*encouragingly*): Yes 'M. (*For the next few minutes she takes* MRS HOLBROOK'S *chair as the goal towards which her tea leaves, etc. are to be swept, till she has finally collected little heaps all around it.*)

MRS HOLBROOK: Well isn't it better for them to leave the Army and Navy and wars with other countries to the men who know all about them? If women had the brains to understand the things men settle in Parliament it might be different, but they haven't. They're clever in another way. You can't combine politics and domestic matters. You – (*Turns first one way and then the other in chair to follow* MRS CHICKY *who is sweeping behind her.*) you see what I mean, don't you?

MRS CHICKY (*pausing again*): You mean as 'ome's one sphere an' Parlyment's another, an they didn't orter be mixed up?

MRS HOLBROOK (*much pleased*): Exactly!

MRS CHICKY (*reflectively*): It just shows you oughtn't to believe 'alf you 'ear! (*Crosses left as she sweeps again.*)

MRS HOLBROOK (*smiling*): What nonsense have you been hearing?

MRS CHICKY (*pausing*): Why I remember Marier Jackson down our Court tellin' me – oh it's some time back now – when 'er baby got pewmonier from sleeping in a banana box, as she didn't never take it to bed with 'er because Parlyment 'ad made a lor about it. I'll give it 'er proper for 'avin' me on like that! (*Sweeps vigorously again.*)

MRS HOLBROOK (*hurriedly*): Oh but I think she was quite right, Mrs Chicky. At least I know there has been some Act passed by Parliament in connection with poor children getting smothered in that way.

MRS CHICKY (*Pausing in surprise*): You don't say, 'M! Why you'd a' most think it was a-mixin' itself up with the 'ome if you didn't know different, wouldn't you?

MRS HOLBROOK (*hotly*): It's a splendid thing that such a law *has* been passed by men!

MRS CHICKY: Oh yes 'M., an' I'm not sayin' that pewmonier an' the Docter's certif'kit aint a sight more respectable than overlayin' an' the Crowner. I 'ope the dust don't worry you 'M.? (*As* MRS HOLBROOK *coughs again.*) Of course I like to see a woman 'ave a voice in settlin' what's best for children meself, but I know some ladies thinks diff'rent. (*Sweeps gradually right, crossing behind* MRS HOLBROOK.)

MRS HOLBROOK: You don't understand, Mrs Chicky! Nobody could feel more strongly than I do that the care of children is a woman's work above everything.

MRS CHICKY: She may care till she's black in the face, but she won't do much good if she's got the lor against 'er!

MRS HOLBROOK: My dear Mrs Chicky, you talk like an ignorant woman! How *could* the law be against her caring for her children?

MRS CHICKY (*a little huffily*): Ho, it's not for me to set my opinion against yours' 'M., bein', as you say, an ignerant woman. An' of course she's got the care of 'em right enough if she ain't got 'er marriage-lines. It's on'y if she's kep' respectable as she can be 'ampered somethin' crool!

MRS HOLBROOK: You seem to have got some extraordinary ideas in your head!

MRS CHICKY: Yus I 'ave. The lor's put 'em there, wot's more.

MRS HOLBROOK: Now my good woman just tell me your difficulties and let me explain them away!

MRS CHICKY (*pauses again and delivers speech very clearly*): Difficulties? Well I guess many a married woman finds it a bit difficult not bein' 'er own child's parent – goin' by the lor, that is. It's a bit difficult for 'er as the lor don't give 'er no voice in 'er child's schoolin' nor religin' nor vaccinatin' nor such like, in the or'nary way. It's a bit difficult for 'er as 'er 'usband can pretty nigh starve 'er an' it if 'e's the mind, but she's got to go the lenth of leavin' 'im before she can get a maint'nance order, an' it's often none too easy to get *that* carried out. It's a bit –

MRS HOLBROOK (*interrupting*): But where have you read all this? I'm quite sure it's nonsense!

MRS CHICKY (*with a laugh*): *Read* it? Bless your 'eart, 'M., women like us don't 'ave to *read* about the lor like you ladies! We're too busy knockin' up against it, as you might say. I don't serpose any o' *your* lady friends comes before the Magistrit onst in a lifetime, but it's diff'rent with mine, though I've kep' clear so far meself, thanks be! (*Begins to poke broom vigorously under* MRS HOLBROOK's *chair which is surrounded by a ridge of tea-leaves.*) Don't you move 'M.! I can sweep under you quite comfortable.

MRS HOLBROOK (*hastily*): No, no, thank you! (*Gets up and steps gingerly over tea-leaves to armchair right and sits down.*) But even if you're right, those difficulties would only arise where a husband and wife weren't doing their duty by living happily together.

MRS CHICKY (*setting broom aside and picking up dust-pan and small brush*): Well, the lor aint made for turtle-doves! (*Goes down on knees and begins to sweep leaves into pan.*)

MRS HOLBROOK: Of course not. But we were talking about votes, weren't we? All this has nothing to do with them.

MRS CHICKY: Votes wouldn't give women a bit of a voice in drorin' up the lors about their own affairs, then?

MRS HOLBROOK: Oh my dear Mrs Hicky –

MRS CHICKY: Chicky!

MRS HOLBROOK: er – Chicky, if the women of England had a voice even in such a roundabout way as that in making laws, what would the homes of England be like?

MRS CHICKY: Maybe you're right 'M. 'Twouldn't never do for those as know most about 'omes to 'ave anythin' to do with fixin' rules for 'em.

MRS HOLBROOK (*testily*): You don't understand what I mean. Fancy giving any woman such a terrible responsibility!

MRS CHICKY: Yes, 'M. You can understand some of 'em wantin' to shirk it, can't you? (*Goes on hurriedly as* MRS HOLBROOK *looks annoyed.*) But after all, there's many would say I 'adn't much call to trouble my 'ead about England. (*Gets up slowly.*)

MRS HOLBROOK (*Rising indignantly*): Anybody who would say such a thing to an Englishwoman ought to be ashamed of themselves!

MRS CHICKY: Yes 'M. But I aint an Englishwoman.

MRS HOLBROOK: You're not an Englishwoman?

MRS CHICKY (*serenely*): No 'M. (*Faces* MRS HOLBROOK *with dustpan in one hand and brush in the other.*) I'm French.

MRS HOLBROOK (*in bewilderment*): *French?*

MRS CHICKY: Yes 'M. My name's Chicky.

MRS HOLBROOK (*Puzzled*): How do you spell it?

MRS CHICKY: Well my 'usband 'e used to spell it C-h-i-q-u-e-with-a-mark.

MRS HOLBROOK (*crossing left*): Oh, *Chiqué!*

MRS CHICKY: Yes 'M. 'E did call it like that onst, but the men in the fact'ry always called 'im 'Chicky' and some'ow we got to writin' it like the poultry, too. 'E was French right enough though, Gawd rest 'im! Talk the langwidge beautiful, 'e could!

MRS HOLBROOK: But that doesn't make *you* French!

MRS CHICKY: Yes 'M. 'E did call it like more's the pity. I don't serpose they'd give me one o' these 'ere votes if I wanted one. They won't let me 'ave one for the Council. 'E's been dead this four year, 'as my 'usband, but 'e never nateralized 'isself, you see.

MRS HOLBROOK: But why haven't you got a Council vote?

MRS CHICKY (*wearily*): Cos I'm French, as I'm tellin' you.

MRS HOLBROOK: But you're *not*! (*Crosses right.*)

MRS CHICKY: Oh yes 'M., the gentleman what come round to arsk Annie Mills to vote for 'im – she's the room below ours – 'e explained it to me. 'E said a wife's what 'er 'usband is – she don't count sep'rit.

MRS HOLBROOK: But you're a *widow*!

MRS CHICKY: 'E said that didn't make no diff'rence. I 'ave to be what Chicky was. (*Puts brush and pan aside and gets hearthbox.*)

MRS HOLBROOK (*moves down towards fireplace*): That *does* seem rather peculiar, certainly.

MRS CHICKY: Yes 'M. (*Comes down right with hearthbox.*) I don't *feel* French!

MRS HOLBROOK (*hurriedly*): Of course not – of course not. (*Pauses, leaning elbow on mantlepiece as MRS CHICKY shakes out hearthcloth, spreads it and kneels down to grate.*) Of course if one thinks a moment one sees the beautiful idea at the back of it. A husband and wife are one, you know.

MRS CHICKY (*docilely*): Yes 'M. Which one? (*Puts on dirty kid gloves and begins to black grate.*)

MRS HOLBROOK (*confusedly*): Oh – er – just *one*. (*Sits down.*) Let's go back to what we were talking about. I was trying to make you see, wasn't I, that all these ideas of women doing men's work are ridiculous.

MRS CHICKY: Well that's as plain to me as (*looks round*) you 'M., sittin' in that chair. I've no patience with the way you'll 'ear some folk settin' women against men as if they were oppersite sides in a battle!

MRS HOLBROOK (*much pleased, leaning forward*): I felt sure you were a sensible woman!

MRS CHICKY: Yes 'M., thank you 'M. There was a lady at my door it'll be a fortnight come Monday, an' me up to my elbers in soap-suds, talkin' a lot o' that nonsense, but she went off quicker'n she'd come, I can tell you!

MRS HOLBROOK (*leaning more forward excitedly*): I'm very glad to hear it!

MRS CHICKY: Yes 'M. 'Woman's spere this, an' Man's spere that,' I says. 'Goin' on for all the world as if one 'ad got four legs an' the other two! The Lord 'E started 'em fair when 'E cremated 'em' I says 'an' 'E didn't lay down no rules about speres, nor make no diff'rence in their jobs. An' I guess thos 'oo go tryin' to parcel 'em off sep'rit I says ' 'ave more'n one muddle to answer for!'

Mrs Holbrook: I – I don't quite –

Mrs Chicky (*glorying in recollection of her own eloquence, waves blacking-brush to emphasize it and hits* Mrs Holbrook *who starts back in annoyance*): 'Besides' I says – oh, beg pardon 'M., I'm shore! – 'besides' I says 'women are doin' men's work, an' men women's, as you call it, all over the shop, an' if you want their speres to be diff'rent at this time o day' I says 'you've got to do more undoin' than'll larst your time an' mine.' She'd got a paper with 'er as she wanted me to put my name to, but I told her straight as I couldn't 'ave no truck with such silliness. (*Gets up and crosses left to fetch pail of water.*)

Mrs Holbrook (*much perturbed*): But Mrs Chicky, you probably misunderstood her entirely. I – I more than suspect she was *against* votes for women!

Mrs Chicky: She was against common-sense, whatever she was. (*Carries pail across right and sets it down near hearth.*)

Mrs Holbrook: And you know it's all nonsense to say women can do men's work. Women can't fight.

Mrs Chicky (*significantly, rolling sleeves higher*): Try 'em!

Mrs Holbrook (*coldly*): I was alluding to fighting for their country.

Mrs Holbrook: Lor bless you, 'M., I guess you an' me wouldn't be so far be'ind the men in that, neether, if it comes to the point! (*Kneels down, wrings out flannel in water and proceeds to wash over hearthstone.*) I'm the last in the world to belittle soldierin' – I'm proud to 'ave two brothers in that line meself – but the way some folks talk about men fightin' you'd think as there wasn't a man in England as didn't stand up to be shot at onst a week! It's a good job they don't 'ave the bearin' of the childring, or they'd be that set up at riskin' their lives so constant there'd be no 'oldin' of 'em in!

Mrs Holbrook: You get so confused, Mrs Chiqué –

Mrs Chicky: Chicky!

Mrs Holbrook: What I mean is that if women were soldiers and sailors there'd be something at once for them to have a vote *for*.

Mrs Chicky: Do soldiers 'ave the vote, then? Well I might 'ave knowed! They will 'ave their joke, will George an' Albert! If you'd 'eard 'em larst Election goin' on like bears with sore 'eads because they 'adn't a vote same as most o' their pals you'd never 'ave serspected it was just a do the 'ole time!

MRS HOLBROOK: You mean your brothers? Oh but it's quite likely that they hadn't.

MRS HOLBROOK: 'Ow's that, 'M.?

MRS HOLBROOK: Well you see to get a vote a man has to be a householder and pay rates and taxes, or a lodger, and stay in the same place a year and – oh, various things that most soldiers and sailors can't do.

MRS CHICKY: Oh then the vote *'asn't* got nothin' to do with fightin' for your country, after all?

MRS HOLBROOK (*testily*): I never met a woman more difficult to explain things to! Can't you see that the right to vote really depends on physical force – strength, you know – and that women haven't got that? (MRS CHICKY *finding* MRS HOLBROOK *in her way gets up and pushes her, chair and all, a foot or so centre with perfect ease*.)

MRS CHICKY (*returning right and kneeling down to hearth again*): Thank you 'M. – I couldn't quite get to this 'ere corner. Strength, is it? There's a parrylised man down our Court what's wheeled to the poll regler. I pushed 'im there meself larst Election, wishin' to oblige.

MRS HOLBROOK: Yes, yes, but you mustn't take everything I say too strictly.

MRS CHICKY: I'm not doin'. (*Dips scouring-stone into water and begins to scour hearth.*)

MRS HOLBROOK: What I want you to see is the broad principle of the thing. A woman's place is in her home, you know.

MRS CHICKY (*sitting back on her heels*): Am I to understand as your brother's not requirin' of me no more?

MRS HOLBROOK: Oh really, Mrs Chiqué – Chicky, then! – (*As* MRS CHICKY *begins to correct her.*) please don't go on narrowing everything I say down to particular cases! Of course I don't mean that you ought to stop going out charing!

MRS CHICKY: Bad job for *my* 'ome if I did!

MRS HOLBROOK (*with brilliant inspiration*): Yes, but don't you see how it all works back to what I said at first? You'd never have time for voting *and* charing, would you?

MRS CHICKY: Well I should say it took me a quarter of a 'our to wheel Tom Welford to the poll an' it was on my way to my work. 'E was took back by motor because 'e'd said 'e wouldn't vote unless. (*Smooths hearthstone over with wet flannel.*)

MRS HOLBROOK: Ah, but it's not just the voting! Look how this Mr Welby had probably *studied* the question, and how he – (MRS CHICKY *emits strangled sounds.*) what's the matter?

MRS CHICKY: On'y – on'y you'll eggscuse me larfin' 'M., but Tom Welford can't read. 'E couldn't do no studyin'. My Josephine runs in now an' again to read 'im the football news – they say 'e was a rare player in 'is young days, pore feller – but 'e don't care to listen to nothin' else. (*The hearth finished, she puts fender back into place and tidies up.*)

MRS HOLBROOK: Very kind of her I'm sure. Well, to go back to what we were talking about –

MRS CHICKY: Yes 'M., we don't seem to be gettin' much forrader, do we? (*Carries hearth box and pail up left.*)

MRS HOLBROOK: But I don't think there's any need for us to argue when in your heart you agree with all I've said. I only wanted to be satisfied that I could put you down as being against votes for women.

MRS CHICKY: An' are you satisfied?

MRS HOLBROOK: Quite. There are hundreds of sensible hard-working women like you who merely want to have the thing simply explained to them and they see its dangers at once. (*Rises and crosses left.*) I don't think I've anything more to ask you Mrs Chicky, thank you.

MRS CHICKY (*coming down centre*): Then can I arsk *you* somethin' 'M.?

MRS HOLBROOK (*a little surprised*): Certainly.

MRS CHICKY: Speakin' straight as one lady to another, an' no offence meant or taken?

MRS HOLBROOK: Certainly.

MRS CHICKY: Well it's this. What are you worritin' about 'em for?

MRS HOLBROOK: About whom?

MRS CHICKY: Why this little 'andful of women you've been a-tellin' me about. What 'arm can they do?

MRS HOLBROOK: Oh they've grown – I don't say they haven't grown. They've such a dangerous way of getting hold of people. You see *they* promise excitement and bands and processions – *we* can only offer dull things like looking after one's children and

258

caring for one's home. (*Crosses right again.*)

MRS CHICKY (*sharply, as she removes dust-sheet from table*): I've never found lookin' after *my* children dull, though (*Looking meaningly at* MRS HOLBROOK.) I know it's what *some* ladies calls it! (*Folds dust-sheet and places same on table.*)

MRS HOLBROOK: You will keep misunderstanding me! I say that the women who want votes think looking after children dull. I believe they'd like to make all women fond of politics instead of children!

MRS CHICKY (*uncovering desk and folding its dust-sheet*): Will they *make* you vote, then, whether you've the mind or not? (*Places dust-sheet on table.*)

MRS HOLBROOK (*dramatically, as she crosses left.*) Never! (*After a little pause.*) I'm not saying that some of us might not think it right to use a vote if it was forced upon us, so that we might counteract all the harm the other women would be doing.

MRS CHICKY (*proceeding to uncover bookshelf and place its dust-sheet on table*): Would they all vote the same way, then?

MRS HOLBROOK: Oh women always herd together!

MRS CHICKY (*with puzzled expression, as she uncovers armchair*): But if you an' your lady friends was all votin' the other way, it don't look as if women *would* be 'erdin' together?

MRS HOLBROOK (*cornered, crossing right*): I – I – oh it's no use trying to explain!

MRS CHICKY (*folding last dust-sheet and putting it on table*): Seems to me this 'ere vote's mighty difficult to understand!

MRS HOLBROOK (*triumphantly*): *Too* difficult – for a woman!

MRS CHICKY (*with apparent relief*): Oh then *you* don't understand it, neether?

MRS HOLBROOK (*with annoyed little laugh*): My good Mrs Chicky, all that *I* don't understand is why any woman should be so ridiculous as to want it!

MRS CHICKY (*quickly*): You don't?

MRS HOLBROOK: I certainly don't!

MRS CHICKY (*Comes down centre, gazes at* MRS HOLBROOK *for a moment, and then speaks as if on a sudden thought*): Now I wonder if it would 'elp you if you saw it writ?

MRS HOLBROOK (*puzzled*): If I saw what written?

MRS CHICKY (*raises her skirt, dives into under-pocket with difficulty, and finally produces red handkerchief knotted at corner, keeping up running*

259

comments the while): It must be 'ere somewhere. I don' know I'm shore why it didn't come to me sooner as I'd got it on me. I know I put it in me 'andkerchief to keep it away from 'Eneryett cos she was wantin' to suck it all the time the lady was a-talkin' – she's my fourth, is 'Eneryett. Never give it a thought till this minit, I didn't. 'Ere it is! Funny 'ow if you onst put a thing in your 'andercher it can go there for days! (*She undoes knot in handkerchief with her teeth, Mrs Holbrook watching her in bewilderment, and discloses small crumpled handbill which she smooths out and from which she proceeds to read.*) 'WHY WOMEN WANT THE VOTE' – that's on top – 'A FEW PLAIN REASINGS IN PLAIN WORDS' – I could 'ave give 'em a few more if they'd 'ave arsked me, but these is put very distink – very distink indeed they are. Praps you'd like to –

Mrs Holbrook (*splutters interruption in horrified amazement.*) You – you – you're a Suffragist?

Mrs Chicky (*looking up from paper with something approaching grin*): What do *you* think?

Mrs Holbrook (*furiously, flopping into chair*): You told me you knew nothing about Women's Suffrage!

Mrs Chicky (*sweetly*): Oh no 'M. You arsk me if I knew what you meant by it, an' I says no. (*Goes on hurriedly as Mrs Holbrook gives angry exclamation.*) I was a-startin' to tell you as I knew what I meant meself right enough, but you stopped me. You said you was 'ere to explain things to *me*!

Mrs Holbrook (*crosses left speaking hotly*): D'you suppose I'd ever have wasted my time over you if I'd known? We – we don't want to talk to people who are against us!

Mrs Chicky: I'm sorry, 'M., I'm shore. You see (*Tapping handbill.*) this lot's so diff'rent. Seems to revel in talkin' to them as don't agree with 'em, they do!

Mrs Holbrook (*looking at paper as if it were poisonous*): May I ask where you got that?

Mrs Chicky: I bring it away from a meetin' larst Tuesday. Praps you'd like to borrer it, 'M.?

Mrs Holbrook (*waving it hastily away*): Oh, if you're going to be taken in by all you hear at meetings –

Mrs Chicky (*interrupting quickly*): Taken in? No 'M., no one don't do no takin' in when Elizer Chicky's about, thankin' you kindly! Why we've 'ad two ladies down our street tryin' to stuff us with argyments that my own cat wouldn't 'ave swallered, an' 'e aint pernickety. 'We've h'always got on very well without women 'avin' the vote' says one. 'Yus' I calls back, '*you* may 'ave, but what price us?

Mrs Holbrook (*coldly*): Mere selfishness never did anybody any good yet!

Mrs Chicky (*apologetically*): Well 'M. I didn't like to call out that for fear she'd think I just wanted to sauce 'er.

Mrs Holbrook (*losing control*): Stupid woman!

Mrs Chicky: So I thought 'M. But praps she was a bit 'ard of 'earin', for she just says over again, 'We've always got on very well without women 'avin the vote'. 'Splendid!' I calls back, 'with some of us makin' blouses at one an' a penny a dozen an' ackcherly managin' to earn six shillins a week for a fourteen hours day! We all keeps our kerridges!'

Mrs Holbrook: But my good woman – (*Crosses right.*)

Mrs Chicky (*unheedingly*): 'Ho' says she, 'there's a lady in the ordyance what makes the mistake of thinkin' the vote's a-goin' to raise women's wages!' 'No' I says, very prompt, 'the lady 'oo's makin' a mistake aint in the ordyance' I says 'but there's a woman there' I says 'oo's got the sense to see that if 'er sex 'as got a vote what's useful to the men they're more likely to listen to 'er than if it 'adn't!'

Mrs Holbrook: But my good woman –

Mrs Chicky (*interrupting earnestly*): Look 'ere 'M., I arsk you before an' I arsk you again – what are you doin' it for?

Mrs Holbrook: Doing what?

Mrs Chicky: Carryin' on this 'ere 'obby of yours – cerlectin' names?

Mrs Holbrook: Why, I want to help to stop this movement! (*Crosses left.*)

Mrs Chicky: You might as well try to stop a leak in a saucepan with sealin'-wax!

Mrs Holbrook: But my good woman –

Mrs Chicky: Yus you might! You take it from me 'M. The first time I 'eard a lady at a street corner sayin' as women orter 'ave votes, I listens for a bit 'an I says 'I'm on this job' I says. I says 'She knows. She's talkin' gorspel. She aint sat in no drorin'-room an' *read* about us' I says. 'She knows.' (Mrs Holbrook *tries to interrupt with little indignant exclamations all through this speech, but* Mrs Chicky

once fairly started, refuses to be baulked.) She didn't waste no time tellin'
women out workin' to keep body an' soul together as they orter be
queens of their 'omes! She didn't go talkin' about a man's 'ome for
all the world as if 'e orter knock at the door an' arsk 'is wife's leave
every time 'e wanted to get inside it! (MRS HOLBROOK *crosses right*.)
She didn't waste no time tellin' women 'oo'd sent their lads off to
fight with their own 'earts breakin' for all their lips were smilin',
as women 'adn't no feelins for their country an' didn't understand
nothin' about war! She didn't waste no time tellin' sweated women
drove on the streets – women 'oo's 'usbands give 'em a drib 'ere an'
a drab there when they're sober, an' the childring goin' 'alf-naked –
women 'oo's 'usbands take up with another woman, an' 'I'm afraid
the lor can't 'elp you my good woman' says 'Is Wushup, in nine
cases outer ten – women 'oo get drove to despair with facin' their
trouble alone while the man 'oo's brought 'em to it gets off scot free
– women 'oo'll take on their 'usband's job when 'e's ill, to keep the
'ome goin', an' get eight or ten shillins docked off for the same amount
of work cos they aint men – she didn't waste no time, I say, jorin' to
women like that about the splendid way their int'rests are pertected
already! She *knew*. (MRS HOLBROOK *crosses left*.) Oh I'm not sayin' this
'ere vote's goin' to set everythin' right, but I do say as anythin' that's
done without it'll be just patchin' an' nothin' more! It's goin' to make
women *count*! It'll make 'em '*ave* to be reckoned with! I've nothin'
against the men. (*Draws hand across eyes*.) I'd the best 'usband as ever
stepped! I believe same as you do that the men want to do what's
best for us, but – *you 'ave to be a woman yourself to know where things
'urt women*! It's Gawd's truth, that is, an' I say Gawd bless the ladies
'oo are 'elpin' us by stickin' out for it!

MRS HOLBROOK (*with satirical little smile*): Well, I'm afraid *you* would
be wasting less time scrubbing your floors than as an orator, Mrs
Chicky.

SERVANT'S VOICE (*heard off*): Mrs Chicky! Mrs Chicky! You're
wanted! (MRS CHICKY *hesitates*.)

MRS HOLBROOK: Oh pray go! Of course you won't understand my
attitude, but nothing that you or anybody else could tell me would
make me alter my mind!

MRS CHICKY (*picking up hearthbox and dust-sheets*): Oh yes 'M., I've
'eard of that before. (*Pauses at door*.) You see 'M. my 'usband lived
in France till just before we was married, an' 'e kep' MULES!

Exit. MRS HOLBROOK *drops on to chair and stares after her in open-mouthed amazement.*
Curtain.

A Chat with Mrs Chicky *by Evelyn Glover was first performed at the Rehearsal Theatre, London in 1912. It was one of the plays written specifically for members of the Actresses' Franchise League, founded in 1908 to perform plays that provided centre-stage roles for women and put across the suffragettes' case.*

THE GREAT SCOURGE AND
HOW TO END IT

This book deals with what is commonly described as the Hidden Scourge, and is written with the intention that this scourge shall be hidden no longer, for if it were to remain hidden, then there would be no hope of abolishing it.

Men writers for the most part refuse to tell what the Hidden Scourge is, and so it becomes the duty of women to do it.

The Hidden Scourge is sexual disease, which takes two chief forms – syphilis and gonorrhoea. These diseases are due to prostitution – they are due, that is to say, to sexual immorality. But they are not confined to those who are immoral. Being contagious, they are communicated to the innocent, and especially to wives. The infection of innocent wives in marriage is justly declared by a man doctor to be 'the crowning infamy of our social life.'

Generally speaking, wives who are thus infected are quite ignorant of what is the matter with them. The men who would think it indelicate to utter in their hearing the words syphilis and gonorrhoea, seem not to think it indelicate to infect them with the terrible diseases which bear these names.

The sexual diseases are the great cause of physical, mental, and moral degeneracy, and of race suicide. As they are very wide-spread (from 75 to 80 per cent. of men being infected by gonorrhoea, and a considerable percentage, difficult to ascertain precisely, being infected with syphilis), the problem is one of appalling magnitude.

To discuss an evil, and then to run away from it without suggesting how it may be cured, is not the way of Suffragettes, and in the following pages will be found a proposed cure for the great evil in question. That cure, briefly stated, is Votes for Women and Chastity for Men. Quotations and opinions from eminent medical men are given, and these show that chastity for men is healthful for themselves and is imperative in the interests of the race.

The use of remedies, such as mercury and '606,' is no substitute for the *prevention* of sexual disease. Drugs and medical concoctions will not wash away the mental and moral injury sustained by the men who practise immorality, nor are they adequate as a cure for the body. The sexual diseases are particularly intractable to cure, and it is never possible to prove that a cure has been effected, so that the disease, while apparently cured, is often only hidden and ready to break out again.

Regulation of vice and enforced medical inspection of the White Slaves is equally futile, and gives a false appearance of security which is fatal. Chastity for men – or, in other words, their observance of the same moral standard as is observed by women – is therefore indispensable.

Votes for Women will strike at the Great Scourge in many ways. When they are citizens women will feel a greater respect for themselves, and will be more respected by men. They will have the power to secure the enactment of laws for their protection, and to strengthen their economic position.

The facts contained in this book constitute an overwhelming case for Votes for Women. They afford reasons more urgent and of greater human importance than any other, that women should have the Vote.

The knowledge of what the Hidden Scourge really is, and of how multitudes of women are the victims of it, will put a new and great passion into the movement for political en-franchisement. It will make that movement more than ever akin to all previous wars against slavery.

From The Great Scourge and How to End It, *1913, by Christabel Pankhurst (1880–1958). She studied law at Manchester University, and her political militancy was further inflamed when she was refused admittance to Lincoln's Inn in 1904 because she was a woman. In 1903 Christabel and her sister Sylvia left the Independent Labour Party and, with their mother Emmeline, formed the WSPU with the slogan 'Votes for Women'. From 1907 Christabel worked as an organizer and orator for the WSPU in London, but in 1912 she fled to Paris to escape a possible conspiracy charge and directed the English campaign through the newspaper* The Suffragette. *She attacked sexual as well as political oppression. Her articles on prostitution and venereal disease were reissued as* The Great Scourge *in 1913.*

THE VOTE WON

Friday 11 January [1918]
Another sedentary day, which must however be entered for the sake of recording that the Lords have passed the Suffrage Bill. I dont feel much more important – perhaps slightly so. Its like a knighthood; might be useful to impress people one despises. But there are other aspects of it naturally. L. to lunch with Ka & a Serbian; I set up, & now find it easily possible to finish a page in an afternoon. L. back, & we took a round by the river, & so home to tea, a great many books. (Life of Keats at last).

From The Diary of Virginia Woolf, *Vol. I, 1915–19, introduced by Quentin Bell, edited by Anne Bell (1977). Virginia Woolf (née Stephen, 1882–1941), the daughter of Julia (Jackson) and Leslie Stephen and sister of the painter Vanessa Bell, was a writer and story-teller from a very early age, but her* History of Women *(c. 1897) is now lost. She suffered the first of several mental breakdowns in 1895, was educated at home and took classes at King's College, London, but envied her brothers their university education. After the death of her father in 1904 and of her brother, Thoby, in 1906, she settled in Bloomsbury with her sister and wrote articles and short stories and*

265

taught at Morley College. In 1912 she married an ex-colonial admin-istrator, Leonard Woolf. Her first novel, The Voyage Out, *was published in 1915. In 1917 the Woolfs set up the Hogarth Press, which published all her books and works by Katherine Mansfield and T.S. Eliot. Her subsequent innovative novels included* Night and Day *(1919),* Jacob's Room *(1922),* Mrs Dalloway *(1925),* To the Lighthouse *(1927),* Orlando *(1928) and* The Waves *(1931). The centre of a literary and artistic coterie in London and Sussex, Woolf, never a politically active feminist, wrote tellingly on the constraints to women's achievement, particularly in* A Room of One's Own *(1929) and the anti-war* Three Guineas *(1938). She killed herself in 1941 after finishing her ninth novel,* Between the Acts.

CHAPTER SIX

WOMEN'S
WAR

The outbreak of war in August 1914 changed the agenda for women's rights. 'We know that a War Government cannot busy itself with franchise legislation,' recognized Millicent Garrett Fawcett of the NUWSS. The Liberal government granted an amnesty to militant suffragettes in prison, and the WSPU announced a suspension of activities in the face of greater violence.

Mrs Pankhurst and her daughter Christabel embraced the patriotic cause. The WSPU journal *The Suffragette* was renamed *Britannia* in October 1915 and called for military conscription, the internment of aliens and a vigorously prosecuted war of attrition. While some of those active in pre-war suffrage threw their energies into war work, organizing the voluntary services and funding ambulances, others embraced pacifism, founding the Women's International League for Peace at The Hague in 1915.

On 6 February 1918, nine months before the end of the war, six million British women over the age of thirty were given the vote. But there were still thirteen million who remained without a voice in the affairs of the nation's government.

The effects of the outbreak of war on women were soon felt: they lost their menfolk to the military, and many women lost their jobs in the early months of the war, with the contraction of the 'luxury trades' created by the sweated labour of dressmakers, milliners and the like.

But by January 1915 around two million men, from a total male labour force of 10.6 million, had joined the armed forces. The war effort needed more soldiers, and it needed the munitions to enable them to fight. So thousands of women who had previously been employed in domestic service or the sweated industries went to work in factories, producing *matériel* for war.

For those women who wanted to do their patriotic duty and for whom earning money was not a necessity, nursing and the medical services provided the answer, in the form of VADs (the War Office scheme for Voluntary Aid Detachments for the Sick and Wounded), who nursed in France, Belgium and in hospitals at home.

Women did not just keep the home fires burning during the First World War: many of them worked outside the home for the first time and enjoyed a degree of responsibility and freedom previously unanticipated. Women worked on the railways, on trams and buses; in farming and forestry; in the Women's Royal Air Force (WRAF), the Women's Army Auxillary Corps (WAAC) and the Women's Royal Naval Service (WRNS); in munition factories, aeroplane factories, the Post Office – anywhere that men had had to march away from for the duration of the war.

Women's voices were raised in wartime to support the war effort in almost every sphere. They were also raised to grieve at the futility, and mourn the dead, of war. Over three-quarters of a million British men were killed in the First World War. It was, indeed, a 'mutilated generation', and few women did not experience the death or serious injury of a husband, lover, father, brother or son. There could be no return to a pre-war world. In so many ways that world had been lost for women, as for men.

AUGUST 1914

For the present at least our arms are grounded, for directly the threat of foreign war descended on our nation we declared a complete truce from militancy which was answered half-heartedly by the announcement that the Government would release all suffrage prisoners who would give an undertaking 'not to commit further crimes or outrages.' Since the truce had already been proclaimed, no suffrage prisoner deigned to reply to the Home Secretary's provision. A few days later, no doubt influenced by representations made to the Government by men and women of every political faith – many of them never having been supporters of revolutionary tactics – Mr. McKenna announced in the House of Commons that it was the intention of the Government, within a few days, to release unconditionally all suffrage prisoners. So ends, for the present, the war of women against men. As of old, the women become the nurturing mothers of men, their sisters and uncomplaining helpmates.

The struggle for the full enfranchisement of women has not been abandoned; it has simply, for the moment, been placed in abeyance. When the clash of arms ceases, when normal peaceful, rational society resumes its functions, the demand will again be made. If it is not quickly granted, then once more the women will take up the arms they to-day generously lay down. There can be no real peace in the world until woman, the mother half of the human family, is given liberty in the councils of the world.

By Emmeline Pankhurst, 1914.

WHAT DO THEY KNOW OF SUCH PLACES?

And all the time boys were being born or growing up in the parish, expecting to follow the plough all their lives, or, at most, to do a little mild soldiering or go to work in a town. Gallipoli? Kut? Vimy Ridge? Ypres? What did they know of such places? But they were to know them, and when the time came they did not flinch. Eleven out of that tiny community never came back again. A brass plate on the wall of the church immediately over the old end house seat is engraved with their names. A double column, five names long, then, last and alone, the name of Edmund.

From Lark Rise to Candleford *(1939) by Flora Thompson (née*

Timms, 1876–1947). The eldest of ten children of an Oxfordshire stone-mason and a former housemaid, Thompson became an assistant postmistress and married a post-office clerk. Lark Rise to Candleford, *a portrait of a fictional hamlet based on Thompson's own village, Juniper Hill, with the central character, Laura, based on herself, was followed by* Over to Candleford *(1941),* Candleford Green *(1943) and* Still Glides the Stream *(published posthumously in 1948). One of her brothers, Edmund, was killed in the First World War.*

I DIDN'T RAISE MY SON TO BE A SOLDIER

I didn't raise my son to be a soldier
I brought him up to be my pride and joy,
Who dares to put a musket on his shoulder,
To kill some other mother's darling boy?

By Adela Pankhurst (1855–1961). Socialist, pacifist, and sister of Christabel and Sylvia Pankhurst, she emigrated to Australia.

SO MANY MOTHERS' SONS

There is, perhaps, no woman . . . who could look down upon a battlefield covered with slain, but the thought would rise in her, 'So many mothers' sons . . . So many months of weariness and pain while bones and muscles were shaped within; so many hours of anguish and struggle that breath might be; so many baby mouths drawing life at woman's breasts; all this, that men might lie with glazed eyeballs, and swollen bodies, and fixed, blue, unclosed mouths, and great limbs tossed – this, that an acre of ground might be manured with human flesh . . .' No woman who is a woman says of a human body, 'It is nothing!'

On that day, when the woman takes her place beside the man

in the governance and arrangement of external affairs of her race will also be that day that heralds the death of war as a means of arranging human differences . . .

It is not because of woman's cowardice, incapacity nor, above all, because of her general superior virtue, that she will end war when her voice is finally, fully and clearly heard . . . it is because, on this one point, and on this point almost alone, the knowledge of woman, simply as woman, is superior to that of man; she knows the history of human flesh; she knows its cost; he does not . . .

It is especially in the domain of war that we, the bearers of men's bodies who supply its most valuable munition, who, not amid the clamour and ardour of battle, but singly, and alone with a three-in-the-morning courage, shed our blood and face death that the battle-field may have its food, a food more precious to us than our heart's blood; it is we especially, who in the domain of war have our word to say, a word no man can say for us. It is our intention to enter into the domain of war, and to labour there till in the course of generations we have extinguished it.

From Woman and Labour, *1911, by Olive Schreiner.*

MANY SISTERS TO MANY BROTHERS

Oh it's you that have the luck, out there in blood and muck:
    You were born beneath a kindly star;
All we dreamt, I and you, you can really go and do,
    And I can't, the way things are.
In a trench you are sitting, while I am knitting
    A hopeless sock that never gets done.
Well, here's luck, my dear – and you've got it, no fear;
    But for me . . . a war is poor fun.

By Rose Macaulay, 1915. Macaulay (1881–1958) was a poet, novelist, travel writer and critic. She wrote twenty-three novels: the first was Abbots Kerney *(1906); the most enduring* The Towers of

Trebizond *(1956)*, Told by an Idiot *(1923) and* Potterism *(1920).*
Dangerous Ages *(1921) won the Femina Vie Heureuse Prize. Her
view of the war changed dramatically after 1915 and in 'Picnic',
written in July 1917, she wrote of staring and peering dizzily
'through the gates of hell'.*

MAKING DO IN WARTIME

There were no ration books and no organized rationing. You
just got what you could. We would queue up for an hour for a
pound of potatoes, seed potatoes so small they had to be cooked
in their jackets. There was no butter or meat for us but sometimes
we would get half a pound of margarine which Mother would melt
and to which she would then add a meat cube in an attempt to
give it a little flavour.

One year at Christmas, there being nothing else to eat, Mother
made a large plain boiled pudding which she served to us with
some golden syrup (saved for an emergency). I thought it quite
funny to be having such a dinner on Christmas Day, but Mother
sat and cried as she watched us eat it. We lived on meatless stews,
which somehow she made quite tasty.

From Behind High Walls: A London Childhood, *1974, by Grace
Foakes.*

THE DREAMS OF ENGLISHWOMEN

That day its beauty was an affront to me, because like most
Englishwomen of my time I was wishing for the return of a
soldier. Disregarding the national interest and everything except
the keen prehensile gesture of our hearts towards him, I wanted

to snatch my cousin Christopher from the wars and seal him in
this green pleasantness his wife and I now looked upon. Of late
I had had bad dreams about him. By night I saw Chris running
across the brown rottenness of No Man's Land, starting back here
because he trod upon a hand, not even looking there because of
the awfulness of an unburied head, and not till my dream was
packed full of horror did I see him pitch forward on his knees
as he reached safety – if it was that. For on the war-films I have
seen men slip down as softly from the trench parapet, and none
but the grimmer philosophers would say that they had reached
safety by their fall. And when I escaped into wakefulness it was
only to lie stiff and think of stories I had heard in the boyish voice,
that rings indomitable yet has most of its gay notes flattened, of
the modern subaltern.

'We were all of us in a barn one night, and a shell came along.
My pal sang out, *"Help me, old man, I've got no legs!"* and I had to
answer, *"I can't, old man, I've got no hands!"* '

Well, such are the dreams of Englishwomen to-day; I could
not complain. But I wished for the return of our soldier.

From The Return of the Soldier, *1918, by Rebecca West.*

SING A SONG OF WAR-TIME

Sing a song of War-time,
Soldiers marching by,
Crowds of people standing,
Waving them 'Good-bye'.
When the crowds are over,
Home we go to tea,
Bread and margarine to eat,
War economy!

If I ask for cake, or
Jam of any sort,
Nurse says, 'What! in War-time?

Archie, cert'nly not!'
Life's not very funny
Now, for little boys,
Haven't any money,
Can't buy any toys.

Mummie does the house-work,
Can't get any maid,
Gone to make munitions,
'Cause they're better paid,
Nurse is always busy,
Never time to play,
Sewing shirts for soldiers,
Nearly ev'ry day.

Ev'ry body's doing
Something for the War,
Girls are doing things
They've never done before,
Go as 'bus conductors,
Drive a car or van,
All the world is topsy-turvy
Since the War began.

By Nina Macdonald.

PRESENT WAR AND FUTURE WOMAN

Education is perhaps the most criticized of all the arts, since it lends itself to that species of criticism which is based on the principle that a tree is known by its fruits, and it requires no specialist to appreciate its products. It was, however, an unusually acute critic who observed, some time ago, that the chief obstacle to the creation of a really satisfactory system of girls' education is the absence of any definite and generally recognized conception of the type of woman it is intended to produce. For boys, the type is pretty well fixed, largely by the great Public Schools, and most parents have a fairly clear idea of the kind of man they wish their son to become; but with girls the case is different. One can only say that the models held up to them reflect in their variety the disorder in the ideals of womanhood which has been so marked a feature of recent years. On the one hand, there are the remains of the system founded on the theory that the aim of a girl's education should be to inculcate the domestic virtues and cultivate a few external graces. On the other, we have the admonition and practice of those who believe that its aim should be to fit a girl to earn her own living; and we are also witnesses of the labours of such as halt between the two opinions. We reserve to the second school the name of vocational educationists, but in reality they both deserve it equally. Neither regards the future woman apart from her vocation; they differ merely as to the nature of the vocation. The first assumes that she will be by profession a woman, the second that she will be a professional woman. Neither chooses to regard her simply as a human being and a citizen.

At the present moment there are symptoms that the hands of the vocational educationists are being strengthened, both by the prospect of economic pressure due to the war and by the casualty lists. Because of the first, there are more families than ever in which the daughters must come to their own aid. And because the casualty lists are so long, and will be longer before the struggle is over, there are fewer girls than before who can assuredly look forward to marriage as their lot. There will be a large preponderance of 'superfluous women' in the immediate future, and their case seems to furnish some of the strongest arguments for a revision of our ideals of womanhood, and the building-up of a more adequate type to set before us as the end of education. To-day we may say that this land is full of child-widows – girls widowed before they have ever heard a word of love. We pity the grown women who have lost husbands or betrothed, but we must not forget the young girls who, in the normal course of events, would have been the wives of the lads of eighteen and twenty who are falling so fast. Allowing for the woman's being usually by a few years the junior of her husband, these unconsciously bereaved, whose experience will be not positive personal loss but diminished chances of marriage, are still girls

275

at school. There lies their hope. For the older women little can be done, but these girls can be prepared for the future that stretches before them. By degrees they will realize that independence, if not solitude and self-support, are their decreed lot. Upon those who have their education in hand lies the responsibility of creating in them the right spirit in which to face it.

What have we to offer them that can be a substitute for the joys that every woman naturally looks for? The best we can give them, it seems to me, is the thought of self-development – whether in the form of definite vocational efficiency or otherwise – for the nation's sake. The suggestion, the reader may say, is not a new one; and the prospect of a career is cold comfort for the loss of domestic happiness. The objection is no newer than the suggestion, and the reply to the criticism is implied in the old saying, that half a loaf is better than no bread. If the metaphor may be varied without becoming a flippancy, I should prefer to say that plain bread is better than no cake. The belief in a right to happiness is, if possible, even more deeply ingrained in women than in men, and a woman's usual synonym for happiness is love. She is less likely than ever to get it; it remains to cultivate her taste for the substitute. And satisfying work is no ill substitute for more ecstatic happiness. It is a sure shield against vain longings and the restlessness of unfulfilment. It is, as many women will agree, the only thing that helps when you come into a strait pass.

But against this it is said that so few careers which provide real interest are as yet open to women that it is small wonder that a girl has no pleasure in looking forward to a working life. The criticism is not unfounded, and opens up large questions, but I venture to think there is a good deal to be said on the other side. Girls are too rarely taught to look for their interest in their work. The need for self-support is still regarded by so many parents as an evil for their daughters, from which marriage will deliver them. The feeling goes so far that girls are allowed to enter half-equipped upon their work, because, forsooth, it is no use spending money on training for an employment which will be merely temporary. We need neither develop that argument nor supply the retort; both are familiar.

And to-day more than ever the professional woman – the self-supporting woman, whose work is not merely her livelihood but her interest – has the force of facts upon her side. We need not fear that by cultivating this type we shall endanger the future supply of wives and mothers. The domestic instincts are not so easily eradicated. Nature will hold her own.

All this is trite enough. It has long been recognized, and to some extent acted upon. But we ought to realize that at present we have a great opportunity in this matter, in the deep stirring of a powerful motive, patriotism and the realization of citizenship. This is what I meant by speaking of *self-development for the nation's sake*. Let our girls to-day be made to feel that they must make the best of themselves, if for no other reason, for the sake of the land that will want good citizens in the future as much as she wants soldiers to-day. The thought will come home to them as it has done to few generations of women in the past.

We hear much of women taking men's places for the duration of the war. Many places will need to be filled for longer than that. The young men that are gone were not only our future merchants, business men, craftsmen, labourers: they were to have been artists, legislators, thinkers, and leaders of thought – our future citizens. Their virtues must be replaced, if their special aptitudes cannot. Here we can appeal to the motive of individual devotion to the memory of the fallen. When Mr. Valiant-for-Truth passed over the river – 'and all the trumpets sounded for him on the other side' – he left his sword to him that should come after him in his pilgrimage, and his courage and skill to him that could get it. The sword is not for a woman's grasp, but surely this legacy of valour, constancy, fortitude, and the lesser virtues of evenness of judgment and 'saving commonsense' is within the reach of every girl who has lost a brother or other relative in the war. England will need wisdom in counsel as much as strength of arm; and shall any one say, that that is something which women cannot give? The women of to-day have already cast off that reproach, and the women of to-morrow must be prepared to carry on and better the tradition. To produce women of such value, of balanced brain and heart, each capable of good work in her own branch and all capable of bringing a sound judgment, based on general knowledge, to the general problems of the community, should be the present aim of female education. Then we may hope that women, being fit for the duties of citizenship, may be recognized by the State as fit also for its full rights; and in this gain, not of political privilege alone, but of a fuller life for half the nation, we shall find in some part the compensation of our present sacrifices.

By D.M. Vaughan in The Englishwoman, *Vol. XXVII, December 1915.*

NON-COMBATANT

Before one drop of angry blood was shed
   I was sore hurt and beaten to my knee;
Before one fighting man reeled back and died
   The War-Lords struck at me.

They struck me down – an idle, useless mouth,
   As cumbrous – nay, more cumbrous – than the dead,
With life and heart afire to give and give
   I take a dole instead.

With life and heart afire to give and give
   I take and eat the bread of charity.
In all the length of all this eager land,
   No man has need of me.

That is my hurt – my burning, beating wound;
   That is the spear-thrust driven through my pride!
With aimless hands, and mouth that must be fed,
   I wait and stand aside.

Let me endure it, then, with stiffened lip:
   I, even I, have suffered in the strife!
Let me endure it then – I give my pride
   Where others give a life.

By Cicely Hamilton, 1916.

THE WORLD WAR AND WOMEN'S WAR WORK

What have I done for you,
  England, my England?
What is there I would not do,
  England, my own?
With your glorious eyes austere,
As if the Lord were walking near,
Whispering terrible things and dear
As the song on your bugles blown,
  England –
Round the world on your bugles blown.

                                    W.E. HENLEY

In the midst of all the plans of organized work, which were certain, as we thought, to lead to speedy victory for the suffrage cause, we were suddenly startled by the trumpet call of war, the world war, the greatest which ever had been waged, and our own country was to be a protagonist in it. The wanton violation of Belgium neutrality by the Germans made this a certainty. Very soon, too, we realized how right the socialists of the allied countries – England, France, Belgium, and Russia – were when they agreed that 'a victory for German Imperialism would be the defeat and destruction of democracy and liberty in Europe,' and we recognized that our cause, the political freedom of women, was but a special case of the still greater cause for which the Allies were fighting. Clearly as we began to perceive this, it will easily be recognized that the time of the outbreak of war was a time of no little perplexity and anguish of mind to nearly all of us. But from the first our duty was quite clear – namely, to help our country and her allies to the utmost of our ability; many of us, however, myself included, believed that the great catastrophe of the world war would greatly hamper and retard the movement to which we had dedicated our lives. It only very gradually dawned upon us that one of the first results of the war would be the emancipation of women in our own and many other countries.

It will be remembered that England entered the war against Germany at midnight on Tuesday, August 4th, 1914. All that day and the previous day the Executive Committee of the N.U.W.S.S. had sat in anxious consultation. We were a tolerably large band of organized women – over 50,000 members, and about 500 societies – scattered all over the country, accustomed to work together in a disciplined, orderly fashion for a common end; we felt, therefore, that we had a special gift, such as it was, to offer for our country's service – namely, our organizing and money-raising power.

From The Women's Victory – and After: Personal Reminiscences, 1911–1918, 1920, *by Millicent Garrett Fawcett (1847–1929), leader of the women's suffrage movement and sister of Elizabeth Garrett Anderson. In 1865 she married Henry Fawcett, Professor of Economics at Cambridge, who was blind. She published* Political Economy for Beginners *in 1870 and campaigned for the passing of the Married Women's Property Act, for moral reform and, above all, for the enfranchisement of women. She became President of the NUWSS in 1897 and worked tirelessly for constitutional reform throughout the period of the militant suffragette campaign.*

PERHAPS

(To R.A.L. . . .)

Perhaps some day the sun will shine again,
And I shall see that still the skies are blue,
And feel once more I do not live in vain,
Although bereft of You.

Perhaps the golden meadows at my feet
Will make the sunny hours of Spring seem gay,

And I shall find the white May-blossoms sweet,
Though You have passed away.

Perhaps the summer woods will shimmer bright,
And crimson roses once again be fair,
And autumn harvest fields a rich delight,
Although You are not there.

Perhaps some day I shall not shrink in pain
To see the passing of the dying year,
And listen to the Christmas songs again,
Although You cannot hear.

But, though kind Time may many joys renew,
There is one greatest joy I shall not know
Again, because my heart for loss of You
Was broken, long ago.

February 1916

By Vera Brittain (1893–1970). A feminist, writer and pacifist, she left Somerville College, Oxford in 1915 to become a VAD nurse during the First World War.. Her fiancé, Ronald Leighton, was killed in France in 1915; her brother died in action in 1918. These experiences were the material for her account Testament of Youth: An Autobiographical Study of the Years 1900–1925 *(1933). After the war Brittain became a prolific journalist and writer and married George Caitlin, a political philosopher.*

TO MY BROTHER*

(In Memory of July 1st, 1916)

Your battle-wounds are scars upon my heart,
Received when in that grand and tragic 'show'

*Captain E.H Brittain, M.C. Written four days before his death in action in the Austrian offensive on the Italian Front, June 15th, 1918.

281

> You played your part
> Two years ago,

And silver in the summer morning sun
I see the symbol of your courage glow –
> That Cross you won
> Two years ago.

Though now again you watch the shrapnel fly,
And hear the guns that daily louder grow,
> As in July
> Two years ago,

May you endure to lead the Last Advance
And with your men pursue the flying foe
> As once in France
> Two years ago.

By Vera Brittain.

A JOURNAL OF IMPRESSIONS IN BELGIUM

And in the end I asked him whether it would bore the wounded frightfully if I took them some cigarettes? (I laid in cigarettes this morning as a provision for this desolate afternoon.)

And – dear Prosper Panne – so thoroughly did he understand my malady, that he himself escorted me. It is as if he knew the *peur sacré* that restrains me from flinging myself into the presence of the wounded. Soft-footed and graceful, turning now and then with his instinct of protection, the orderly glides before me, smoothing the way between my shyness and this dreaded majesty of suffering.

I followed him (with my cigarettes in my hand and my heart in my mouth) into the big ward on the ground floor.

I don't want to describe that ward, or the effect of those rows upon rows of beds, those rows upon rows of bound and bandaged bodies, the intensity of physical anguish suggested by sheer force of multiplication, by the diminishing perspective of the beds, by the clear light and nakedness of the great hall that sets these repeated units of torture in a world apart, a world of insufferable space and agonizing time, ruled by some inhuman mathematics and given over to pure transcendent pain. A sufficiently large ward full of wounded really does leave an impression very like that. But the one true thing about this impression is its transcendence. It is utterly removed from and unlike anything that you have experienced before. From the moment that the doors have closed behind you, you are in another world, and under its strange impact you are given new senses and a new soul. If there is horror here you are not aware of it as horror. Before these multiplied forms of anguish what you feel – if there be anything of *you* left to feel – is not pity, because it is so near to adoration.

If you are tired of the burden and malady of self, go into one of these great wards and you will find instant release. You and the sum of your little consciousness are not things that matter any more. The lowest and the least of these wounded Belgians is of supreme importance and infinite significance. You, who were once afraid of them and of their wounds, may think that you would suffer for them now, gladly; but you are not allowed to suffer; you are marvellously and mercilessly let off. In this sudden deliverance from yourself you have received the ultimate absolution, and their torment is your peace.

From A Journal of Impressions in Belgium, *1915, by May Sinclair (1863–1946), a novelist influenced by the work of Freud. It was Sinclair who coined the phrase 'stream of consciousness' when reviewing Dorothy Richardson's* Pilgrimage *in 1918. Her many and important novels include* The Divine Fire *(1904),* The Helpmeet *(1907),* The Three Sisters *(1914, reflecting the life of the Brontës), the semi-autobiographical* Mary Olivier *(1919) and* The Life and Death of Harriett Frean *(1922). Sinclair was a member of the Women Writers Suffrage League and worked for the relief forces in Belgium during the First World War.*

LAMPLIGHT

We planned to shake the world together, you and I
Being young, and very wise;
Now in the light of the green shaded lamp
Almost I see your eyes
Light with the old gay laughter; you and I
Dreamed greatly of an Empire in those days,
Setting our feet upon laborious ways,
And all you asked of fame
Was crossed swords in the Army List,
My Dear, against your name.

We planned a great Empire together, you and I,
Bound only by the sea;
Now in the quiet of a chill Winter's night
Your voice comes hushed to me
Full of forgotten memories: you and I
Dreamed great dreams of our future in those days,
Setting our feet on undiscovered ways,
And all I asked of fame
A scarlet cross on my breast, my Dear,
For the swords by your name.

We shall never shake the world together, you and I,
For you gave your life away;
And I think my heart was broken by the war,
Since on a summer day
You took the road we never spoke of: you and I
Dreamed greatly of an Empire in those days;
You set your feet upon the Western ways
And have no need of fame –
There's a scarlet cross on my breast, my Dear,
And a torn cross with your name.

December 1916

*By May Wedderburn Cannan (1893–1973), novelist and poet who
served in the Voluntary Aid Detachment and the Intelligence Service*

during the war. Her fiancé, Bevil, son of Sir Arthur Quiller-Couch,
died of influenza soon after the Armistice, having survived the war.

VADs AT WAR

Pain . . .

To stand up straight on one's feet, strong, easy, without the surging of any physical sensation, by a bedside whose coverings are flung here and there by the quivering nerves beneath it . . . there is a sort of shame in such strength.

'What can I do for you?' my eyes cry dumbly into his clouded brown pupils.

I was told to carry trays from a ward where I had never been before – just to carry trays, orderly's work, no more.

No. 22 was lying flat on his back, his knees drawn up under him, the sheets up to his chin; his flat, chalk-white face tilted at the ceiling. As I bent over to get his untouched tray his tortured brown eyes fell on me.

'I'm in pain, Sister,' he said.

No one has ever said that to me before in that tone.

He gave me the look that a dog gives, and his words had the character of an unformed cry.

He was quite alone at the end of the ward. The Sister was in her bunk. My white cap attracted his desperate senses.

As he spoke his knees shot out from under him with his restless pain. His right arm was stretched from the bed in a narrow iron frame, reminding me of a hand laid along a harp to play the chords, the fingers with their swollen green flesh extended across the strings; but of this harp his fingers were the slave, not the master.

'Shall I call your Sister?' I whispered to him.

He shook his head. 'She can't do anything. I must just stick it out. They're going to operate on the elbow, but they must wait three days first.'

285

His head turned from side to side, but his eyes never left my face. I stood by him, helpless, overwhelmed by his horrible loneliness.

Then I carried his tray down the long ward and past the Sister's bunk. Within, by the fire, she was laughing with the M.O. and drinking a cup of tea – a harmless amusement.

'The officer in No. 22 says he's in great pain,' I said doubtfully. (It wasn't my ward, and Sisters are funny.)

'I know,' she said quite decently, 'but I can't do anything. He must stick it out.'

I looked through the ward door once or twice during the evening, and still his knees, at the far end of the room, were moving up and down.

It must happen to the men in France that, living so near the edge of death, they are more aware of life than we are.

When they come back, when the post-war days set in, will they keep that vision, letting it play on life . . . or must it fade?

And some become so careless of life, so careless of all the whims and personalities and desires that go to make up existence, that one wrote to me:

'The only real waste is the waste of metal. The earth will be covered again and again with Us. The corn will grow again; the bread and meat can be repeated. But this metal that has lain in the earth for centuries, the formation of the beginning, that men have sweated and grubbed for . . . that is the waste.'

What carelessness of worldly success they should bring back with them!

Orderlies come and go up and down the corridor. Often they carry stretchers – now and then a stretcher with the empty folds of a flag flung across it.

Then I pause from laying my trays, and with a bunch of forks in my hand I stand still.

They take the stretcher into a ward, and while I wait I know what they are doing behind the screens which stand around a bed against the wall. I hear the shuffle of feet as the men stand to attention, and the orderlies come out again, and the folds of the flag have ballooned up to receive and embrace a man's body.

286

Where is he going?
To the mortuary.
Yes . . . but where else . . . ?

Perhaps there is nothing better than the ecstasy and unappease-
ment of life?

. . . The gallants have been saying unprofessional things to me,
and I haven't minded. The convoy will arm me against them.
'Soldiers are coming into the ward.'

Eight o'clock, nine o'clock . . . If only one could eat something! I took a sponge-finger out of a tin, resolving to pay it back
out of my tea next day, and stole round to the dark corner near
the German ward to eat it. The Germans were in bed; I could see
two of them. At last, freed from their uniform, the dark blue with
the scarlet soup-plates, they looked – how strange! – like other
men.

One was asleep. The other, I met his eyes so close; but
I was in the dark, and he under the light of a lamp.

I knew what was happening down at the station two miles
away; I had been on station duty so often. The rickety country
station lit by one large lamp; the thirteen waiting V.A.D.'s; the
long wooden table loaded with mugs of every size; kettles boiling;
the white clock ticking on; that frowsy booking clerk . . .

Then the sharp bell, the tramp of the stretcher-bearers through
the station, and at last the two engines drawing gravely across the
lighted doorway, and carriage windows filled with eager faces,
other carriage windows with beds slung across them, a vast Red
Cross, a chemist's shop, a theatre, more windows, more faces . . .

The stretcher-men are lined up; the M.O. meets the M.O.
with the train; the train Sisters drift in to the coffee-table.

'Here they come! Walkers first . . . '

The station entrance is full of men crowding in and taking
the steaming mugs of tea and coffee; men on pickaback with
bandaged feet; men with only a nose and one eye showing, with
stumbling legs, bound arms. The station, for five minutes, is full
of jokes and witticisms; then they pass out and into the waiting
chars-à-bancs.

A long pause.

287

'Stretchers!'

The first stretchers are laid on the floor.

There I have stood so often, pouring the tea behind the table, watching that littered floor, the single gas-lamp ever revolving on its chain, turning the shadows about the room like a wheel – my mind filled with pictures, emptied of thoughts, hypnotized.

But last night, for the first time, I was in the ward. For the first time I should follow them beyond the glass door, see what became of them, how they changed from soldiers into patients . . .

The gallants in the ward don't like a convoy; it unsexes us.

Nine o'clock . . . ten o'clock . . . Another biscuit. Both Germans are asleep now.

At last a noise in the corridor, a tramp on the stairs . . . Only walkers? No, there's a stretcher – and another . . . !

Now reflection ends, my feet begin to move, my hands to undo bootlaces, flick down thermometers, wash and fetch and carry.

The gallants play bridge without looking up. I am tremendously fortified against them: for one moment I fiercely condemn and then forget them. For I am without convictions, antipathies, prejudices, reflections. I only work and watch, watch . . .

Our ward is divided: half of it is neat and white and orderly; the other half has khaki tumbled all over it – 'Sam Brownes,' boots, caps, mud, the caked mud from the 'other side.'

But the neat beds are empty; the occupants out talking to the new-comers, asking questions. Only the gallants play their bridge unmoved. They are on their mettle, showing off. Their turn will come some day.

Now it only remains to walk home, hungry, under a heavy moon.

It was the first time I had heard a man sing at his dressing. I was standing at the sterilizer when Rees's song began to mount over the screen that hid him from me. ('Whatever is that?' 'Rees's tubes going in.')

It was like this: 'Ah . . . ee . . . oo, Sister!' and again: 'Sister . . . oo . . . ee . . . ah!' Then a little scream and his song again.

I heard her voice: 'Now then, Rees, I don't call that much of a song.' She called me to make his bed, and I saw his left ear was full of tears.

O visitors, who come into the ward in the calm of the long afternoon, when the beds are neat and clean and the flowers out on the tables and the V.A.D.'s sit sewing at splints and sandbags, when the men look like men again and smoke and talk and read . . . if you could see what lies beneath the dressings!

When one shoots at a wooden figure it makes a hole. When one shoots at a man it makes a hole, and the doctor must make seven others.

From A Diary without Dates, *1918, by Enid Bagnold (1889–1981), playwright, novelist and autobiographer. She studied painting with Walter Sickert, then nursed in 'a vast, weary military hospital' (the Royal Herbert Hospital, Woolwich) in the First World War, which she described in* A Diary without Dates. *She married Sir Roderick Jones, head of Reuters News Agency, in 1920. Her several books include the children's novel* National Velvet *(1935),* The Squire *(1938) and* The Chalk Garden *(1953).*

THE EAST END AT WAR

War hardships arose immediately. The women in trouble came at once to the Women's Hall and asked for 'Sylvia'. I was deeply impressed by their faith in the Federation and in me. They had fought with us and made sacrifices: I would strive to mitigate for them the burden of war. Our staff and members rose bravely to the occasion, the poor gallantly helping the poor. The [East London] Federation [of Suffragettes] acted as a Trade Union or a family solicitor on behalf of the people in need, approaching Government departments, magistrates, and local authorities as the case might require, and meanwhile, if other assistance were lacking, supplying the immediate sustenance required.

Prices rose in the first week to famine height; factories were shut down in panic; men and women thrown out of employment.

289

Reservists were called up. Separation allowances were slow in coming, and when they came how meagre! Despairing mothers came to us with wasted infants. I appealed through the Press for money to buy milk, but the babies were ill from waiting; doctors, nurses, and invalid requirements were added, of necessity. Soon we had five Mother and Infant Welfare Centres in East End districts, and a toy and garment factory for unemployed women...

Before August 1914 was out we had opened our Cost Price restaurants, where two-penny meals to adults and penny meals to children were served to all comers, with free meal tickets for the destitute. The Gunmakers' Arms,* a disused public house, was turned into a clinic, day nursery, and Montessori school...
We regarded our relief work as a lever for securing similar institutions from public funds, and were amongst the first to organize such work. We agitated by meetings, processions, and deputations to Government departments to protect the people from exploitation by profiteers, to secure that wages should rise with the cost of living, to gain, for the women soon flocking from all quarters into what had hitherto been masculine occupations, a rate of pay equal to that of men. We set up a League of Rights for Soldiers' and Sailors' Wives and Relatives to strive for better naval and military pensions and allowances... We toiled for the preservation of civil liberties, always so gravely attacked in war times. Votes for Women was never permitted to fall into the background. We worked continuously for peace, in face of the bitterest opposition from old enemies, and sometimes unhappily from old friends. To us came many tried militant stalwarts of the W.S.P.U. We were giving the lead to a substantial share of the Labour, Socialist, and Suffrage organizations. Much of this activity hung on me. I had often a stiff fight to keep going with the broken health left to me from the hunger-strikes.

When I first read in the Press that Mrs. Pankhurst and Christabel were returning to England for a recruiting campaign, I wept. To me this seemed a tragic betrayal of the great movement to bring the mother-half of the race into the councils of the nation.

From The Suffragette Movement, *1931, by Sylvia Pankhurst.*

*Renamed the Mothers' Arms.

THE JINGO-WOMAN

Jingo-woman
(How I dislike you!)
Dealer in white feathers,
Insulter, self-appointed,
Of all the men you meet,
Not dressed in uniform,
When to your mind,
    (A sorry mind),
    They should be,
    The test?
The judgment of your eye,
That wild, infuriate eye,
Whose glance, so you declare,
    Reveals unerringly,
Who's good for military service.
Oh! exasperating woman,
I'd like to wring your neck,
    I really would!
    You make all women seem such duffers!
    Besides exemptions,
    Enforced and held reluctantly,
    – Not that you'll believe it –
    You *must* know surely
Men there are, and young men too,
Physically not fit to serve,
Who look in their civilian garb
    Quite stout and hearty.
And most of whom, I'll wager,
Have been rejected several times.
How keen, though, your delight,
    Keen and malignant,
Should one offer you his seat,

291

In crowded bus or train,
Thus giving you the chance to say,
In cold, incisive tones of scorn:
  'No, I much prefer to stand
  As you, young man, are not in khaki!'
Heavens! I wonder you're alive!
  Oh, these men,
These twice-insulted men,
  What iron self-control they show.
  What wonderful forbearance!
But still the day may come
For you to prove yourself
As sacrificial as upbraiding.
So far they are not taking us
But if the war goes on much longer
  They might,
  Nay more,
  They must,
When the last man has gone.
And if and when the dark day dawns,
You'll join up first, of course,
Without waiting to be fetched.
But in the meantime,
Do hold your tongue!
You shame us women.
Can't you see it isn't decent,
To flout and goad men into doing,
  What is not asked of you?

By Helen Hamilton, 1918.

Statement from the War Office, September 1916

The formation of large armies has necessarily had a far-reaching effect on the industrial and commercial life of the Nation, and in view of the increasing demand for men of military age to bear arms in the defence of liberty, it is incumbent on those not engaged in Military Service to make a supreme effort to maintain the output of Articles required for the War and the export trade.

It is considered that a more widespread knowledge of the success which has been attained by Women in nearly all branches of men's work is most desirable, and will lead to the release of large numbers of men to the Colours who have hitherto been considered indispensable.

Employers who have met the new conditions with patience and foresight readily admit that the results achieved by the temporary employment of Women far exceed their original estimates, and even so are capable of much further extension. If this is true in their case, how much greater must be the scope for such substitution by those Employers who have not attempted it from reasons of apprehension or possibly prejudice? The necessity of replacing wastage in our Armies will eventually compel the release of all men who can be replaced by women, and it is therefore in the interests of Employers to secure and train temporary substitutes as early as possible, in order to avoid any falling off in production.

Women of Great Britain, employers of labour, remember that:

(a)   No man who is eligible for Military Service should be retained in civil employment if his place can be temporarily filled by a woman or by a man who is ineligible for Military Service.

(b)   No man who is ineligible for Military Service should be retained on work which can be performed by a woman (for the duration of the War) if the man himself can be utilized to release to the Colours one who is eligible for Military Service, and who cannot be satisfactorily replaced by a woman.

293

WOMEN AT WAR

'They're saving the country. They don't mind what they do. Hours? They work ten and a half, or with overtime, twelve hours a day, seven days a week. At least that's what they'd like to do. The Government are insisting on one Sunday – or two Sundays – a month off. I don't say they're not right. But the women resent it. *"We're* not tired!" . . . '

First of all we visit the 'danger buildings' in the Fuse Factory, where mostly women are employed. About 500 women are at work here, on different processes connected with the delicate mechanism and filling of the fuse and gaine, some of which are dangerous. Detonator work, for instance. The Lady Superintendent selects for it specially steady and careful women or girls, who are paid at time and a quarter rate. Only about eight girls are allowed in each room. The girls here all wear – for protection – green muslin veils and gloves. It gives them a curious ghastly look, that fits the occupation. For they are making small pellets for the charging of shells, out of a high explosive powder. Each girl uses a small copper ladle to take the powder out of a box before her and puts it into a press which stamps it into a tiny block, looking like ivory. She holds her hand over a little tray of water lest any of the powder should escape. What the explosive and death-dealing strength of it is, it does not do to think about. In another room a fresh group of girls are handling a black powder for another part of the detonator, and because of the irritant nature of the powder, are wearing white bandages round the nose and mouth. There is great competition for these rooms, the Superintendent says! The girls in them work on two shifts of 10½ hours each, and would resent a change to a shorter shift. They have one hour for dinner, half an hour for tea, a cup of tea in the middle of the morning – and the whole of Saturdays free. To the eye of the ordinary visitor, at least, they show few signs of fatigue.

From England's Effort: Six Letters to an American Friend, *1916, by Mrs Humphry Ward (Mary Augusta Ward, 1851–1920). An untiring advocate of education for women, Ward was the author of twenty-eight novels and a moving spirit in the Anti-Suffrage League, founded in 1908. Her most famous novel was* Robert Elsmere *(1888);* Marcella, *published in 1894, was an instant success; and* Delia Blanchflower *(1915) a sharp portrait of the suffrage movement.*

THE WAR-WORKERS

Mrs. Willoughby, in Miss Vivian's private office, reversed all rules of official precedent.

'Sit down again, my dear child – sit down!' she cried cordially, at the same time establishing herself close to the table. 'I hear you're doing wonderful work for all these dear people – Belgians and the dear Tommies and everyone – and I felt I simply *had* to come in and hear all about it. Also, I want to propound a tiny little scheme of my own which I think will appeal to you. Or have you heard about it already from that precious boy John, with whom, I may tell you, I'm simply *madly* in love? I'm always threatening to elope with him!'

'I'm afraid,' said Char, disregarding her visitor's pleasantry, 'that I can really hardly undertake anything more. We are very much understaffed as it is, and the War Office is always —— '

'I can turn the *whole* War Office round my little finger, my dear,' declared Mrs. Willoughby. 'There's the dearest lad there, a sort of under-secretary, who's absolutely devoted to me, and tells me all sorts of official tit-bits before anyone else hears a word about them. I can get anything I want through him, so you needn't worry about the War Office. In fact, to tell you rather a shocking little secret, I can get what I want out of most of these big official places – just a little tiny manipulation of the wires, you know. (*Cherchez la femme* – though I oughtn't to say such things to a girl like you, ought I?)'

Char looked at Mrs. Willoughby's large, heavily powdered face, at her enormous top-heavy hat and over-ample figure, and said nothing.

But no silence, however subtly charged with uncomplimentary meanings, could stem Mrs. Willoughby's piercing eloquence.

'This is what I want to do, and I'm told at the camp here that it would be simply invaluable. I want to get up a Canteen for the troops here, and for all those dear things on leave.'

'There are several Y.M.C.A. Huts already.'

'My dear! I know it. But I want to do this all on my little own, and have quite different rules and regulations. My Lewis, who's been in the Army for over fifteen years, poor angel, tells me that they all – from the Colonel downwards – think it would be the greatest boon on earth, to have a *lady* at the head of things, you know.'

'My time is too much taken up; it would be quite out of the question,' said Char simply.

'Darling child! *Do* you suppose I meant you – a ridiculously young thing like you? Of course, it would have to be a married woman, with a certain regimental position, so to speak. And my Lewis is second in command, as you know, so that naturally his wife ... You see, the Colonel's wife is an absolute dear, but an invalid – more or less, and no more *savoir faire* than a kitten. A perfect little provincial, between ourselves. Whereas, of course, I know this sort of job inside out and upside down – literally, my dear. The *hours* I've toiled in town!'

'But I'm afraid in that case you oughtn't to leave —— '

'I must! I'm compelled to. It's *too* cruel, but the doctor simply won't answer for the consequences if I go back to London in my present state. But work I *must*. One would go quite, quite mad if one wasn't working – thinking about it all, you know.'

'Major Willoughby is – er – in England, isn't he?'

'Thank God, yes!' exclaimed Lesbia, with a fervour that would have startled her husband considerably. 'My heart bleeds for these poor wives and mothers. I simply thank God upon my knees that I have no son! When one thinks of it all! England's life-blood —— '

Char did not share her mother's objection to eloquence expended upon the subject of the war, but she cut crisply enough into this *exaltée* outpouring.

'One is extremely thankful to do what little one can,' she said, half-unconsciously throwing an appraising glance at the files and papers that were littered in profusion all over the table.

'Indeed one is!' cried Lesbia, just as fervently as before. 'Work is the only thing. My dear, this war is killing me – simply killing me!'

Miss Vivian was not apparently prompted to any expression of regret at the announcement.

'As I said to Lewis the other day, I must work or go quite mad. And now this Canteen scheme seems to be calling out to me, and go I must. We've got a building – that big hall just at the bottom of the street here – and I'm insisting upon having a regular opening day – so much better to start these things with a flourish, you know – and the regimental band, and hoisting the Union Jack, and everything. And what I want you to do is this.'

Lesbia paused at last to take breath, and Char immediately said:

'I'm afraid I'm so fearfully busy to-day that I haven't one moment, but if you'd like my secretary to —— '

'Not your secretary, but your *entire* staff, and your attractive self. I want you *all* down there to help!'

'Quite impossible,' said Char. 'I wonder, Mrs. Willoughby, if you have any idea of the scale on which this Depôt is run?'

'*Every* idea,' declared Lesbia recklessly. 'I'm told everywhere that all the girls in Questerham are helping you, and that's exactly why I've come. I want girls to make my Canteen attractive – all the prettiest ones you have.'

'I'm afraid my staff was not selected with a view to – er – personal attractions,' said Miss Vivian, in a voice which would have created havoc amongst her staff in its ironical chilliness.

'Nonsense, my dear Char! I met the sweetest thing on the stairs – a perfect gem of a creature with Titian-coloured hair. Not in that hideous uniform, either.'

Miss Vivian could not but recognize the description of her typist.

'I don't quite understand,' she said. 'Do you want helpers on your opening day, or regularly?'

'Quite regularly – from five to eleven or thereabouts every evening. I shall be there myself, of course, to supervise the whole thing, and I've got half a dozen dear things to help me: but what I want is *girls*, who'll run about and play barmaid and wash up, you know.'

'Couldn't my mother spare Miss Bruce sometimes?'

'*Is* Miss Bruce a young and lively girl?' inquired Mrs. Willoughby, not without reason. 'Besides, I need dozens of them.'

'Yes, I see,' said Char languidly. She was tired of Mrs. Willoughby, and it was with positive relief that she heard her telephone-bell ring sharply.

There was a certain satisfaction in leaning back in her chair and calling 'Miss – er – Jones!'

Miss Jones moved quietly to answer the insistent bell.

From The War Workers, *1918, by E.M. Delafield (Edmée Elizabeth Monica de la Pasture, 1890–1943). Daughter of 'Mrs Henry de la Pasture', and herself a novelist, short story writer, playwright and journalist, Delafield spent several years as a postulant in a Belgian convent, which she described in* Brides of Heaven. *She served as a VAD nurse in Devon during the First World War and published her first novel,* Zella Sees Herself, *in 1917. A wry observer of the nuances of women's complicity in their own subjection, Delafield's most celebrated novel was* The Diary of a Provincial Lady *(1931), comprising pieces that were first commissioned by Lady Rhondda for the feminist periodical* Time and Tide.

IF WOMEN COULD COMBINE

To MISS E. HOBHOUSE.   LONDON [? 1915].

. . . Yes, there is a change of tone – it is principally caused by the rise of prices. This war will probably go on for another year and a half or two years. France and Germany would long ago have made peace, but England and probably Russia won't let them. She wants German traid [? trade] and colonies. If the Imperialists were severely [? beaten] in German West and in Egypt peace would probably come very soon, but as this is most unlikely to happen, it won't. I don't think that feebly gushing over the war does any good. To combine, as the labour party under Keir Hardie and some Social Democrats are doing in Germany, to protest against the action of *their own* government, *is* immense good. If women could combine – which they won't – in their millions to defeat the politicians of their own country at the next elections, and to prevent their husbands and sons from enlisting, that would do good, and anything one individual ever does to diminish this hideous nation-hatred does do good.

From The Letters of Olive Schreiner, 1876–1920, *edited by S.C. Cronwright Schreiner (1926).*

EDUCATION

The rain is slipping, dripping down the street;
The day is grey as ashes on the hearth.
The children play with soldiers made of tin,
    While you sew
    Row after row.

The tears are slipping, dripping one by one;
Your son has shot and wounded his small brother.
The mimic battle's ended with a sob,
    While you dream
    Over your seam.

The blood is slipping, dripping drop by drop;
The men are dying in the trenches' mud.
The bullets search the quick among the dead.
    While you drift,
    The Gods sift.

The ink is slipping, dripping from the pens,
On papers, White and Orange, Red and Grey, –
History for the children of tomorrow –
    While you prate
    About Fate.

War is slipping, dripping death on earth.
If the child is father of the man,
Is the toy gun father of the Krupps?
>> For Christ's sake think!
>> While you sew
>> Row after row.

By Pauline Barrington, 1918.

REGRET TO INFORM YOU

Then the blow fell. On the afternoon of September 4th – too late to get married that day – a further telegram arrived ordering Jack to leave Victoria for service overseas early on the 7th. There was nothing to be done, but to cancel the honeymoon plans, while one of Jack's friends discovered a farm which would be willing to take us after the wedding next day. This was near Haslingfield, a village about six miles from Cambridge, where in my school days I had often sat reading by a stream on solitary bicycle rides.

So, after our marriage on the 5th, to Haslingfield we went in the autumn sunshine, with the last of the corn stooks standing in the fields. Jack was twenty-six and I was twenty, and both of us were, I think, very young for our ages. In the tense emotional climate of the time, we had little conception of what we were doing, and little idea of what we might be committing ourselves to. We were indeed strangers and afraid in a world we never made.

The next afternoon we took the train to London, staying overnight at the Rubens Hotel so as to be near the station for Jack's departure next day. Early the following morning, a day and a half after our marriage, I saw him off from Victoria along with a train-load of other cannon fodder.

Five weeks later the War Office 'regretted to inform me' that Capt. J.W. Wootton of the 11th Battalion Suffolk Regiment had died of wounds. He had been shot through the eye and died forty-eight hours later on an ambulance train; and in due course his blood-stained kit was punctiliously returned to me.

300

From In a World I Never Made, *1967, by Barbara Wootton. An economist and educator, Wootton was Professor of Social Studies at the University of London, 1948–52.*

THE FEVER CHART OF WAR

'The women are splendid . . . ' How tired we are of hearing that, so tired that we begin to doubt it, and the least hostile emotion that it evokes is the sense that after all the men are so much more splendid, so far beyond praise, that the less one says of anyone else the better. That sentence is dead, let us hope, fallen into the same limbo as 'Business as Usual' and the rest of the early war-gags, but the prejudices it aroused, the feeling of boredom, have not all died with it. Words have at least this in common with men, that the evil they do lives after them.

Let me admit that when those in authority sent for me to go to France and see what certain sections of the women there were doing, I didn't want to go. I told them rather ungraciously that if they wanted the 'sunny-haired-lassies-in-khaki touch' they had better send somebody else. I am not, and never have been, a feminist or any other sort of an 'ist, never having been able to divide humanity into two different classes labelled 'men' and 'women.' Also, to tell the truth, the idea of going so far behind the lines did not appeal. For this there is the excuse that in England one grows so sick of the people who talk of 'going to the Front,' when they mean going to some safe château at a base for a personally conducted tour, or – Conscientious Objectors are the worst sinners in this latter class – when they are going to sit at canteens or paint huts a hundred miles or so behind the last line of trenches. The reaction from this sort of thing is very apt to make one say: 'Oh, France? There's no more in being in France behind the lines than in working in England.' A point of view in which I was completely wrong. There is a great deal of difference, not in any increased danger, but in quite other ways, as I shall show in the place and order in which it was gradually made apparent to me.

Also, no one who has not been at the war knows the hideous boredom of it . . . a boredom that the soul dreads like a fatal miasma. And if I had felt it in Belgium in those terrible grey first weeks of her pain, when at least one was in the midst of war, as it was then, still fluid and mobile, still full of alarums and excursions, with all the suffering and death immediately under one's eyes still a new thing; if I had felt it again, even more strongly, when I went right up to the very back of the front in the French war zone for the Croix Rouge, in those poor little hospitals where the stretchers are always ready in the wards to hustle the wounded away, and where, in devastated lands only lately vacated by the Germans, I sat and ate with peasants who were painfully and sadly beginning to return to their ruined homes and cultivate again a soil that might have been expected to redden the ploughshare, how much the more then might I dread it, caught in the web of Lines of Communication . . . I feared that boredom.

And there was another reason, both for my disinclination and my lack of interest. We in England grew so tired, in the early days of the war, of the fancy uniforms that burst out upon women. Every other girl one met had an attack of khakiitis, was spotted as the pard with badges and striped as the zebra. Almost simultaneously with this eruption came, for the other section of the feminine community, reaction from it. We others became rather self-consciously proud of our femininity, of being 'fluffy' – in much the same way that anti-suffragists used to be fluffy when they said they preferred to influence a man's vote, and that they thought more was done by charm . . .

With official recognition of bodies such as the V.A.D.s and the even more epoch-making official founding of the W.A.A.C.s, the point of view of the un-uniformed changed. The thing was no longer a game at which women were making silly asses of themselves and pretending to be men; it had become regular, ordered, disciplined, and worthy of respect. In short, uniform was no longer fancy dress.

But the feeling of boredom that had been engendered stayed on, as these things do. It is yet to be found, partly because there still are women who have their photographs taken in a new

302

uniform every week, but more because of our ignorance as to what the real workers are doing. And, like most ignorant people, I was happy in my ignorance.

I was at the Headquarters of the British Red Cross – which is what the letters H.Q.B.R.C.S. stand for – and I was being shown some very peculiar and wonderful charts. They are secret charts, the figures on which, if a man is shown them, he must never disclose, and those figures, when you read them, bring a contraction at once of pity and of pride to the heart. For, on these great charts, that are mapped out into squares and look exactly like temperature charts at a hospital, are drawn curves, like the curves that show the fever of a patient. Up in jagged mountains, down into merciful valleys, goes the line, and at every point there is a number, and that number is the number of the wounded who were brought down from the trenches on such a day. Here, on these charts, is a complete record, in curves, of the rate of the war. Every peak is an offensive, every valley a comparative lull.

Sheet after sheet, all with those carefully-drawn numbered curves zigzagging across them, all showing the very temperature of War. . . .

With this difference – that on these sheets there is no 'normal.' War is abnormal, and there is not a point of these charts where, when the line touches it, you can say – 'It is well.'

As I looked at these records I began to get a different vision of that tract of country called 'Lines of Communication,' which I had come to see. This, where War's very pulse is noted day by day, is the stronghold of War himself. Here he is nursed, rested, fed with food for the mouths of flesh and blood, and food for the mouths of iron; here, the whole time, night and day, as ceaselessly as in the trenches, the work goes on, the work of strengthening his hands, and so every man and woman working for that end in 'L. of C.' is fighting on our side most surely. Something of the hugeness and the importance of it began to show itself.

And, as regards that particular portion which I had come out to see, I began to get a glimmering of that also, when it was told me that, of those thousands of wounded I saw marked on the charts, a great proportion was convoyed entirely by women. There are whole districts, such as the Calais district, which includes many towns and stations, where every ambulance running is driven by a woman. Not only the fever rate of War is shown on those charts, but, to the seeing eye, other things also; just as behind any temperature chart in a hospital, is the whole construction of the great scheme – doctors, surgeons, nurses, food, drugs, money, devotion, everything that finds its expression in that simple sheet of paper filled in daily as a matter of routine, so behind these charts of War's temperature kept at H.Q. is the whole of the complex organization known as the British Red Cross. And outstanding, even amongst so much that is splendid, are certain bands of girls behind the lines, who, not for a month or two, but year in, year out, during nights and days when they have known no rest, have, they also, had their fingers on the pulse of war.

From The Sword of Deborah: First-hand Impressions of the British Army in France, *1918, by F. Tennyson Jesse, novelist, playwright, journalist and crime writer. Jesse was one of the handful of women war correspondents during the First World War, but The Sword of Deborah was not released by the Ministry of Information until after the war ended. She edited several volumes of the* Notable British Trials *series, and in her compelling account of the Thompson/Bywater case,* A Pin to See the Peepshow (1934), *she suggested that it was her adultery, rather than the crime, that led to Edith Thompson's conviction for murder.*

THIS LONELIEST HOUR

When the sound of victorious guns burst over London at 11 a.m. on November 11th, 1918, the men and women who looked incredulously into each other's faces did not cry jubilantly: 'We've won the War!' They only said: 'The War is over.'

From Millbank I heard the maroons crash with terrifying clearness, and, like a sleeper who is determined to go on dreaming after being told to wake up, I went on automatically washing the dressing bowls in the annex outside my hut. Deeply buried beneath my consciousness there stirred the vague memory of a letter that I had written to Roland in those legendary days when I was still at Oxford, and could spend my Sundays in thinking of him while the organ echoed grandly through New College Chapel. It had been a warm May evening, when all the city was sweet with the scent of wallflowers and lilac, and I had walked back to Micklem Hall after hearing an Occasional Oratorio by Handel, which described the mustering of troops for battle, the lament for the fallen and the triumphant return of the victors.

'As I listened,' I told him, 'to the organ swelling forth into a final triumphant burst in the song of victory, after the solemn and mournful dirge over the dead, I thought with what mockery and irony the jubilant celebrations which will hail the coming of peace will fall upon the ears of those to whom their best will never return, upon whose sorrow victory is built, who have paid with their mourning for the others' joy. I wonder if I shall be one of those who take a happy part in the triumph – or if I shall listen to the merriment with a heart that breaks and ears that try to keep out the mirthful sounds.'

And as I dried the bowls I thought: 'It's come too late for me. Somehow I knew, even at Oxford, that it would. Why couldn't it have ended rationally, as it might have ended, in 1916, instead of all that trumpet-blowing against a negotiated peace, and the ferocious talk of secure civilians about marching to Berlin? It's come five months too late – or is it three years? It might have ended last June, and let Edward, at least, be saved! Only five months – it's such a little time, when Roland died nearly three years ago.'

But on Armistice Day not even a lonely survivor drowning in black waves of memory could be left alone with her thoughts. A moment after the guns had subsided into sudden, palpitating silence, the other V.A.D. from my ward dashed excitedly into the annex.

'Brittain! Brittain! Did you hear the maroons? It's over – it's all over! Do let's come out and see what's happening!'

Mechanically I followed her into the road. As I stood there, stupidly rigid, long after the triumphant explosions from Westminster had turned into a distant crescendo of shouting, I saw a taxicab turn swiftly in from the Embankment towards the hospital. The next moment there was a cry for doctors and nurses from passers-by, for in rounding the corner the taxi had knocked down a small elderly woman who in listening, like myself, to the wild noise of a world released from nightmare, had failed to observe its approach.

As I hurried to her side I realized that she was all but dead and already past speech. Like Victor in the mortuary chapel, she seemed to have shrunk to the dimensions of a child with the sharp features of age, but on the tiny chalk-white face an expression of shocked surprise still lingered, and she stared hard at me as Geoffrey had stared at his orderly in those last moments of conscious silence beside the Scarpe. Had she been thinking, I wondered, when the taxi struck her, of her sons at the front, now safe? The next moment a medical officer and some orderlies came up, and I went back to my ward.

But I remembered her at intervals throughout that afternoon, during which, with a half-masochistic notion of 'seeing the sights,' I made a circular tour to Kensington by way of the intoxicated West End. With aching persistence my thoughts went back to the dead and the strange irony of their fates – to Roland, gifted, ardent, ambitious, who had died without glory in the conscientious performance of a routine job; to Victor and Geoffrey, gentle and diffident, who, conquering nature by resolution, had each gone down bravely in a big 'show'; and finally to Edward, musical, serene, a lover of peace, who had fought courageously through so many battles and at last had been killed while leading a vital counter-attack in one of the few decisive actions of the War. As I struggled through the waving, shrieking crowds in Piccadilly and Regent Street on the overloaded top of a 'bus, some witty enthusiast for contemporary history symbolically turned upside down the signboard 'Seven Kings.'

Late that evening, when supper was over, a group of elated V.A.D.s who were anxious to walk through Westminster and Whitehall to Buckingham Palace prevailed upon me to join them. Outside the Admiralty a crazy group of convalescent Tommies were collecting specimens of different uniforms and bundling their wearers into flag-strewn taxis; with a shout they seized two of my companions and disappeared into the clamorous crowd, waving flags and shaking rattles. Wherever we went a burst of enthusiastic cheering greeted our Red Cross uniform, and complete strangers adorned with wound stripes rushed up and shook me warmly by the hand. After the long, long blackness, it seemed like a fairy-tale to see the street lamps shining through the chill November gloom.

I detached myself from the others and walked slowly up Whitehall, with my heart sinking in a sudden cold dismay. Already this was a different world from the one that I had known during four life-long years, a world in which people would be light-hearted and forgetful, in which themselves and their careers and their amusements would blot out political ideals and great national issues. And in that brightly lit, alien world I should have no part. All those with whom I had really been intimate were gone; not one remained to share with me the heights and the depths of my memories. As the years went by and youth departed and remembrance grew dim, a deeper and ever deeper darkness would cover the young men who were once my contemporaries.

For the first time I realized, with all that full realization meant, how completely everything that had hitherto made up my life had vanished with Edward and Roland, with Victor and Geoffrey. The War was over; a new age was beginning; but the dead were dead and would never return.

From Testament of Youth: An Autobiographical Study of the Years 1900–1925 *by Vera Brittain (1933).* Testament of Friendship *(1940) told of her close friendship with the novelist Winifred Holtby and* Testament of Experience *(1957) completed the trilogy, recounting Brittain's growing feminism and pacifism.*

VISTAS OF DEATH

7 Oct. 1918

I am beginning to rub my eyes at the prospect of peace. I think it will require more courage than anything that has gone before. It isn't until one leaves off spinning round that one realizes how giddy one is. One will have to look at long vistas again, instead of short ones, and one will at last fully recognize that the dead are not only dead for the duration of the war.

From Lady Cynthia Asquith: Diaries 1915–1918, *with a foreword by L.P. Hartley (1968). Lady Cynthia Asquith (née Charteris) was the daughter of the 11th Earl of Wemyss and the daughter-in-law of Herbert Asquith, Prime Minister in the first year of the war. She acted as J.M. Barrie's secretary for a time and wrote novels, children's books and biographies.*

PEACE

London, [*November 1918*]

... These preparations for Festivity are too odious. In addition to my money complex I have a food complex. When I read of the preparations that are being made in all the workhouses throughout the land – when I think of all those toothless old jaws guzzling for the day – and then of all that beautiful youth feeding the fields of France – Life is almost too ignoble to be borne. Truly one must hate humankind in the mass, hate them as passionately as one loves the few, the very few. Ticklers, squirts, portraits eight times as large as life of Lloyd George and Beatty blazing against the sky – and drunkenness and brawling and destruction. I keep seeing all these horrors, bathing in them again and again (God knows I don't want to) and then my mind fills with the wretched little picture I have of my brother's grave. What is the meaning of it all?

From The Collected Letters of Katherine Mansfield, *edited by Vincent O'Sullivan and Margaret Scott (1984).*

AFTERWARDS

Oh, my beloved, shall you and I
Ever be young again, be young again?
The people that were resigned said to me
– Peace will come and you will lie
Under the larches up in Sheer,
Sleeping,
And eating strawberries and cream and cakes –
       O cakes, O cakes, O cakes, from Fuller's!
And quite forgetting there's a train to town,
Plotting in an afternoon the new curves for the world.

And peace came. And lying in Sheer
I look round at the corpses of the larches
Whom they slew to make pit-props
For mining the coal for the great armies.
And think, a pit-prop cannot move in the wind,
Nor have red manes hanging in spring from its branches,
And sap making the warm air sweet.
Though you planted it out on the hill again it would be dead.

By Margaret Postgate Cole, 1918. A Cambridge professor's daughter, educated at Girton College, Cambridge, Cole (1893–1980) taught classics at St Paul's Girls School before going to work in the Fabian Research Department in 1917. She wrote several books – including detective fiction – some in collaboration with her husband, the economist and labour historian, G.D.H. Cole.

ACKNOWLEDGEMENTS

Permission to reproduce material in this book is gratefully acknowledged. Every effort has been made to locate the copyright-holders, but should any have been inadvertently omitted, they should contact the publisher, who will be pleased to credit them in any further editions.

Excerpts on pp. 47, 155-7 and 159-60 from *The Diary of Beatrice Webb, Vol. 1: Glitter Around: Darkness Within, 1873-1892*, edited by Norman and Jeanne Mackenzie (1982), are reprinted by permission of Virago Press; the papers of Teresa Billington-Greig on pp. 47-51 are reprinted by permission of the Fawcett Library; the excerpt on p. 64 from *The Memoirs of Ethel Smyth*, edited by Ronald Crichton, is reprinted by permission of Viking; *Marriage as a Trade* by Cicely Hamilton (pp. 65 and 175-9) was published by Chapman & Hall in 1909; the excerpts on pp. 70-5, 111-13 and 272 from *My Part of the River* and *Behind High Walls* by Grace Foakes are reprinted by permission of Shepheard-Walwyn (Publishers) Ltd; *The Getting of Wisdom* by 'Henry Handel Richardson' (pp. 75-7, 91-2, 99-103, 171-2) was published by William Heinemann in 1910; the excerpt on pp. 117-19 from *Fenland Chronicle: Recollections of William Henry and Kate Mary Edwards, collected and edited by their daughter*, Sybil Marshall, is reprinted by permission of Sybil Marshall and Cambridge University Press; the letters of Katherine Mansfield on pp. 148-9, 204 and 308, from *The Collected Letters of Katherine Mansfield*, edited by Vincent O'Sullivan and Margaret Scott (1984), are reprinted by permission of Oxford University Press; the letters of Olive Schreiner on pp. 153-5 and 172-3, from *Olive Schreiner Letters, Vol. 1: 1871-1899*, edited by Richard Rive (1988), are reprinted by permission of Oxford University Press; the excerpts on pp. 163, 174 and 208-9 from *Dear Girl, The diaries and letters of two working women, 1897-1917*, edited by Tierl Thompson (1987), are reprinted by permission of the Women's Press; Dora Carrington's letter on pp. 194-5 is taken from *Carrington: Letters and Extracts from her Diaries*, edited by David Garnett (1979), published by the Hogarth Press; the excerpt on pp. 225-8 from *The Hard Way Up. The Autobiography of Hannah Mitchell, Suffragette and Rebel*, edited by Geoffrey Mitchell (1968), is reprinted by permission of Faber and Faber Limited; 'The Life of Emily Davison' on pp. 239-45 by Rebecca West is reprinted by permission of the Peters Fraser & Dunlop Group Ltd; the poem 'Many Sisters to Many Brothers' on p. 271 by Rose Macaulay is reprinted by permission of the Peters Fraser & Dunlop Group Ltd; 'Sing a Song of War-Time' on pp. 273-4 by Nina Macdonald is taken from *War-time Nursery Rhymes*, published in 1918 by Routledge & Kegan Paul; 'Non-Combatant' on p. 278 by Cicely Hamilton is taken from *Poems of the Great War*, edited by J.W. Cunliffe, published in 1916 by the Macmillan Company, New York; the excerpt on pp. 304-7 from *Testament of Youth* by Vera Brittain is included with the permission of Paul Berry, her Literary Executor, and Victor Gollancz Ltd. Her poems 'Perhaps . . .' (pp. 280-1) and 'To My Brother' (pp. 281-2) from *Verses of a VAD* (Erskine MacDonald, 1918) are copyright her Literary Executor; *A Diary Without Dates* by Enid Bagnold (pp. 285-9) was published by William Heinemann in 1918; 'Education' on pp. 299-300 by Pauline Barrington is taken from *Poems Written During the Great War, 1914-1918*, edited by Bertram Lloyd, published in 1918 by George Allen & Unwin; *The Sword of Deborah: First-hand Impressions of the British Army in France* by F. Tennyson Jesse (pp. 301-4) was published in 1918 by William Heinemann; 'Afterwards' on p. 309 by Margaret Postgate Cole is taken from *Poems*, published in 1918 by George Allen & Unwin.